"Kurek's passionate, raw honesty will take your breath away, and his infinite ability to love will stir the very depths of your soul and enable you to realize your greatness."

—MINNA, singer/songwriter and founder of the Pixie Revolution

"I read it on the subway and kept reading as I walked home from the station in a daze, unable to stop reading or walking, trying to stop my eyes welling up . . . given me a new and powerful way to walk through life."

—SCOTT WALKER, writer/director

"This book is (Kurek) throughout—his devotion is his passion for life, and the love he brings forth is in all he does. . . . Here, he opens the door for all to learn; all you have to do is walk through."

—DEBORAH LAMIA DENAVER, Academy Award–nominated and Emmy-winning make-up artist

"This book is certainly inspiring, and I could not put it down once I started; it is not only Kurek's story and thoughts, it's also our journey with him, and I am grateful that he walks on this earth the same time as me."

—HARRI KOLOKOTAS, founder of Harri K Connex

"If you want more than the average person, then please read Kurek Ashley's *How Would Love Respond?* Packed with life-changing advice, tips, and strategies that I found simple to understand, I am now more motivated to achieve my goals than ever before. . . . I am definitely giving this book to everyone I know."

—ANNETTE SYM, bestselling author of the Symply Too Good To Be True cookbook series, listed in the BRWeekly magazine as one of the top 50 entrepreneurial women in Australia

"... Kurek gives you effective strategies that create positive change. His candor is so refreshing, you'll feel you have a new best friend after you finish this book. Very powerful information!"

—SKIP LA COUR, six-time National Bodybuilding champion

"To come across somebody who has had the life experience of Kurek Ashley, then shares his experiences with us in this book, is truly a wonderful gift. All who read this amazing book will be left with life-changing thoughts and results and an empowering new outlook on many aspects of their life. No matter what it takes, read it from cover to cover. Kurek Ashley has made a massive difference in my life and those around me—allow him to do the same to you!"

—MARTIN AYLES, author of *You need a Rocket*

"Kurek's story of 'beaten to unbeatable' highlights how any situation can be transformed when you ask the simple question "How Would Love Respond?" This book is sure to inspire and empower readers around the world."

—SANDY FORSTER, International Prosperity Mentor

"Truly transformational! Kurek's new work is a joyous gift of insight, clarity, and inspiration."

—STEVE McGLOTHEN, producer of *I, Robot*

"*How Would Love Respond?* is sure to become an international bestseller. No matter where you are in your life right now, this book gives you the tools to transform it into the life that you desire. It is a personal development masterpiece."

—BRIAN KLEMMER, author of the international bestseller
The Compassionate Samurai

"I've been privileged to have known and toured the world with Kurek Ashley for decades. The biggest blessing of our shared adventures by far has been the sage-like wisdom I've been able to benefit from just by being in his presence. [*How Would Love Respond?*] is the distillation of this warrior-poet's journey through the very fires of hell, and what he's realized has always been his compass' true north through the highs and lows every life possesses. I'm proud to be able to call Kurek my friend and mentor . . . and I'm grateful to him for being brave enough to share his story with the world."

—GUNNAR NELSON, quintuple platinum rock star, more than 5 million albums sold, #1 hit songwriter/author, Guinness World Record holder

"After finishing Kurek's book I found myself reliving the amazing journey I had with Kurek in the last 18 months before the Olympic Games in Sydney. There is absolutely no doubt that Kurek was the missing link in terms of Natalie's and my success. We wouldn't have been able to do it without him. I devoured each page of the book as if it was the first time I was learning it all. It's so true and it's so inspirational. Thank you, Kurek, for teaching me the skills to take on the challenges that I previously thought were impossible. Thank you for doing it in such a caring and understanding way. I highly recommend reading Kurek's book, but only if you're ready to improve and be the person you've always wanted to be!"

—KERRI POTTHARST OAM, Olympic gold medalist, Sydney 2000

"*How Would Love Respond?* is an amazing true story about extraordinary challenges that have eventually led to an intense spiritual experience, the Gift of Life. This is the turning point in Kurek's life and the source of his divine inspiration to others that stems from an infinite intelligence."

—BARBARA PEASE, bestselling author and international speaker

HOW WOULD Love RESPOND?

KUREK ASHLEY

*Imagine If You Were Given a Gift So Powerful That
You Knew You Had to Share It With the World*

BENBELLA

BENBELLA BOOKS, INC.
Dallas, TX

BENBELLA

BenBella Books, Inc.
6440 N. Central Expressway, Suite 503
Dallas, TX 75206
Send feedback to feedback@benbellabooks.com
www.benbellabooks.com

Printed in the United States of America
10 9 8 7 6 5 4 3 2

Library of Congress Cataloging-in-Publication Data is available for this title.

ISBN 193377138-0

Proofreading by Maggie McGuire and Stacia Seaman
Cover design by Laura Watkins
Text design and composition by PerfecType, Nashville, TN
Printed by Bang Printing

Distributed by Independent Publishers Group
To order call (800) 888-4741
www.ipgbook.com

For special sales, contact Robyn White at Robyn@benbellabooks.com

CONTENTS

*"Your mind is like a parachute.
It works much better when it's open!"*

Trust in the fact that there are no accidents and that there is something in this book that you're searching for in your life. And even if you don't yet know what it is you're searching for or maybe you didn't even know that you are searching, have faith that it will be revealed to you, and that's why you chose this book.

1

Life Doesn't Turn Out the Way It Should

*H*alf a mile from our target and hundreds of feet in the air, like a bird of prey waiting for the kill, we hover above the jungle in our camouflaged attack helicopter. Only the pilot and copilot's seats remain—the rest of the cabin's been stripped clean. Even the carpeting is gone. This is a military vehicle with a specific purpose, and beauty and comfort isn't it. Back-to-back on opposite sides of the helicopter, Rob King, the other door gunner, and I are poised for action.

As I stand in the open doorway gripping the M60 machine gun in front of me, I can feel every joint in my body rattling from the engine's vibration and the giant rotors spinning overhead. It's a clear and sunny day, yet the humidity is so thick and heavy you could cut it and put it in a storage bag. One last time, we make sure our weapons are locked and loaded. We're here to do a job.

More commandos are on the ground, poised and ready to move. From our bird's-eye view, the soldiers patrolling the house and compound of the infamous Columbian drug lord Ramon Cota look like ants scurrying around their mound. Little do Ramon and his men know they are about to be squashed.

Our pilot, Jojo Imperial, receives a call over the radio. The voice on the other end is clear and precise. "Delta one, you have a green light. I repeat, you have a green light and are a go."

Jojo turns his head in our direction, yelling over the engine's roar. "Hang on, we're going in!" No sooner does he say that than he drops the nose of the 'copter. We feel the instant shift in momentum as we accelerate into a 45-degree dive, heading for the compound at high speed.

The Dolphin helicopter has a shrouded tail rotor like the ones the Coast Guard uses. As it maneuvers through the air, it makes this eerie, screaming noise, like a banshee coming to steal a soul. Jojo flicks open the safety cover for the weapons button on the joystick. Knowing exactly when the moment is right, he presses the buttons, freeing two rockets that race away from us. He hits the button again, and two more sail away.

In a matter of seconds all hell breaks loose as the rockets explode on contact. The compound goes into instant chaos. As we come roaring across the grounds, Rob and I open fire on anything that moves. Soldiers fly backward through the air and land on the ground with a thud. Rat, tat, tat, tat, tat! Exploding lines trace across the dirt. Our bullets chase the fleeing soldiers, catch up with them, and take them out. Other parts of the compound explode in balls of flame.

As we soar past the compound, Jojo pulls up on the controls, and the helicopter quickly noses us up toward the sky. Then, just before the forward momentum is about to slow down to the point where we stall, he executes a hammerhead maneuver without warning. The 'copter spins around 180 degrees and heads straight back down on almost the exact line it came up. It sends us racing toward the compound for a second run. It's a hairy maneuver. The g-force is intense.

Coming in for a second pass, Jojo unleashes another onslaught of rockets. Again Rob and I cut a path of death and destruction from both sides of the 'copter as brass rains down from our machine guns. Not one soldier is left standing, but that doesn't stop us unleashing a fury of gunfire until we have flown out of range of the compound again.

Jojo's ready to do another wild maneuver, but he gets word over the radio that our mission is done for now. He turns the 'copter around, and we slowly approach the grounds of Ramon Cota's citadel.

Hovering above the helipad, Jojo brings us to a soft landing. Rob and I look at each other. He smiles and says, "Wow, what a rush that was." I nod and reply, "I hope we get to do it again." We climb out of the helicopter. It feels good to be back on the ground.

———

Aaron Norris, the director, walks up to congratulate us. He informs us that we will have to do some more after lunch. My buddy Mike slaps me a high five. "Man, you looked awesome hanging out the door firing that gun! I'm jealous! I wish I got to do some of that stuff."

Don, another friend of mine, shakes my hand and says, "Welcome back to the Palace in the Sky!"

The Palace in the Sky is a palatial mansion located in Tagaytay City. Former Philippine president Ferdinand Marcos and his wife Imelda built it as a summer home. The house is perched high up on a rim of the Taal Volcano. The views are awe-inspiring. From one side of the property you can look straight into the massive crater of the volcano. The immense blue lake in the center of the crater has a small island in the middle of it. There are days when waterspouts form like tornadoes and cut across the lake. Looking down on them is a unique perspective. Seeing the inside of a tornado is a fascinating experience. A tornado inside a volcano is something else again! On the other side of the property is a cliff with a sharp drop down the side of the mountain. A winding road leads up to the house. Bordering the estate is lush, green, dense jungle where gangs of monkeys play high in the trees.

For the past ten weeks, we have been at the house filming the movie *Delta Force 2: The Columbian Connection*, starring Chuck Norris. In the movie, Chuck plays Col. Scott McCoy. He and his Delta Force team go in to bust up the drug cartel of Ramon Cota, played by Billy Drago. I began work on the film a couple of weeks later than everyone else because I'd been finishing up another movie, *Lock Up* with Sylvester Stallone, in which I played the role of a convict in the main bad guys' gang, who is also Stallone's character's nemesis. They had cut my shoulder-length hair into a long Mohawk so I looked more demented for the role.

When I got the call to work as an actor/stuntman on *Delta Force 2*, I was supposed to play a bad guy, but I really didn't feel like stepping off the plane in Manila with that crazy hairstyle, so I cut it all off. Now it was shaved on the sides and 1/16 of an inch on top. I looked like a brand-new marine recruit. When I arrived on the set and met Aaron, he took one look at me and changed my role from a bad guy to one of the elite Delta Force team members.

———

At this time, I'm twenty-seven years old and have been in Hollywood for nine years trying to find acting work in films and TV. I've done a few small roles on different projects before, but now I feel like I've made it to the big time. Ever since seeing *Rocky* I'd wanted to work with Sylvester Stallone. And I just have. In the same month I land another job working with Chuck Norris, and to top it off, I get flown to this exotic location!

I'm thinking, "*It doesn't get better than this*"—that is, until I arrive on the set and see a bunch of my friends also working on the show, including the lighting director Don Marshall, his brother Ralph, stuntman Geoff Brewer (Pierce Brosnan's stunt double), and one of my very best friends, the key grip, Mike Graham. The reason I know so many of the crew members is because during the rest of the year, when I wasn't getting acting jobs or doing stunts, I worked behind the camera as a "grip." And because Mike is a "key grip"—the head of the department—he hired me on the films he worked on. When you spend fifteen to eighteen hours a day working with your grip crew, they end up being close friends.

I don't think there could be a more fun job for a young guy to have than the one that I do, working on this film. They dress me up in a black military jumpsuit, black beret, and combat boots. Then they hand me a fully automatic machine gun loaded with live blank ammo. My job is to blow things up, fly in a helicopter, shoot, stab, and kill people, then pick them up, wipe them off, and have lunch with them. After lunch I get to kill them again! It's a great job—it's like being a kid again, except the toys are way better, and they pay me to play. They're even paying me an extra $400 hazard pay for every flight I take in the helicopter, and there are days when I do ten to fifteen flights.

So I'm making good money and having a great time spending it. This particular week, I've bought myself a nice camera in Manila so I can capture everything I'm seeing and experiencing in the Philippines to show everyone back home. One of my favorite things is to take pictures of the Filipino crew members and the local people who live nearby, especially the local kids. Every night after work I go to the photo shop near my hotel and have the pictures printed up so I can give them to the people I photographed the day before. Money is hard to come by for these wonderful people; the cost of buying a camera is just too big a luxury for them. Most have never even seen themselves in a photo before. So when I hand them a picture of themselves they're over the moon.

Today I take a great shot of Chuck Norris and me for my mom. She loves all the pictures of me with the stars I work with. She has quite a collection. I also get a unique shot today. In all the years Mike and I have known each other, we've never had our picture taken together. I hand my camera to one of the other stunt guys, and he snaps a great shot of us together in front of the mansion.

It's the last day of our work week. We're all looking forward to having a day off to get drunk and disorderly in Manila. Every weekend we find trouble to get into. Most of it includes plenty of alcohol and late hours in nightclubs.

We're getting ready to shoot the last scene of the day, which is going to be an easy one. In this scene, the Delta team has already boarded the helicopter. Geoff Brewer runs up and reports to John P. Ryan's character, saying, "Col. McCoy [Chuck Norris] is nowhere to be found. What should we do?"

"We can't wait for him," John says. "We'll have to take off without him."

Geoff jumps into the helicopter, and we take off. Because we've already shot the rest of the scene, we only need to get the couple of pieces of dialogue between Geoff and John. Then the helicopter will just take off, go up about fifteen feet, and that will be the cut. All in all it will take only a few minutes to complete this sequence. Then we can party in Manila.

This is the only time since filming began that I've gotten a chance to fly with Mike and Don in the helicopter, because they've always been on the ground watching while we've been filming. But for this brief scene the camera needs to be inside the helicopter, so some of the crew has to ride with us. Don's holding a portable light, Gadi is operating the camera, Rami is the camera assistant, and Mike's securing the camera crew. Including Jojo (the pilot), there are now ten of us in the helicopter.

We feel the chopper vibrate under us as Jojo starts the engine. The noise and wind from the whipping blades is exhilarating. As we lift off, we feel the blood pumping through our bodies. Jojo takes the helicopter off the ground a couple of feet to rehearse for the camera, then softly brings it back to the ground.

Gadi is looking through the eyepiece of the camera trying to find the shot he wants. He slides the camera over to the right about four inches. He gives everyone the thumbs-up. Because of the new camera position and the direction it is facing, I figure out that I probably won't be in the shot. I ask Gadi if I'm in or not. He looks through the eyepiece again and tells me I'm out, and so is Rob King. Rob and I step out of the helicopter. I turn to Mike and we slap a high five, signifying the weekend party is going to be starting in about five minutes.

Leo, the first assistant director, calls out, "Roll camera!"

Rami flips on the camera. He yells, "Speed!"

Aaron shouts, "Action!"

Right on cue, Geoff runs to the open door of the helicopter and delivers his lines to John, who completes his dialogue back to Geoff. Geoff jumps into the 'copter as rehearsed. A second later, Jojo lifts the 'copter off the ground and levels off about fifteen feet over our heads. Mike looks down from the open doorway at me, smiling from ear to ear and giving me the thumbs-up sign. From where they're hovering over the corner of the estate grounds, the view is probably incredible, with the volcano crater on one side and the cliffs and jungle on the other.

A brisk breeze comes over the top of the mountain. It's impossible to tell which direction it's coming from. It feels like it's blowing in from everywhere at the same time. Between the breeze and the blast from the helicopter blades, it's like having two giant fans blowing on you, and a welcome relief from the humid heat we've endured all day.

For some reason I can't explain, I get a strange feeling in the pit of my stomach, as if something is wrong, or we're in danger. As a drip of sweat slowly runs down the center of my back, I scan the set and the estate grounds to see if anything's out of place, anything that might warrant this feeling.

Everything seems to be just fine, except it feels as though someone has pressed the slow-motion button on a DVD player while watching a movie that we all seem to be trapped in. Everything moves in slow motion around me—the helicopter blades, people moving or talking, each second ticking by. Even the loud thump, thump, thump, thump of the helicopter blades is muddled and slowed, as if it's happening under water. The next few minutes feel like months. In my head, I can hear every breath I take. It feels like someone has drugged me. When I take a few steps, it feels as if I'm walking in glue.

Jojo is working the controls of the 'copter as it hovers over our heads, making small adjustments to compensate for the wind. The helicopter stays at the same altitude but seems to slide sideways about twenty feet, placing them directly above where the estate ends and the cliffs begin. Still no concern there; after all, it is a helicopter. Since it is now off to the side of us, I have a better angle and can see all the guys inside. Everything seems to be fine with them too, and, as always, Mike is smiling from ear to ear. He shoots me another thumbs-up.

No one else on the set or in the helicopter seems to be concerned. Why is it, then, that I have such deep, foreboding feeling? Is it just me? Maybe I ate something that isn't agreeing with me. Maybe I've been working too long in this extreme heat and humidity for too many days and it's taking a toll. I know what I'm feeling, and I just can't seem to shake it or justify it.

What I don't know is that this is about to become the most powerful event of my life, changing the way I look at it and experience it forever.

The noise is something I'll never forget—a loud *pop,* so loud it seems to have made me temporarily deaf, because even though I'm still looking at the helicopter, I can't hear the roar of the engine anymore.

Everything seems to go quiet—too quiet. The thump . . . thump . . . thump of the blades has changed to a dry-sounding whoosh . . . whoosh . . . whoosh. The blades seem to slow down so I can see each individual one. For a moment, no one on the set looks too troubled. I can see the faces inside the helicopter. None of them is acting as if anything is wrong—until I catch the look on Jojo's face.

I feel like I'm experiencing vertigo and my head is being pulled through a funnel. The hair on the back of my neck stands straight up. Jojo has a look of terror on his face and seems to be fighting with the controls. I look at Rob standing ten feet away from me. Our eyes lock. He's feeling the same thing I am. For the first time since I've known him, this seasoned stuntman who faces his own death every time he goes to work has a look in his eyes of sheer panic. I quickly raise my eyes back up to the helicopter. Seeing the look of alarm on the guys' faces, I know now that the secret is out. Our worst nightmare is unfolding, and there is nothing any of us can do about it.

Now I realize what that strange quietness is: the sound of the engine is missing. The engine has stalled and shut off.

The nose of the helicopter dips straight down toward the ground hundreds of feet below, over the side of the cliff. It seems to hang there frozen in space for another few seconds. I have never felt so completely helpless. I can't reach out and pull it back to us. Then, as if someone has cut a string, the helicopter drops out of sight down the side of the cliff.

At the same moment, everything goes back into real time. Rob and I run to the edge of the cliff, attempting to chase after the helicopter as it soars into the abyss, as if there is something we can do to stop it, but we quickly realize the futility.

In circumstances like this, everything your mind tells you to do doesn't help—not catching the falling 'copter in your arms, or jumping on the rails like Rambo and pulling everyone out to safety. Your mind races through its files, searching for ways to stop what's happening.

I know I have to get to the bottom of the mountain so I can be there to help the guys. I run as fast as I can across the grounds of the compound, heading for the road that will take me there. As I run past other members of the crew, I'm yelling, "The chopper's going down! The chopper's going down!"

I make it to the road. My running speed seems to increase because of the slope, but it doesn't make it any easier. My lungs are burning, crying out for more oxygen in the hot and humid air. I ignore the painful signals my body is giving me, trying to tell me to stop running. I run faster than I've ever run before. I couldn't stop if I wanted to. I'm being driven by the love I have for my friends and the terror pumping through every vein in my body. I keep telling myself over and over, "Just a little bit further—keep going!"

Coming around a bend in the road, I still can't see the bottom of the cliffs. But what I hear will echo through the caverns of my soul for the rest of my life: an orchestra of horrifying noises all coming to a crescendo at the same time. It's the sound of the major impact you might hear if a speeding train collided with a truck sitting on the tracks: shattering glass, metal crunching and tearing.

My body is burning pure adrenaline, and it helps me find another gear which gets me running even faster. I'm already imagining what I'm going to see. Fear is already taking over, yet I can't let it slow me down. I also have to ignore the pain in my lungs and my muscles. I can't remember my body ever hurting this much before.

I finally clear the last bend in the road. What I see stops me in my tracks. The helicopter is on its side with smoke billowing out. It had nosedived straight down the side of the mountain, crashing headfirst into the road below, then falling over onto its side, a crumpled mess of twisted steel and broken glass.

Its four rotor blades are still attached, but now they are stacked on top of each other. Luckily they hadn't shattered and gone flying like shrapnel, because congregated fifty feet away from where the helicopter has landed are fifty or sixty Filipino men who have been working on the movie as background extras. By sheer luck, the helicopter hadn't landed right on top of them, and the rotor blades hadn't sheared off. It would have been a massacre.

They seem to think this is all part of the movie, because they're all just standing around, looking at the smoking carcass of the helicopter.

I quickly scan the area. Twenty feet past the wreckage, Rami is on the side of the road on his hands and knees. He's conscious and moving, and he's yelling in a language I can't understand. He's from Israel. In between every few words he says in Hebrew, there is a swear word or two in English. I don't care what he's saying. He's alive and well, which means the rest of the guys are too. My level of fear drops considerably. I run past the helicopter to see what I can do to help him. He's bleeding a little from several different areas, and he's in some pain, but basically he looks okay.

"Rami, where are the rest of the guys?" He extends his arm, blood dripping from his fingers, and points back to the helicopter. I slowly pivot 180 degrees. I look inside the helicopter through what used to be the windshield. My heart drops.

Through the smoke pouring out of the large hole in the shattered front windshield lie the bloody, motionless bodies of my friends. Jojo is pinned by the crushed fuselage. The control panel is embedded in his chest. Mike is unconscious, still seat-belted to where he was sitting on the floor, but because the helicopter is now lying on its side, he appears to be suspended in the air, stuck to the wall. John is upside down, his bloodied face contorted and pressed up against the windshield. The rest of the bodies are all piled on top of each other. My first reaction is to just sit down and cry, but I know there's no time. I begin ripping out what's left of the windshield so I can start getting the guys out of the wreck. Right away a bunch of the Filipino guys come over and help. There's no time to check who's alive or who's dead. We just want to get them out before the helicopter catches fire and explodes.

One of the guys helps me lift John, and we run over to a grassy area where Rami is lying. I see a caravan of vehicles and people racing down the hill. As we're fighting to free Jojo from the wreckage, a small fire starts in the grass near the tail. In a matter of seconds, it grows as it ignites the tall grass and brush around it. We fight even harder to free Jojo. I yell to Mike, telling him not to worry, that we're coming for him. I promise him I won't leave him behind. I know he is unconscious and probably can't hear me, but it makes me feel better to say it.

As a few of us rip away the fuselage and control panel pinning Jojo in, a couple of other guys lift him out and carry him into a waiting vehicle. Other guys load John into another vehicle. One by one, we pull our friends out of the wreckage as another group of guys tries to put out the brush fires. Some are using fire extinguishers; others are trying to stamp them out with their feet.

No one sees the fuel from the tanks spraying inside the 'copter. Without warning, the fuel ignites, and helicopter is engulfed in flames. People quickly back away and take cover, fearing it might explode. I go in the opposite direction. Mike is still in there, and I have to get him out. Through the smoke and flames I'm trying to get a visual on him to determine his condition. My nightmare is only getting worse. There are no fire hoses, all of the fire extinguishers are running low, and to my horror I see that Mike's clothes have now caught fire. The only way to get Mike out is to go in and get him, and it has to happen now!

Guys are holding me back, warning me not to get any closer because it could explode at any moment, but I pull away. I can't just leave Mike in there without at least trying to get him out. Luckily we've gotten everyone else out, so it's only Mike we have to focus on. Everyone with a fire extinguisher is now spraying inside the cabin, trying to keep the flames away from him, but because of the intensity of the fire and the amount of smoke, it's hard to see if they are being effective or not. For me there's no time to think of a plan to get Mike out; every second that passes is another second that Mike could be suffering. So I do the only thing I know how to do: jump into the middle of it all. With just a few small steps, my environment is completely transformed.

Inside the helicopter it's what I imagine hell to be like. When I first go in, I hold my breath without knowing it, because as soon as I attempt to inhale, I begin to choke: it's like trying to breathe under water. There's no usable oxygen. Even the sunlight has vanished from my world. The smoke and the airborne powder from the fire extinguishers are so dense that they're squelching it out. It's like being in a black hole in space, because it seems as though not even the fires are giving off any light, but they are radiating intense heat. My skin is being baked. My natural instinct is to get out and run, but I hear a voice in my head say, "If you leave now, you won't be able to get back in again to help Mike."

I feel around in the claustrophobic blackness, stumbling over debris. When I reach the back of the compartment, I finally see Mike, who is engulfed in flames. Most of his clothes are already burnt off. He appears to be levitating above me as if I'm in a scene from some demonic movie. Some of his limbs are so badly charred that they are almost burned completely off. I yell to the guys with the fire extinguishers to zero in on Mike, but it's about as effective as throwing a glass of water on a bonfire. I pray to God to get us out of here as I fight with his burning seat belt, but his body weight is causing too much pressure on the buckle, and I can't get it undone. Then, as if by divine intervention, the seat belt burns through, and Mike falls into my arms.

His skin is as hot as a frying pan, charred black and brittle. Because of the way he lands in my arms, I have to set him down for a moment so that I can get him in a better position. I grab his wrist to prop him up so I can get my arm underneath him, but he is so badly burned, his arm almost comes off in my hands.

This is where I almost lose my sanity. I let God know that I need some help right now, and having this happen is not it. I tell Him they will have to shoot me if Mike's arm comes off, because I will be insane. I scoop my arms underneath Mike and lift him up. My journey of only a few feet feels like the length of a football field. His body feels like it's coming apart in my hands as I carry him over the debris in the cabin.

As quick as I can, I find the exit. In one step the world goes from pitch black to bright and sunny. I hand Mike to someone waiting outside the fuselage. My lungs gasp for air as if I have just broken the surface after being underwater too long. I'm hunched over, holding my knees, coughing up my guts. Even though my jumpsuit is soaked in fuel, for some unknown reason, it hasn't caught fire. Yet my skin is burning from contact with the fuel. I feel relieved that Mike and I are out of there, but my break is short-lived.

I look around and notice a few of the Filipino guys trying to move the wreckage. Then I see why. Trapped under the wreckage is the body of Gadi, the cameraman. He must have fallen out on impact, and then as the 'copter fell over on its side, it landed on top of him. I had only met Gadi a few weeks earlier. As soon as I worked with him, I knew we were going to be friends for life. He was such a genuine guy.

I know that we just can't leave him there. We owe it to him to get him out so that at least his family can have a proper funeral for him. I join the five other men trying to lift the helicopter. The fire's raging inside the wreckage and in the brush around us. In the blink of an eye, the fire flares up, and the heat forces us to back.

He's trapped underneath the wrecked helicopter, and it seems everyone else has decided it's impossible to get him. They're all backing away from the area, terrified the helicopter is going to explode at any moment. I just can't bring myself leave him there. I know he's dead and there isn't anything any of us can do to change that, but I still feel his family deserves the opportunity to see him and say good-bye to him. I make the decision then and there. I don't know how I'm going to get him out. All I know is that I'm going to do it anyway.

I know I only have one shot. I squat and find solid places that I can grip with my hands. I summon every bit of courage, strength, personal power, love, hate, rage, and whatever else I can use to move that helicopter enough to get Gadi free. I take a deep breath, and on the count of three, grunt out every ounce of strength that I can muster. At first it feels like nothing is happening and nothing is moving. Then I feel the 'copter move a few inches, then a couple more, just enough to settle in a new position. Something underneath it must have shifted because as I let go, it stays in the new spot. I quickly grab Gadi under his armpits and pull on him. I tug on him a few times; each time he's a couple inches closer to being freed. Finally, I give him one last jerk, and his body breaks free. I land on my rear end with him in my arms. Guys rush over, pick him up, and carry him away. It's the last time I ever see him.

As I get to my feet, it feels like someone has pulled the plug out of my bathtub. All the adrenaline I used to free Mike and Gadi from the helicopter comes rushing out of my body. Every muscle burns from the strain I just put it through. Again I find myself hunched over, coughing and gasping. I feel I'm never going to ever get enough air to breathe. This hero stuff isn't how it is portrayed in the movies. I have never been in so much pain in so many places on my body all at the same time. My self-pity break is interrupted when I feel a hand on my shoulder. It's stuntman Kinnie Gibson.

"You okay?" he asks.

I nod.

"Do you know CPR?" He has a very concerned look. There's something else he wants to say.

I answered, "Yeah, I know CPR. What's up?"

Kinnie takes a deep breath and slowly lets it out before saying anything. It's as though he's searching for the right words.

I ask again, "Kinnie, what's going on?"

Kinnie takes another breath. There's a look in his eyes of real sadness. In a gentle and kind voice he says, "I know you and Mike have been close friends for a long time."

He's really struggling to finish his sentence. I say, "Kinnie, don't pull any punches. What's going on?"

"Mike's in real bad shape, and I think you should be with him now."

I stand frozen, looking at Kinnie. I heard what he said, but I don't know what to do, or how to respond. I fight back the urge to cry.

"Kurek, Mike needs you to be with him now. Right now!"

He leads me by the arm to where they have placed Mike on the side of the road. When I see him, my heart drops into my stomach. He is lying in the fetal position, barely breathing on his own, almost completely naked because everything has been burned off. His skin is charred and smoking. All of a sudden, reality comes rushing up and slaps me in the face. This day is not over yet. Actually, it's just about to start. We have to get these guys to a hospital somewhere, but where? We are out in the middle of nowhere. There's only one ambulance on the set, and we have eight badly injured men who need emergency care. Yet with all the commotion and chaos, the scene still seems well orchestrated. Different teams have taken responsibility for making sure that each one of the men is being cared for.

I pick up Mike and carry him to where Rico, my private driver, is standing near his car. I had hired Rico the first week in Manila to take care of me while I was working. Without me even asking, Rico opens the back door so I can get in with Mike. As soon as I get him into the car, Bob, the second assistant director, gets in the front seat next to Rico. We join the convoy of vehicles carrying the other guys down the road in search of a hospital. Bob has a walkie-talkie so he can contact all the other vehicles. The communication going back and forth is in Tagalog, the most widely known language of the Philippines. Even though I can't understand what is being said, I can hear that the words are filled with confusion and frustration. We are too far away from Manila to make it to a hospital there, and no one is really sure where the closest one is. We are speeding down a country highway filled with other cars, buses, motorbikes, oxen, cows, people walking on the side of the road, and bicycles. None of the people around us are aware of what has happened up at the Palace in the Sky, or what is going on inside our vehicles. They're just going about their daily lives at the slow speed they are accustomed to.

Mike is lying across my lap in the backseat. His lower legs and feet are hanging out of the window. His breathing is getting weaker with every breath. I keep my hand on his chest so I can feel his heart. It's growing weaker by the second. I know that the time to test my CPR skills is about to begin. His breathing is fading away. I tilt his head back and pinch his nose with my thumb and forefinger. Mike's face is covered with soot and the residue of the jet fuel. It's the only part of his body that didn't get burned.

As I begin giving him mouth-to-mouth, I have to fight the urge to vomit because I can taste the smoke and burnt tissue coming from his lungs. As I'm holding Mike's nose closed with one hand, I'm pushing on his chest trying to keep his heart going with the other. During the long drive to hospital, his heart and breathing keep stopping, and I keep getting them restarted. Five times he dies; five times I bring him back. Each time it gets more difficult. After driving for forty-five minutes, we're only a block away from the hospital. Mike opens his eyes. I tell him to hang on, we're just about there. He looks up at me. His gaze goes straight through me. I think I can hear him speaking to me even though his mouth isn't moving. There is no doubt what he is telling me. Mike's saying good-bye! That's when his breathing and heart stop for the sixth time.

I get this strange feeling that something's just rushed through me, like a wind. There's no other way to describe it. That's how I know this is the end for him. I keep trying to revive him right up until we pull up to the emergency room doors and the trauma staff come rushing up to the car. Even as they open the back door, I keep giving Mike mouth-to-mouth. The doctors have to physically carry him out of the car before I give up on him.

Because all of them are already being used, there are no beds or gurneys left in the emergency room. They lay Mike on a wooden bench from the lobby, using it as a makeshift stretcher. Four of them pick him up and rush him into the emergency room.

I already know it isn't going to make a difference. No matter what happens, he isn't coming back.

On the 15th of May, 1989, my dear friend Mike Graham, twenty-nine years old, died in my arms pulling into the driveway of a hospital in some town I don't know the name of in the Philippines.

The backseat of Rico's car was soaked in Mike's blood. So was I. I sat there for a moment, numb from everything that had happened so far that day, totally drained and tapped out.

I didn't think I had anymore in me. I was already contemplating what I was going to say to Mike's fiancée, Susan, and his mom when I got back to the States. How could I justify the fact that I couldn't do a damn thing to save him? How would I explain to the guys on Mike's American crew that I failed them and let him die?

As I looked up, I saw that they were still bringing some of our guys into the emergency room. I would have to finish this discussion with myself later. It was too late to help Mike, but not too late for the other guys. As I climbed out of the car, Rico stood looking at me. With tears in his eyes he said, "I loved Mr. Mike too, and I am very sorry for your loss. I am honored that I was able to be of service to you both in your time of need." I hugged Rico and thanked him. I told him I would pay for the damage to his car. He said it would be an insult to him if I did. "Mr. Mike was my friend too," he said.

I told him how grateful I was to him for him being there, and that I had to go into the emergency room to help those who were still fighting for their lives. Rico said he would be there when I came out, no matter how late that was. In that moment, Rico represented all of the wonderful Filipino people I had met. They are such a warm and loving nation of people. I gave Rico a grateful smile and then went into the emergency room.

As I walked in, they were pulling a sheet over Mike, who was still lying on the bench. I stopped them so I could have a moment with him. I knelt down next to him. I leaned over him and kissed him on the forehead. I said my good-byes. As I stood up, a staff member finished pulling the sheet over his head. He put his hand on my shoulder and said, "I'm sorry." Then we went right over to assist the doctors working on the other guys.

By the end of the day, the death toll had risen to four. A few days later, it climbed to five. The other three guys—Rami, Mateo, and John—were in seriously bad shape, getting medical care at the hospital at the Clark Air Force Base, an American base in the Philippines. Once they were stable enough to be moved, they were flown back to Los Angeles and admitted to Cedars-Sinai Medical Center until they recovered. I went to see them once while they were there. I haven't seen them again since.

If you get a chance to see *Delta Force 2*, the very last credit roll says, "This film is dedicated with fond remembrance to: Geoff Brewer, Don Marshall, Mike Graham, Gadi Danzig, and Jojo Imperial."

The photograph of Mike and me that was taken that day, just hours before the crash, is the only picture ever taken of us together. If you want to see that photo, and the one of Chuck Norris and me that was also taken that day, go to the gallery section of the *How Would Love Respond?* Web site, www.howwouldloverespond.com.

2

The Promise

*E*verything I have told you so far can be researched. It's in the public domain. What I'm going to tell you next isn't. It's the untold story. It's something I used to share with only my closest friends. These are my most personal and private experiences connected to the friendship I had with Mike and the events that transpired over the years following his death. If parts of my experiences seem hard to believe, I can understand that. As it was happening, it was hard for me to believe it too. Yet it did happen. I know it's true, and I have peace in knowing it. I'm not asking you to change your beliefs in order to understand my story. Just open your mind to it, and know this: the universe works in mysterious ways!

For years after the accident, I wondered why I had stepped out of the helicopter when I did, since staying on would have earned me the easiest $400 I would have made during the filming. I had already completed all the dangerous stunts in the helicopter earlier that day, and the last flight was only supposed to go up fifteen feet. Yet, for some reason, I didn't stay on the helicopter. If I had, I would most likely have died too.

What made me decide to step out? I have always described my decision at that moment as being guided by some force. By the end of this chapter, you will understand why.

Through the powerful, wonderful, and often challenging encounters I had over the two years after the accident, I was given a gift. I feel obligated to share this gift with everyone I can to ensure it will continue to be passed on long after I am gone.

Whether you believe the story or not is up to you, and honestly, that's not what is really important anyway. What's most important for *you* is the message—a message so powerful it has not only changed my life, but it has also positively changed the lives of tens of thousands of people I have worked with through my seminars and workshops. I have never told the people at my programs how I received the message. I used to only deliver the teaching without disclosing where it actually came from. The time has now come for me to share the untold story behind that life-changing message.

Trust in the fact that you didn't pick up this book by accident. When you accept the possibility that there's something in here for you, you will discover what that is. I promise you that it will be worth the investment of time you put into reading this book.

Two Weeks Before the Helicopter Crash

Mike and I were in a Manila bar in Mabini, the nightclub district. It was our night off, and we were having a few drinks. On my way back from the men's room, I saw some guy hassling Mike, getting in Mike's face, trying to pick a fight with him. Mike hated fighting, and, being his normal polite self, he was trying to calm the guy down. But the guy wasn't buying it, and he shoved Mike against the wall.

I raced through the crowd, came up behind the guy, and had him in a choke hold so fast he didn't know what hit him. I was so enraged that I didn't realize how hard I was actually choking him. Seeing the guy was about to lose consciousness, Mike urged me to let him go. He wasn't even upset at the guy for starting the fight. He checked to see if he was all right and apologized for the misunderstanding. The guy walked away, grateful his life was saved.

"Looks like you could use a drink," Mike said and walked me over to the bar. I ordered a scotch straight up, and quickly gulped it down in one swig.

"What! No time for 'cheers'?" Mike laughed.

Across the room I could see the guy who hassled Mike talking with another guy. Every once in a while, they would look in our direction. I guessed they were planning retaliation, or maybe that was just the story I was telling myself. Either way, I was sitting there stewing in my own anger, so instead of it dissipating, it kept growing stronger. All of a sudden, the glass in my hand exploded and shattered into a hundred different pieces. Blood started dripping from the bottom of my hand. My anger had been so intense, my hands clenched with such force, that without even thinking about it I crushed the glass.

"How dramatic," Mike chuckled, checking my hand to see how bad the cut was. It wasn't a serious injury, only a good bleeder. He handed me a cocktail napkin and told me to apply pressure to the wound, then shook his head, laughing, "I can't take you anywhere!" Then he reached over the bar and grabbed an olive fork.

"What are you doing?" I asked. He smiled broadly and then, without answering, jabbed himself in the hand.

"Let's not waste it," he said, grinning like a little boy. "Now we can be blood brothers."

I thought Mike must have watched too many movies when he was a kid. It was a bit over the top, but I liked his style, so I went along with it. Thumb to thumb we grabbed each other's hands, mixing our blood, making the ceremony official. Now this probably wasn't the smartest idea in the world, and when you have a few drinks in you, the desire to make things more dramatic comes into play. I looked Mike in the eye and said, "Mike, as my friend, I love you. And to me, my friends are the most important things in my life. When I call someone my friend, it means I will always be there for them, and with you, Mike, I promise you right now that if the shit ever hits the fan, and we were in any kind of danger together, I will be there with you until the very end!"

Mike nodded. "I know that about you, and I know you mean it when you say it." We gave each other a hug. "Have we had enough melodrama for the night?" he added. We both laughed and went back to drinking and having fun.

Later that night Mike invited me to work with him on the next movie he was booked to do, *Wings of the Apache* (a.k.a. *Fire Birds*), with Nicolas Cage. It involved military helicopters again, and he wanted me to do all the camera mounts with him. This was really turning out to be the biggest year of our lives so far. We were finally making the transition from low-budget to big-budget films and the better pay that goes with them.

For the rest of that night, Mike and I had a great time going from bar to bar. We caught up with some of the other stunt guys and crew members and stayed out until early morning. All we had to do was get showered to get ready for the work day ahead, since a private bus would pick us up for work at 4 A.M., so all we had time to do to prepare for the workday ahead was get showered and get on the bus on time. We knew we could sleep during the three-hour bus ride to location and that there would also be enough time during the day to catch up on extra sleep, so it didn't really bother anyone that we didn't get any sleep that night. After all, this was what being on location was all about.

About a Week after the Helicopter Crash

I'd asked the production company if they could fly me to San Francisco so I could escort Mike's body to his mother's house. He was an only child, and I knew his mother would be taking it very hard. His fiancée, Susan, was also flying up from Los Angeles to meet us. I wanted to be there to answer any questions they might have. The media were already doing their job of misinforming people, and I didn't want Susan or Mike's mom to be fed any rumors. It was only two weeks earlier that I had promised Mike I would take care of him no matter what. I was committed to keeping my promise. At the time, I believed that bringing him home to be buried would be the end. I would soon find out I was mistaken.

There was a mix-up as I was leaving the Philippines. Mike's casket and I got put on different flights home, and then my plane was delayed a full day due to mechanical problems. By the time I finally made it to San Francisco, I had already missed Mike's funeral service. It was okay with me. I had already said my good-byes.

Susan and Mike's mom picked me up at the airport and drove me straight to the cemetery. Seeing his grave wasn't that emotional for me; to me, it was just a mound of dirt and a headstone. I didn't associate it with Mike, since I hadn't been to the funeral. I placed on his grave a little American flag, a rubber chicken, and a flag I'd made from a T-shirt Mike had printed in Manila. Susan understood the significance, but I had to explain it to Mike's mom. Since I was the only one of Mike's crew to come to San Francisco, I represented us all. The rubber chicken was a mascot we took to every movie we worked on. We were famous for sneaking it into different scenes in each of our movies. We would surreptitiously put it in the background in places only the most observant viewer would notice. One of our best examples is the movie *Crack House*. We were over the moon when we went to the screening and saw the chicken in fifty-two different places! It was our own private joke that bonded us as a crew.

On the shirt Mike had printed was the rubber chicken with the caption, "Mike and the Griptamizers on the paradise tour." He had one printed for every crew member in the Philippines and for each member of his L.A. crew as well. He had designed the chicken to look really fat. When I'd asked why, he'd said that since we were starting to work on big-budget movies, we would all be eating better, including the mascot chicken. It was also the shirt Mike was wearing the day he died. So I cut the shirt he had given me into the shape of a flag, stapled it to a stick, and stuck it into the mound of his grave, along with his personal rubber chicken.

Susan hugged me and said, "That's the way Mike would have wanted it to be."

I spent a day with them before they dropped me off at my hotel. That past week had been the longest of my life, and, at the same time, it was so surreal that it didn't feel as if any of it was really happening at all.

That evening I was sitting on my bed in the hotel room reading with the TV on. In my peripheral vision, I noticed something move near the hallway leading to the bathroom and the front door. I thought I'd locked the door, but obviously not, because someone had just walked in. Without looking up from my book, from the corner of my eye, I could see someone standing in the room by the hallway. I didn't feel threatened or scared. I just figured it must be someone who worked for the hotel, so I kept reading to finish the paragraph I was on.

Suddenly it struck me as strange that they didn't knock or announce themselves as they came in, and now they were just standing there. I glanced over to see who it was. It wasn't someone from room service. It wasn't someone who worked for the hotel. It was the person I least expected to be standing in my room. I knew I wasn't dreaming, because I wasn't asleep! I even shook my head a few times to make sure.

In plain view, Mike stood in the doorway of my room, wearing the same T-shirt and khaki shorts he'd been wearing the last time I'd seen him. The only difference was that he wasn't burned or injured in any way. He looked the same as he always had prior to the crash. With his curly blond hair and big ear-to-ear smile, there was no mistaking him. It was Mike!

Back in the Philippines, it was normal for us guys to just walk into each other's rooms; we always left our doors propped open. So when I saw Mike walk in, it didn't seem that out of place at first. I suddenly thought that the entire last week had been a figment of my imagination. Relieved, I started explaining it to Mike.

"Man, you wouldn't believe this terrible nightmare I had," I began. "I dreamed we were all in a helicopter crash, and the real messed-up part is that you and some of the other guys were killed. Damn, Mike—it was so real, it felt like it really happened."

A smile came across Mike's face.

"What's so funny?" I asked.

He didn't answer. I looked around to see what was so amusing, and then I glanced out the window and saw the city skyline. It took me a moment, and then it hit me: I wasn't in my hotel room in Manila anymore. It was San Francisco outside my window. It wasn't a bad dream after all. It had really happened, and I was here to escort Mike's body home to his mother. But if that were true, how could he be standing right here, in my room?

I slowly turned my head back to look at Mike. His smile grew even bigger. Obviously he was amused by my discovery. I was glad he thought it was funny, because I was having a harder time with it. At no time did I feel scared—just really confused. I had so many things to say, and so much to ask, yet no words were coming out of my mouth. I must have looked like a deer staring into the headlights of an oncoming car. Mike didn't say anything, but I had a feeling he wanted to.

Neither of us made the first move to speak up. We just looked at each other for a moment, and then he turned away and walked down the hallway. I jumped off the bed as fast as I could, wanting to grab him before he got to the door. But as I came around the corner, he was gone. I threw open the door, yelling out to him, "Mike, wait, don't go!" I looked down the hallway in both directions. He wasn't there. The only person visible was a housekeeper, and you should have seen how startled she was! I tried to come up with an excuse for my behavior but couldn't think of one, so I retreated to my room, closing the door behind me.

I leaned back against the door and tried to take in what had just transpired. Maybe I was temporarily insane because of all the stress. But that didn't make sense, because I knew I really had seen Mike standing in front of me. I quickly flipped on the light to the bathroom, as if I might find him hiding there. Then I opened the closet. Again no luck. My mind struggled to get a handle on the situation.

I had absolutely no doubts that I had just seen Mike standing here. He was as real as the TV across the room, and even though we didn't talk with each other, we still interacted. On the other hand, I knew this was impossible. Only a few hours earlier I placed the rubber chicken on his grave. Totally perplexed, I walked across the room and sat on the floor with my back against the bed so I could face the hallway in case Mike decided to visit again. The next morning, I woke up cold with kinks in my body from sleeping on the floor in the same position all night.

Without seeing Mike again, I flew home to Los Angeles.

If seeing Mike in San Francisco that day were only an isolated incident, I most likely would have passed it off as stress-related, and I probably wouldn't be writing about it now. But it wasn't. It was only the beginning of the most challenging and traumatic two years of my life.

At the end of those two years, the entire experience would culminate in a wonderful and powerful event that would radically change the direction of my life.

What I do with my life now—helping people from all walks of life to achieve more and realize their dreams—is a direct result of what this event gave to me. I now know that the reason I was compelled to step off the helicopter that day, the reason I am still alive, was to experience those two years with Mike following his death in the crash, and to follow through on all the insights that resulted from our time together.

I have come to understand that *you always get what you ask for and that it rarely comes in the package you think it is supposed to.* Who could have predicted that a helicopter crash in which five men lost their lives would be the catalyst that facilitated such a positive change in so many people's lives, including mine?

Yours, too, when you let it!

———

Back in Los Angeles, I wasn't coping too well. Depression had set in. I started having nightmares about the crash. Every night they would play over and over in my mind. What really made them scary was that the whole scenario seemed to be from someone else's point of view—it wasn't what I saw or experienced that day at all. Instead of looking up at the helicopter, I would be in the cabin, belted in, and experiencing the crash from the inside. I would glance out the open doorway and see the people on the ground looking up at us. I'd even recognize myself as one of the people looking up from down there.

Then all of a sudden the 'copter would radically accelerate, nosediving toward the ground below. There was no doubt as to what would happen next. I'd feel my body tense up as I tried to prepare for the inevitable. A few seconds later, I'd feel my body violently jerk forward, I'd hear loud noises of metal crushing and glass breaking, and then, in a flash, it would all go black and silent.

I would feel as if I had woken up and opened my eyes, but everything would still be dark. I wouldn't be sure where I was. Had I survived? Was I still in the nightmare, or was I dead? I'd be soaked in sweat, my heart pounding as if it was trying to jump out of my chest. It would take me a moment to get my bearings. Then when I finally did, I'd be relieved and grateful to discover I was back in my bedroom in Los Angeles.

These flashbacks or nightmares left me perplexed because I had always heard that if you die in one of your dreams, you'll die in real life. Yet night after night I'd keep having the same dream, and each time I'd have the dream, it would always end the same way: I'd die.

Thinking about these dreams, I was at a loss to explain why I was experiencing the crash from the inside. And how could it be, I wondered, that I also saw myself on the ground, looking up at the sky? None of it made any sense.

3

The Encore

Two months after the crash, I received a call from the production company asking me to return to finish filming the movie. Regardless of the fact that people had died, business is business, and, as they say in Hollywood, "The show must go on." None of us who had been in the Philippines had any desire to go back there, so the company decided to change locations. We wound up in Johnson City, Tennessee. The set designers went to work, adding palm trees and set pieces to make the mountains of Tennessee look like the jungles of the Philippines. When you see the movie, it's almost impossible to tell the difference.

When those of us who had been in Manila saw each other again, we had mixed feelings. On one hand, we were happy to see each other; on the other, it was discomforting to be reminded of all we had been through, and those we lost.

We all lost the same friends, and we all found our own ways of dealing with it—or, for some of us, temporarily blocking it out.

As I arrived on set for my first day back, I discovered the first thing I would be working on was re-shooting the scene we were working on when the helicopter crashed.

"Redoing the scene? What do you mean?" I asked. It never occurred to me that we would have to face that scene again. Aaron explained that the camera, along with the film inside it, was destroyed in the crash, so we'd have to redo the scene to complete the movie. There would be one difference, though: this time the camera would be on the ground, and it would film us in the helicopter, taking off and flying away.

I wasn't afraid of flying or of being in the helicopter again because I'd already lived through one crash. What were the odds of it happening again?

I walked over to where we were going to shoot and saw another helicopter painted to look just like the one we'd had in the Philippines. We were on top of another mountain with the helicopter perched close to the edge of the cliff, the same way as before at the Palace in the Sky. Putting on my best game face, I climbed into the back of the 'copter, sat with my legs hanging out the doorway, and mounted the machine gun attached to the rail. Rob climbed in on the other side and straddled his M60 there. They put a dummy dressed up like John in the copilot seat because he was too injured to finish the movie. For safety reasons only Rob, Mischa (the pilot), and I took this flight to keep the weight down on board. Plus, they thought that if anything went wrong this time, the number of casualties would be minimized. Now there's an encouraging thought!

The helicopter began to rumble and vibrate as Mischa started the engines and the blades began their high-speed rotation. The inside of the helicopter, the smell of exhaust coming from the engine, the wind from the spinning blades—I remembered it all too well. The last time I had been in a helicopter was that fateful day. I tried to fight off the memories flooding my mind. I knew I couldn't let them get to me.

It dawned on me that I had been reliving these exact events over and over again in my nightly dreams. I quietly began scrutinizing the faces of everyone around me, searching for some kind of sign that they too might be having a hard time. Were they having nightmares too? I couldn't see it. Everyone seemed to be behaving as if nothing had ever happened. I started to wonder: Why was I such a wreck? Why was I feeling so much anxiety? I began to notice where this line of questioning was taking me. I was getting worked up, so I quickly changed my internal dialogue to something a little more motivating. I told myself, "If you want to freak out, save it for later. Right now you have a job to do."

Aaron told everyone to get ready because he was set to shoot. Mischa pulled up on the throttle as the helicopter began to lift off. The rumbling inside intensified as the rotor blades picked up speed. Cameras were rolling. Rob and I got into character.

Aaron yelled out, "Action!" It happened that fast, and we were back making the movie. The 'copter lifted about twenty feet off the ground. My machine gun was pointed directly at the cameras below us, as if they were the bad guys we were trying to kill. As I pulled the trigger, brass ammo casings started pouring out the side of the machine gun, and I remembered why I liked this job so much. The toys I got to play with were awesome!

The 'copter glided horizontally, simulating a real military maneuver. Without noticing, we drifted out over the edge of the cliff, and then, without any warning, we immediately started to drop, nose first, down the side of the mountain. Before we fell out of sight, I saw the looks on the faces of the crew members standing near the camera, including Aaron. I recognized shock and helplessness written all over them. Jaws dropped open in horror, and I could read some lips as they mouthed, "Oh no!" and, "Oh my God!"

I remembered how it felt to be one of those people on the ground, totally powerless to do anything about it. Now I was one of the people in the helicopter feeling what the guys must have felt that day in Manila. Suddenly I was overcome with the sensation of déjà vu. Once again, I got the feeling of my head being pulled through a funnel. It was as though I knew everything that was going to happen next.

That experience of looking out the helicopter door and seeing the people staring at us with terror on their faces—I knew I'd seen it all somewhere before. I knew that as we dropped out of sight over the ridge, I would look up to see the film crew rush to the edge of the cliff and stare down at us.

Right on cue, it happened. As I looked out the front windshield of the 'copter, I saw the ground rushing up to meet us. Sweat was pouring down my face as we nose-dived toward earth. I was actually trapped in a live version of the nightmares I had every night for the past two months.

I remembered once seeing an episode of *The Twilight Zone* in which three astronauts came back from space and were in the hospital talking about their experience. One by one, they started to disappear, to cease to exist, because they weren't supposed to have made it back. They were supposed to have died out there in space and somehow slipped through a crack in time. But the universe made up for the mistake and wiped them out because the rule is, "What is supposed to be must be."

I was thinking maybe this was about to happen to Rob and me. Maybe we weren't supposed to have stepped off that helicopter two months ago. Maybe we weren't supposed to have survived.

Tomorrow's headlines started running through my head: "Stuntmen Survive Helicopter Crash Only to Be Killed in Same Crash Two Months Later!"

Mischa was handling the control sticks. Rob and I were now lying on our backs on the floor of the cabin, our arms locked to make sure neither of us would fall out. We felt the helicopter pick up speed as we raced toward the ground. Rob was one of the toughest stuntmen I knew. When I saw the same look of fear on his face that I was sure I had on mine, it did nothing to boost my confidence. It was clear we were in real trouble. I knew that impact was only seconds away.

Right at the moment I was expecting the crash, it suddenly felt as if someone had placed big blocks of cement on my chest. I was pinned down and couldn't get up. The tail rotor screamed under the strain. Rob and I started to slide back headfirst across the floor toward the rear until we were pressed up against the back wall. Then it felt like being on a roller coaster racing up a giant hill. I tried to look out the windshield to see what was happening. All I could see were the tops of trees as we roared over them.

Mischa had pulled a rabbit out of his hat and managed to stop us from crashing.

He knew exactly how to handle the situation. As we went out over the cliff, he had used the increased air speed of the helicopter to create lift and pull it out of the dive.

As soon as we had leveled off and Rob and I knew that we were out of danger, we rose back to our feet and resumed our position in the doorway, manning our guns again. We glanced back at each other, smiling.

"I won't tell if you don't," Rob said, referring to our holding on to each other, fearing for our lives. It's one of those stuntman codes: don't let anyone see you're scared.

Mischa safely landed the helicopter in the same spot where we had started. After shutting down the engines, he and Rob disembarked. I stayed on board for a few extra minutes, sitting in the position I had assumed when I thought we were going crash. I was still mystified as to why everything that just happened had matched up so perfectly with my recurring bad dreams. Everything looked the same, only the location was different.

That's when the realization hit me like a ton of bricks. The spot I was sitting in is the exact spot I occupy in my dreams. Everything that I see happening in my dreams is from that spot and point of view. It was also the exact same spot where Mike had sat the day he lost his life! They might have been dreams, but the fact was that I had been seeing all my flashbacks through his eyes, through his perception. Yet could that be? I wasn't in the helicopter with Mike when it crashed. How *could* I see everything happening from where he was sitting? And why?

4

Rock Bottom

After ten more weeks filming in Tennessee, I returned to my life in Los Angeles. The nightmares were still waking me up, and I was getting used to living on only a few hours of sleep every night. It reached the point where I was doing whatever I could to avoid going to sleep altogether.

Being tired seemed less painful than going through all of those flashbacks. I'd stay up all night watching TV and only sleep the very minimum needed to survive. Most days I walked around in a funk, exhausted from lack of sleep and numb with depression.

Just when I thought it couldn't get any worse, the bottom dropped out, and my world came crashing down even further.

Someone from the media called Mike's mom in San Francisco and told her a lie. They said on the day of the crash, I had driven off and left Mike on the side of the road to die. Being in such a fragile emotional state, Mrs. Graham believed their story. I tried to defend my integrity and my actions, but she didn't want to hear my side of the story. She was convinced that what they said to her was true. It hurt horribly to listen to her accusations. It felt like being stabbed in the chest. After pleading my case over and over, I finally managed to calm her down, but I knew she wasn't convinced. I had to surrender to the notion that this would have to be a good enough result, because I just didn't have anymore strength left.

With each passing day, I felt my life falling apart. My brother, Steve, came up with an accurate way to describe my life at the time. He would say, "Kurek, if you didn't have bad luck, you wouldn't have any luck at all." That's exactly how it felt.

One night, after finally falling asleep, I awoke to the sense that there was an intruder in my house. I could hear someone moving. As my eyes were adjusting, I thought I could make out a silhouette standing in the doorway of my room. I squinted, trying to get a clearer view. I was afraid to say anything, fearing it might be someone breaking in to rob or kill me. I stayed frozen in my bed wondering if someone was really standing there, or if it was just my eyes playing tricks. It didn't take long for me to find out. The silhouette took a step toward me. There was definitely someone there. My heart started racing even faster as I slowly reached for the pistol I kept by the side of my bed. The shadowy shape took another step.

I knew that if I was going to move, now was the time. With all the courage I could muster, I leapt out of bed with my pistol pointing straight at the intruder's chest. By now I could see his shape more clearly.

"Who are you?" I asked. "What are you doing in my house?"

No answer. The intruder just stood there. Then, without saying a word, he turned and slowly walked out of my bedroom and into the living room. I made my way across my bedroom in pursuit. As I reached the doorway, I felt around the wall for the light switch. With nervous anticipation, I flicked on the lights. I looked around my bedroom to see if someone else might be hiding there. No one.

Slowly, I made my way into the living room, my gun still pointing in front of me. I perused the room. No one! The doors were still closed, and so were all the windows. Nothing seemed to be tampered with or out of place. I turned on every light in the house as I cautiously checked every room. Nothing was moved or disturbed, and still I found no one. But I knew what I had seen. Where was he?

Needless to say, I was a little freaked out. Even though I didn't find anyone in the house, something still didn't feel right. I felt as though I wasn't alone, as though I was being watched. I didn't get anymore sleep that night. I just stayed up like a sentry on guard duty, waiting for the intruder to come back.

After a few days, I concluded the whole experience was just a product of being tired and stressed out. After a couple of weeks, I forgot about it.

Until it happened again.

This time I awoke when I felt someone actually sitting on the foot of my bed. I froze, pretending to be asleep. Slowly, I peered out of one eye. Sure enough, sitting on the edge of my bed was what appeared to be the same silhouette. Every muscle in my body tensed up. My brain was racing to find a way to handle this situation.

I waited for the person to say or do something, but he didn't. Gradually my fear morphed into curiosity, then subsided altogether. I started feeling very calm. Somehow I knew I wasn't in any danger. Although I couldn't make out who it was in the dark, I could feel his energy, and it felt familiar. I thought it might be my roommate, Dave, who lived in an adjoining part of the house. Maybe it was one of my friends sneaking into my house as a joke. Whoever it was, I somehow had the feeling I was going to be all right.

I had learned my lesson after the incident a couple weeks earlier. This time I was better prepared. I slowly glided my hand across the sheet under the covers and felt down the side of the bed for the flashlight I had placed there. As soon as I turned it on, the beam of light filled the entire room with a soft glow.

Sure enough, I was right. There *was* someone sitting at the foot of my bed. It took me a few moments to register who it was. We both sat there in silence, looking at each other. I closed my eyes, thinking that when I opened them everything would be back to normal. When I opened them, he was still there.

He finally spoke up. "Are you okay?"

I really didn't know how to answer. I just sat there calmly looking at him. By this point I was already resigned to the fact that I had lost my mind. I just figured that since I thought I was seeing him, I might as well go along with it. What did I have to lose? Finally I broke my own silence by asking the only question I could think of asking.

"Mike, what are you doing here?"

The flashlight started to flicker, then went out. Instantly the room was dark again. I tried to get the flashlight to work. Nothing happened, so I got out of bed and found my way to the light switch on the wall. When I turned it on, Mike was gone. I slid to the floor, tears welling up in my eyes. I didn't know if I was crying because I thought I had just seen Mike or because I thought I was cracking up. Both possibilities overwhelmed me.

I had mixed feelings about my situation. If I really had seen Mike, that could be a good thing because I'd get to spend more time with him. I couldn't believe I was thinking this way. I knew he was dead!

I thought, "Have I just turned into one of those people you see walking down the street talking to someone who isn't there?" Then I wondered, "Do they see the person that they're talking to as clearly as I see Mike? Is this what going insane feels like?"

I stayed on the floor for the rest of the night, my arms wrapped around one of the legs of my desk, trying to hold on to something that felt solid, because nothing else in my life seemed to be.

I tried to tell some of my friends that I had seen Mike, and the response I got from them was pretty much the same. They'd say, "You just went through a traumatic experience, so it's understandable that your mind might be playing tricks on you."

The more the days and weeks passed, the worse I seemed to be dealing with it all. Even though I knew I tried to do my very best for all the guys at the time of the accident, I still felt I failed by not being able to save my friends. To make matters worse, I was starting to feel tormented about another incident that occurred five or six days after Mike's death.

I was sitting in my hotel room in Manila feeling numb from the Valium injection the hotel doctor gave me the day before. Apparently a bunch of stunt guys returning to our hotel after a day in town found me curled up in the middle of the hotel lobby, crying like a baby after I'd collapsed, unable to get up.

Because of the state I was in, no one from the hotel wanted to deal with me, so they'd just left me there sobbing and talking gibberish until the stunt guys found me and picked me up. They'd carried me to my room. Then they had the hotel doctor give me the Valium shot so I couldn't do anything to harm myself.

The next day when the phone rang in my room, I was startled into consciousness. It was the stunt coordinator, Dean Ferrandini, calling me from the Clark Air Force Base Hospital where he was looking after the four guys who had survived the crash. Dean had been there every day and night since the crash. His voice sounded strained and tired. Out of all of the guys, Geoff was in the worst shape. He was in a coma. Dean sat next to Geoff's bed every night keeping vigil over him. All of the other stunt guys had already taken turns watching over Geoff. Dean asked if I would come to the hospital to do the final night shift tonight. He knew that Geoff and I had been friends for a long time, and that there was no way I would turn him down. It was to be the last shift, because Geoff's wife, brother, and father were flying in from the United States and would be at the hospital in the morning.

At around 5 P.M. that day, I arrived at the base and met Dean in the lobby of the hospital. He looked more tired than he had sounded on the phone. He was running purely on reserve energy. As we rode up in the elevator, he explained that Geoff was stable and breathing on his own. The only thing that I had to do was sit in the room, keep him company, and make sure he was cared for.

Geoff's room was directly across the hallway from the elevator. It only took me a few steps to see him lying unconscious in his bed, connected to all kinds of machines and with tubes coming out of his nose and mouth. As I stood in the doorway of his room, a feeling of helplessness engulfed me again. Dean put his hand on my shoulder and just said, "Thanks." Then, with what appeared to be the last of his energy, he made his way to the elevator.

As the elevator doors closed, I walked back into Geoff's room and sat down next to his bed. I couldn't get over the fact that Mike, Don, Gadi, and Jojo were dead, and now I was watching Geoff fight for his life. It didn't seem fair that such a young, good-looking guy, whose son had turned two years old only a few days ago, could be in a situation like this.

I remembered hearing somewhere that if you talk to someone in a coma, he might be able to hear you and that sometimes it can help. At this point, I was willing to try anything or believe anything that might give me a shimmer of hope. I talked to Geoff about anything and everything I could think of. There were times when it seemed to work. I would talk about certain things, and it seemed he would respond. More than likely it was just my wishful thinking or, maybe more appropriately, my wishful hoping!

All night long, I sat in that chair talking to Geoff until the sun came through the window. I must have fallen into a sort of trance, babbling away about nothing, because I was startled into consciousness when the phone rang.

"Is this Kurek?" asked a voice.

"Yes, it is," I replied. The caller identified himself as Charlie Brewer, Geoff's brother. He said he was downstairs at reception with Geoff's wife and their father, and asked me how Geoff was doing. I told him he was still in a stable condition and must be getting better, because he was responding with his breathing when I talked to him.

Charlie said this was very good news and then informed me they were on their way up. Just hearing they were already there gave me the ray of hope I'd been waiting for. Knowing his family was there made me feel everything was going to get better. As soon as I hung up, I started to tell Geoff the great news. Again his breathing seemed to become less labored and smoother, as if he was responding.

Across the hall I heard the elevator bell ring. In less than thirty seconds they would be walking into the room. I turned to tell Geoff the news. His family was here. Halfway through my sentence, Geoff took a full single deep breath in, and then peacefully let it out. Then, without any notice or fanfare, he stopped breathing altogether. The monitor measuring his heartbeat stopped beeping and produced a solid, steady tone.

I begged him, "Oh no, please, Geoff, not now! Please don't die now!" I recognized the look on his face. I had seen it only a few days before on Mike: the look of surrender. Geoff's fight was over. He chose to let go, and I knew he wasn't coming back.

As I was lifting up the remote unit to press the call button, Geoff's wife and family walked in. I couldn't move or say anything. I was paralyzed. I stood staring at them as the tears started rolling down my cheeks. They approached the bed, not realizing what had happened. They didn't notice Geoff wasn't breathing. They saw me crying.

"Are you okay?" Charlie asked. "What's the matter?"

"I'm sorry."

At first they didn't understand. There was an awkward moment of silence. No one said a word, no one moved.

I could see the realization slowly register on their faces. They turned to look at Geoff. All of a sudden, the steady drone coming from the heart monitor stuck out like a burglar alarm.

Charlie took a deep breath and turned to look at me still holding the call button. The tone in his voice had changed. He was no longer concerned about my feelings or well-being. "I spoke to you less than two minutes ago, and you said Geoff was doing fine! You even told me you thought he was going to make a full recovery! What the hell happened? Why didn't you call for help?"

I tried to reply, but I was choking on my tears. I didn't know how to tell them that I knew Geoff had surrendered his fight to live.

"After I hung up the phone with you, I started talking to Geoff," I said. "I told him you guys were here and on your way up to see him."

"Then what happened?" Charlie asked.

"I don't know," I said. "He was here a minute ago, and now he's not. I'm sorry!"

Without warning, Geoff's wife slapped me hard across the face. There was hate in her eyes.

"It's because of you that my husband is dead," she sobbed. "You killed my husband."

"But I didn't do anything, I was just talking," I began, but she cut me off.

"That's right, you didn't do anything, and now he's dead. Get out!"

She pointed toward the door. I didn't know what to do. I wanted to apologize, but for what?

She repeated her command, "Get out!"

I was still very confused as I looked back at Geoff lying there, then at his dad and brother.

"Now!" she demanded.

I know she wasn't really mad at me or blaming me. She was in shock, and she was just looking for some way to take away her pain. It still didn't make me feel any better about what had just happened.

Feeling emotionally pummeled, I walked out.

———

With every day that passed, I became consumed with depression. From the moment my eyes opened in the morning, I was depressed. I must have been depressed even while I slept—that is, when I slept. The nightmares did a good job of making sure I wasn't doing much of that.

As a result of the depression, I started indulging in a lot of disempowering behavior. All my life I had tried to get my parents to stop smoking because I thought it was such a nasty habit, yet now I started smoking myself because the nightmares were getting worse, and I was terrified of sleeping.

During the day I was clean and sober because I had to work. The nights were a different story. I would go into the gang neighborhoods of Los Angeles in the middle of the night to buy cocaine. It reached the point at which I was snorting three to five grams up my nose every night. Then I would drink excessive amounts of alcohol to balance out the hyped-up feeling from all the cocaine I was using.

It was like I was living my life in a washing machine. It was a vicious circle that kept going round and round, and there seemed to be no way to get out of it.

I wasn't doing these things to party. I was doing them in an attempt to stop myself from thinking. I was trying to get myself weak enough to kill myself.

The strange thing about all of this is that I had already been reading personal development books and going to seminars for ten years prior to the crash. I was the one who would help other people when they were depressed or grieving, and now I couldn't even help myself. My entire world felt like it was imploding, and I was being crushed in the middle.

My friends and family attempted to help me through my emotional funk. It wasn't working. It finally reached the point at which most of them gave up trying because it was so frustrating for them to watch me spiral out of control in front of them. My life was in a terrible tailspin, and tonight it was about to take a turn for the worse.

———

It was about 1 A.M., and like every other night, I was still up watching television. I was such an emotional wreck I found myself crying at commercials, cartoons, and reruns of old shows. I felt completely lost. I just couldn't see how anything was going to change. There seemed to be no light at the end of the tunnel. Every tomorrow was going to be a repeat of the painful day I had suffered through today. I was so physically and mentally tired that the only thing I could think about was how to stop this merry-go-round. I couldn't take it anymore.

That night I made a decision to stop my suffering.

I walked into my bedroom. I looked around to see if there was anything that might change my outlook—something that would show me I was worth being spared. There was nothing. I walked over to the side of my bed, reached underneath it, and pulled out what I thought would be my ticket to freedom. I opened the cylinder to make sure the chambers were loaded. It was really just an exercise in redundancy because I knew that it was always loaded.

I knelt down at the foot of my bed, leaning on it with my elbows as if it was a pew in a church. I could taste the gunpowder, the cleaning solution, and the cold steel of my Smith & Wesson .357 Magnum as I put the barrel in my mouth. I cocked the hammer and placed my finger on the trigger. Now came the hard part—getting up the courage to take the next step.

Actually, I take that back. It's not courage you need. Suicide isn't an act of courage; it's a display of weakness. In order to commit suicide, you have to weaken your inherent survival system to the point at which it loses its ability to protect you from your own self-destruction. That's why when so many people actually go through with it they have to get drunk or high first. It's the only way they can get their bodies to override their own defense systems.

I was no different. With the help of cocaine and alcohol, I had finally weakened enough to take the first step. I squeezed my eyes shut, anticipating how bad this was going to hurt when the bullet penetrated my skull. I was trying to think about what excuse I was going to use when I faced the Creator to explain why I took my life. Sweat was streaming down my forehead. My hand holding the gun was trembling with fear.

I told myself I would count to three, and that when I got to three, it was time to pull the trigger. Yes, that was it! I'd do the clichéd three-count routine. It always worked before when someone dared me to do something stupid, like jump into a cold lake or pool in the middle of winter in Chicago.

I was about to start the countdown when I decided to take the gun out of my mouth for a moment. I started talking to the empty room. I told my mom and dad that I loved them. I also told them how sorry I was for turning out to be such a disappointment. Then I started thinking about my five brothers and my sister. I sent them a mental good-bye message. Once I finished, I placed the gun back in my mouth. Once again, I squeezed my eyes shut as if it was somehow going to make what I had to do easier. Then I started my countdown.

"One." Then a long pause. "Two." Another long pause. "Three." And then nothing. There was nothing but dead silence.

I couldn't do it. I had chickened out. I knelt there breathing hard with the gun still in my mouth. I couldn't believe I'd actually gotten to three. That seemed like a big feat to me. I didn't think I'd even get that far. Slowly, I took the gun out of my mouth and laid it on the bed. I made sure to release the hammer, gently easing it back into the safety position so it wouldn't go off by accident. I remained kneeling at the foot of the bed, contemplating how and when I would make my next attempt.

Again I was torn between two worlds. On one hand, I was embarrassed that I didn't follow through, and on the other, I was relieved that I was still here.

Suddenly, from behind me, I heard someone standing at the door of my room. I thought it might be my roommate Dave. I had been so involved in my own world that I hadn't even heard him walk up. My body blocked his view as I slipped my pistol under the blankets in front of me.

"What are you doing?" he asked me.

"Oh nothing, I was just sitting here." It was the only response I could come up with quickly. "What are you doing up at this hour?" I asked.

He didn't answer. I began to feel uncomfortable. How much had he seen?

I turned around to look at him.

Dave was nowhere to be seen. Instead it was Mike standing in the doorway with a big smile on his face again. This time there was no mistaking what I was seeing. This time all the lights were on. And I wasn't sleeping either. I know for a fact that I heard him talk to me.

The only thing I could think to say was, "Why are you here?"

He took a moment before saying anything. "Do you remember what happened in the Philippines?"

I got up and sat at the foot of my bed. I could feel the shape of my gun tucked under the blanket. Considering that just moments ago I had it in my mouth, and knowing that I had it there because I was trying to escape the nightmare of the crash, I thought his question was a bit ridiculous.

Mike seemed as if he too was embarrassed by his question. Seeing each other in this context was a new experience for us both, and neither one of us was really ready for it. There was a question I was aching to ask, but I didn't know any tactful way to frame it, so I just came out with it.

"Mike, do you know that you're dead?"

Mike clearly did know, and he wasn't happy about it. He didn't think it was fair that he was dead at twenty-nine. There were so many other things he wanted to do that he wouldn't get to do now. He was upset because he felt there were so many other things he wanted to do that would never happen now. He was most upset at the fact that he hadn't seen Susan for months because he had been on location working on the film, and because he hadn't gotten the chance to say good-bye to her properly because of the crash.

I felt frustrated because I knew there was nothing I could do to ease that pain for him. Instead, I tried to change the direction of the conversation.

"Mike, you're my great friend, and I love you being here. You know that, right?" He nodded yes. "Well, since you know you're dead, and I know you're dead, then what are you doing here, and why do you keep visiting me?"

Mike sat down at my desk and began to tell me everything he knew about the crash. To my amazement he knew everything about it. He said that right after the helicopter hit the ground, he was already floating out of his body, looking down. I couldn't hold back my tears as he recalled my going into the helicopter to get him out, and everything that happened while we were inside the burning fuselage.

"I was counting on you as my friend to get me out," he said, "and you played your part just the way you were supposed to— right on cue."

Floating above the crash site, he said, he could see everything everyone was doing. He even knew about the car ride to the hospital and how it ended.

"Mike, since we both know you died in my arms," I persisted, "what are you doing here?"

"That's what I want to talk to you about," he said. "I don't know how else to tell you, so I'm just going to come right out with it. At the moment I died, I rushed you."

"What do you mean?"

Mike explained that as his body was dying, he attached his soul energy to me because he thought it would be his only chance to say good-bye to Susan. I thought back to the time in the car in the Philippines when I was trying to resuscitate Mike. Just as he died for the last time, I'd felt a fresh breeze flowing right through me. Listening to Mike, I just figured out what caused that feeling.

That's also when the flashbacks of the crash from inside the helicopter started to make sense. I had been seeing it all from Mike's actual point of view. He agreed and added that he had been giving me the flashbacks as a way to communicate with me.

"But why? Why would you do that to me?" I asked.

"Because I'm not ready to go yet."

"Mike, it's a little late," I argued. "You *are* dead, and there's nothing I can do about that."

"I know that. There's something else I need your help with."

"What's that?"

"I want the chance to say good-bye to Susan," Mike began, "and I want you to help me to do that."

I suggested that he go visit her like he's been visiting me. He said he had tried numerous times already, but for some reason it wasn't working. Then I suggested the logical solution—that I'd see her and convey his message. He disagreed, saying that wasn't good enough.

Feeling a little frustrated, I said, "Mike, if you have already tried and it didn't work, and my going over there isn't good enough either, then what is it you want? I don't know how else to handle this for you!"

"*Please* help me find a way to say good-bye to her," he pleaded. "I can't leave like this. I have to find a way, and I need your help."

Totally at a loss, again I tried to talk my way out, but Mike came straight back at me.

"Didn't you promise me that you would *always* be there for me if I ever needed you?" Mike had hit me right between the eyes, holding me to the promise I had made in that bar in Manila.

"Yes, but—"

Mike stopped me. "But nothing," he said. "Are you a man of your word or not?"

I nodded yes.

He continued, "I need you now more than ever. I don't want to leave this Earth without saying good-bye to Susan. I'm asking you again: please help me do that!"

He had me over a barrel. There was no way I could see to turn down his request. I had no idea how I was going to do it, and I knew I had to keep my promise. The only idea I could come up with was to make him another promise that I would do everything in my power to fulfill.

Mike smiled, content. Then he got up and walked into the living room. This time, I didn't get up to see where he was going. I already knew he wouldn't be there, and, in any case, I knew I would be seeing him again.

———

You'd think that seeing Mike again might have provided some relief from some of the stress and depression I was going through, but it didn't. It actually made it worse. It made me feel sorry for him because he wasn't able to experience his life anymore. He and I both knew he was dead, and there was nothing either of us could do about it. For Mike, it must have been like being locked up at Alcatraz. Imagine being so close that you can see the lights of San Francisco, and even hear the sounds of music being played and people enjoying themselves, and yet knowing, at the same time, that you'll never be able to get there because there's something in between that's keeping you away. How frustrating must that be?

Seeing Mike also made me feel guilty for still being alive. Questions kept plaguing me about why I stepped out of the helicopter. What was it that made me check with Gadi to see if I was in the camera frame or not? And why hadn't I just stayed on for the ride? It was only supposed to go up fifteen feet and then come right back down. I should have stayed on board. Why didn't I die with the rest of my friends? I felt like a coward for living. Why did the Creator hate me so much that He did this to me?

No wonder I wound up sucking on the barrel of my pistol every night. When you ask bad questions, you get bad answers, and those answers dictate how you feel. It works the same way with positive questions: ask positive questions, and you get positive answers. Except I didn't know that back then.

Another thing I didn't understand was that just because you can think up a question doesn't mean there's any truth or validity to it. For instance, I questioned how the Creator could hate me so bad that He'd torture me. Think about it. Because I can frame those words, does it necessarily mean that the Creator hates me and is torturing me? No! When you ask negative questions like that, you can only get negative answers, and so the downward spiral begins. Because I was in the middle of it all, I couldn't see that it was actually my own self-talk—the negative stories I was telling myself—that was trapping me in that negative emotional state.

No wonder then that even after the encounter with Mike, my cocaine use continued, and so did the nightly episodes of putting my gun in my mouth. I thought it would end the guilt and the nightmares. Most of all, I thought I would be free of the painful world I was living in.

Before the helicopter crash, I had thought I could do anything, and that I would always find a way to come out on top of any situation. After the crash I felt as if my Superman cape had been ripped away from me. I no longer felt invincible. I was faced with the reality that I was mortal, and that some day I too would be dead. I felt my life was no more valuable than that of an ant or a cockroach. You're born, you live, you die, and you never come back—end of story. These kinds of thoughts left me feeling so hollow I figured it would be better to end my life on my terms.

Every night I would count to three. Somehow, by the grace of God, I was too strong to do it. My survival instincts were still in place. Every night I would put my gun away until the next night arrived.

Mike was starting to make regular visits and wasn't impressed with my antics. He was dead and would do anything to be alive again, and here I was doing stupid things like toying with my own life. He was also irritated because I wasn't actively doing anything to fulfill my promise and help him complete his quest.

He was frustrated by that fact that he could go and see Susan but she couldn't see him, and he couldn't even find a way to communicate with her. He told me how difficult it was to see her going through so much pain, and to feel so helpless. I told him I didn't know what to do to satisfy his request.

"Besides," I said, "I have my own dramas to deal with."

"I thought you promised that as my friend, you would be there to help me when I needed you," Mike reiterated.

"That's true. I did."

"Well," Mike shot back, "what happened to that promise?"

"I was always there for you," I replied defensively. "I was the good friend I promised I would be. Remember: I'm the guy who climbed into the burning helicopter to get you out and stayed with you right up until the point where you died in my arms. How much more do you want from me?"

Mike wasn't ready to give up. "Are you saying that your promise had conditions attached to it?"

"What are you talking about?" I said, growing very frustrated. "Weren't you listening when I told you I was there for you until the very end?"

My answer wasn't good enough for Mike. He still had one more strategic arrow left. "You keep saying, 'I *was* with you until the very end.' What happened to, 'I *am* with you until the very end'? I need your help now more than ever, and you're going to tell me that your promise isn't a promise anymore just because I'm dead?"

I was completely floored. I couldn't believe what I was hearing. No matter how defensive I became, though, I knew he was right. When I'd made the promise, I had assumed it stood for the rest of our lives. What I was quickly discovering now was that it doesn't really end there. It can go beyond that. And a promise is a promise!

At that moment I experienced an awakening. I didn't know what I was going to do to make Mike's goal a reality. And I decided I was going to make it happen anyway. Right then I discovered that making a decision is the first step in creating change in your life. Even if you don't know what to do, as long as you have a big enough purpose, the "how" will eventually reveal itself to you. The next step is to take action. Mike had just reminded me of my purpose. I had made the promise to my friend, and a promise is a promise. All I had to do now was figure out a strategy to fulfill that promise. This was going to take some real contemplation.

5

Into the Light

$\mathscr{F}$or more than a year, I searched for answers as to how I might help Mike with his request. Finally my research led me to a concept I'd heard only a little about: "out-of-body experiences." I was excited to discover that some people claim they are able to get their spirits to leave their bodies for short periods of time, and that many different cultures, including the American Indian shamans, believe this is possible.

The trouble was that most of these people seemed to live in far-off lands or had faded into history along with their long-forgotten cultures. What I needed was someone in my neck of the woods to teach me about it. Through Lisa, a friend of mine, I located a young woman named Carol who knew how to do it, and who could help others do it as well. If I could do this, and have Susan do it too, then when she was out of body, she and Mike would be able to communicate—that is, if she would actually agree to participate!

I called her up and talked to her about the plan. It went a lot smoother than I anticipated. She actually seemed keen to give it a try, unless she was merely humoring me because she thought it might help with my depression. I didn't really care why she was doing it. I was just focused on getting my objective completed so I could get my life back into some kind of order. At this stage of the game, I was willing to believe in anything. So I made an appointment to have Carol meet me at Susan's apartment.

Carol thought it was the best place to do this because it had also been Mike's apartment. She said it helps to do the process in an environment where the person you're trying to contact has a lot of personal effects, because those things have a lot of the person's residual energy attached to them. I had my doubts as to whether this was real or a sham. Yet I kept an open mind because I really wanted it to work for Mike, for Susan, and for me. Anything was worth a try.

When Carol was eighteen, she was shot and killed during a robbery attempt. She said that when she was on the operating table in the hospital, she could see everything going on in the room as she floated up near the ceiling. She described how she watched the doctors and nurses frantically working to revive her. After about two minutes, she was brought back to life and was back in her body. After that experience, she realized she had some special gifts. She went and studied with some American Indian shamans who helped her cultivate those gifts, and that's how she came to do what she does these days. To me, she seemed very sincere. Even Susan felt comfortable with Carol when she met her.

Carol had Susan gather up some of Mike's personal belongings, including some things that had belonged to both of them, like photographs of them together. Carol spread them across the coffee table in Susan's living room. She then held on to each item for an extended moment to see if it had the right energy, and decided that all the items Susan chose were good, with lots of Mike's energy still attached to them. Carol also said she could feel Mike's presence in the room. That was one thing she didn't need to tell me. I already knew he was there. It was the same feeling I would get whenever he was about to make one of his appearances. I was expecting him at any moment, except he never did appear—well, not in the way he normally did when I saw him.

Carol's intention was to guide Susan and me through the out-of-body experience. She said, "An out-of-body experience is where your soul takes a short trip outside your body. It's like being in a dream, except that you have control over what you do in the dream."

Susan had invited a lady friend of hers to be with us because she had also been good friends with Mike. We all found comfortable places to sit in Susan's living room, then Carol instructed us to close our eyes and relax. Once we all got settled, she guided us through a visualization process. It wasn't long before I was out of my body and sitting right next to Mike in what seemed like a room of grey fog, devoid of any identifiable features. It was claustrophobic and lifeless. This must be purgatory, I thought—the space between the two dimensions of life and death.

I understand if you're having trouble believing any of this really happened. Put yourself in my shoes and imagine how I felt! Here I was at the age of twenty-seven. I grew up in Chicago, lived a middle-class life, and considered myself quite normal. I wasn't into Ouija boards, séances, tarot cards, or psychic hotlines. As a matter of fact, up until that moment, if someone had tried to tell me about an experience like that, I might have had a hard time believing it too. Yet I really didn't have any choice in the matter. I didn't try to make it happen. I was thrust into the middle of the experience as it unfolded in front of me.

During the out-of-body experience, I saw Mike and Susan standing face-to-face about two feet apart from each other. It was obvious to me they were able to see each other but for some reason weren't able to talk or communicate. I could see how frustrated they were getting trying to find a way. I sat there and watched the entire exchange between them, feeling so helpless for them.

When we came out of the experience, Carol asked us what had happened. I spoke first and told her what I saw. Instantly Susan became really upset and broke into tears. When I asked what was wrong, she said that what I was describing was exactly what she had experienced.

"How do you know what happened in my dream?" she asked. I explained that I was standing right next to them both and could see it all happening. Susan sat there frozen in shock, listening to me describe the details of what I had saw.

Afterward, Carol took us through another meditative process she said was necessary to shut down the pathway between the two dimensions. Then she reached into her bag and produced a large tuning fork about eight inches long. She said its sound would re-align our energies in the aftermath of the experience. When she struck the tuning fork against the table, it rang a steady and consistent tone. Then she passed the tuning fork around Susan's body. The sound stayed the same. She did the same procedure with Susan's friend, and the results were the same. But when Carol repeated the procedure with me, the tuning fork went crazy. It sounded like a British police car siren. Everyone in the room was a little freaked out by this, including Carol.

She explained that I hadn't shut down the channel between myself and the other side, and that this could set up a situation in which other entities could travel through the open channel and cause problems in my life. I told her I didn't care, and that I would do whatever it took to get Mike delivered to where he had to go. I told Carol I wouldn't shut down the channel between Mike and myself because it wasn't over yet.

"I know what you're going to do," Carol said.

"What's that?"

"You're going to go back and try it again," she replied. I told her she was right.

Seeing my determination, Carol thought she'd better warn me of the dangers, and she gave me strict instructions not to go into the light myself, as this was a place only for people who are passing over. She warned me that I could set up some serious problems for myself if I tried to cross over before my time.

I knew I had to try again to get Mike into the light, and I knew that before I could do this, I first had to find a way for him to have his meeting with Susan.

That night when I got home, I had another visit from Mike. He was still upset about what had happened with Susan earlier that day. Right then I had an idea. I told him to go visit Susan that night in her dreams while she was asleep. This way she wouldn't be so connected to her human form, and maybe she would be more receptive to the idea of breaking through her fears and limiting beliefs. We agreed that it was worth a shot.

For the first time in many months, I finally got a good night's sleep without having any nightmares. Then, on the one day I could have actually slept in, I was jolted awake at 6 A.M. by the phone ringing. Grudgingly I answered, "Hello."

To my surprise, it was Susan, and she was crying so much that I could barely make out what she was saying.

"Susan, what's wrong?" I had to ask twice. "What's wrong?"

It took her a few minutes to finally gain her composure. She said that Mike showed up at her place, and they spent the entire night together, talking. I couldn't believe my ears. Our plan actually worked! The sense of relief was huge. Already I could feel some stability returning to my life. I guess I wasn't as crazy as I had thought. Susan described how Mike showed up while she was sleeping and sat down on the end of her bed. They said everything they needed to say to each other, and then they hugged as they said their good-byes. She felt she was at peace with it all. I was so happy and relieved I wanted to scream with joy.

I felt elated for Mike and Susan. Mike's mission was accomplished, but his presence was still a powerful influence in my life, and I knew something had to be done about it. The visits from Mike continued for a couple more weeks until, eventually, I decided to do another out-of-body experience, this time by myself.

I followed Carol's instructions to the letter. I went into a deep meditative state. Breathing slowly and deeply, I walked myself through the process, remembering what Carol had done with us. It didn't seem to take much time at all, and before I knew it, I was back with Mike in the void space of grey fog.

I explained to him that it was time to move on. He told me he was afraid about where he would go and also sad that he would never be able to return. I didn't have any real answers as to how I could change that for him. I did tell him the only possible way for him to return that I could think of would be for him to go into the light first to be reprocessed and then sent to wherever he was supposed to go next. Yet if he stayed here, he would be trapped in this void between the two places. I told him he had to trust me and that this wasn't where he wanted to stay. I assured him that I would be with him every step of the way and that he needed to do it for me as well as for himself, because I needed my life back.

If I had to go through this for much longer, I would lose my mind. After all, here I was having meetings with a friend who just happened to be dead. Maybe I had already lost it. With a little convincing, he agreed, saying that he trusted me, and then he thanked me for making the meeting with Susan happen. I told him that I loved him and that it was my honor.

Where Mike and I started our passage together the air was stagnant. I escorted him through this void, a nothingness with no discernable features or colors, a monotonous corridor of nonexistence. Fear of the unknown touched us both as we moved forward, step by cautious step. We didn't know where we were going or how to get there. I just followed my natural intuitions.

I say step by step, but really we seemed to be moving without walking or using our legs at all. In fact, it was hard to tell whether we were traveling of our own volition or being drawn along. It was also hard to tell if we were covering any distance, as there were no landmarks or physical features to gauge our progress. Yet somehow I still knew we were in motion. Suddenly we found an infinite wall of light right in front of us. Though it appeared without warning, we were not startled. It went from not being there to being only one step away, as if it had been there the whole time.

Mike stopped just inches away from this endless portal of light, frightened to go any further, afraid of what might await him on the other side. I recalled Carol's instructions that I must not enter into the light myself because it could cause serious repercussions. It wasn't my time yet.

Mike turned his back to the light. We stood looking at each other, knowing this was going to be a crossroads in our friendship. I gave him the biggest hug I could. I assured him everything would be all right and that this was the only way forward for us all. It had to be done for everyone involved, himself included.

"I know what has to be done," Mike agreed, "but I'm still worried that I'll be gone forever and won't be able to come back."

"The only way to come back," I told him, "is to first go through the door of light."

Knowing this was the last time we would see each other, we hugged even tighter.

"I promised I would be with you to the very end," I whispered in his ear, "and I'm keeping my promise. We'll always be together, and I promise I won't let anything happen to you."

With that, I took a step forward, backing him into the aura of light until he was completely enveloped by it. Following Carol's instructions, I made sure not to enter the light completely, yet I couldn't help allowing the front half of my body to touch the aura as I gently backed Mike in. I instantly felt the light, warm and comforting on my body, yet without any real sensation of heat or temperature, like the way it feels when you're a child and you get a loving hug from your mom. The light was the purest, whitest, brightest light I had ever experienced—a million times brighter than the desert sun, and yet there was no need to squint my eyes. Instead, it was soothing to view. I felt love in every cell, every atom of my being. I felt I was being freed from darkness, and I knew I was in the presence of the most powerful force in the universe. Pure love is the only way to describe it. Pure, unconditional love!

As soon as my Mike made contact with the light, his body began fragmenting into millions upon millions of bits of effervescent energy that seemed to become one with the rest of the light. It was like pouring a bucket of water into an ocean. As these fireflies of magical energy sparkled off in every direction, I could still see his eyes and his smile. He was finally at peace, surrounded by and immersed in the light.

That's when I was given the gift from the light. It spoke to me, not through words or sounds; it was as though the message was being infused directly into my mind. It was clear and specific. It would take me a few years to truly understand the meaning of the message and what I was supposed to do with it. First, though, I understood that I had to clean myself up and put effort into evolving myself before its true meaning would come to light for me.

One day, a few years later, it hit me like a blinding flash of the obvious. All of a sudden, the meaning of the message and what I was supposed to do with it became crystal clear. Now there is absolutely no doubt. I was given this gift, and it's not for me to keep. It's so powerful that I am obliged to share it.

When you use the insights and strategies laid out in the pages of this book, you too will have possession of this gift. It will give you the ability to make your life, and the lives of everyone you come into contact with, golden!

In my heart I know that what I experienced was real, and that's how I'll always feel about it. Whether you believe it is up to you. Yet even getting caught up in thinking about this takes us away from focusing on what's really important: the gift itself, the message.

Since those early days, this message has changed my life forever, and sharing it with others has had a positive impact upon millions of lives. I deliver the message through the way I live my life, the people I have taught, and the contributions I have made. Until now I have not publicly shared how the message was given. I have been guarded about telling people about the source of the information I teach; I was afraid people wouldn't believe me. Now I know that whether they do or don't doesn't matter anymore. I have an obligation that I must live up to, and I am excited to fulfill that responsibility in the pages of this book.

Mike didn't make any more visits after that. At least not in the same way. He did appear to me one other time, years later, while I was participating in a group meditation, but it was a different kind of visit. I saw him in my mind as I was meditating. He was standing in front of the wall of light, but this time even the light was different. Instead of Mike being outside the light and separate from it, it was as if the light was a presence, or a being of energy, that was supporting him from behind, backing him up. Without saying a word, he told me he was very happy and that everything was as I had promised him it would be. He thanked me for everything I had done for him.

The Gift:
Everything in this life is borrowed. You have to give it all back. The only thing you get to keep is the love you gave, the love you received, and the experiences your soul got to have.

The message may appear to be a bit simple, and perhaps it's not what you were expecting. That's exactly why it took me a few years to finally figure out the true magnitude of its meaning. I have written this book to help you figure it out sooner than I did and to help you enjoy the results this gift can bring you along the way to that discovery. I know this book isn't really from me. It's written through me for you.

We all have the chance and ability to live our lives in the light— the light of unconditional love. We came from love, we will go to love, and our journey between those two events is about living the same path. This is a book about learning how to experience the joy and happiness you desire every day of your life, no matter what is happening around you.

As you start to read the next chapter, you may notice that it seems like you have begun reading a completely different book from the original one. The reason I have organized the book this way is so I could first show you where I have come from and what's the driving force for me to write it. As you have already learned, after the helicopter crash, my life spiraled out of control, and I lived each day in what felt like the darkest depths of hell. Since then I have completely turned my life around to enjoy a holistically successful life, and I have also helped tens of thousands of people to do the same for themselves. So, for the rest of the book, I am going to show you how I have moved forward with my life and how you can do the same in your own.

I'm not going to tell you that I created all of these strategies myself because I haven't. They have been on the planet for thousands of years and have been taught by many different teachers in many different ways. What I have done is compiled the best of the best strategies that I know, without a doubt, universally work for whoever chooses to put them into action.

If there are times while you're reading that you feel I am repeating a couple of things, I am, and trust that there is a method to my madness. The truth is that I don't have any desire to just teach content.

My intention is to help you make real lasting changes for yourself and for the people that you love and care about. There is a big difference between just reading something and really knowing it. When you really get it, you will be able to utilize it.

The more you read on, the more you will see how everything I've shared fits together. Remember what I said at the very beginning of the book: trust in the fact that there are no accidents and that there is something in this book that you're searching for in your life. And even if you don't yet know what it is you're searching for or maybe you didn't even know that you are searching, have the faith that it will be revealed to you and that's why you chose this book.

6

The Formula for Creation

*F*or two years after the helicopter crash, I lived in a dark, suffocating world, cruising the gang neighborhoods of Los Angeles night after night to buy my fix of cocaine and marijuana. Even though I was a regular customer, I didn't get any loyalty points with the drug dealers, who would sometimes sell me laundry washing powder, baby laxative, or some other foreign chemical instead of the real thing. Luckily I was spared the rat poison substitutes and somehow always escaped with my life, even when some gang members pulled guns or knives attempting to rob me.

One time a gang member shot off the side mirror of my truck, cracking the windscreen. As scary as it all was, I still found myself driving back into the dangerous, seedy neighborhoods every night to get my fix of the Dream Stealer. That's what I call cocaine now, because that's what it does. It steals your dreams. It was definitely stealing away every one of mine.

The Dream Stealer also turns you into a liar. I was renting a house in Studio City when Mom came out from Chicago to stay awhile. She slept in my room, so I slept on the living room floor. Every night I would wait up until around 2 A.M., when I thought she'd be asleep, and then slip out to make my nightly drug run. She always heard me leave. Every morning she asked me where I'd been, and every morning I lied to her. I lied even though I could see that she knew I was lying. I lied even though I could see how much her heart was breaking and how much she was blaming herself because she felt helpless to save her son. I felt her pain, and that still didn't stop me from sneaking out every night and then waiting out the dark hours in a haze of drug-induced paranoia, watching junk on TV.

One night there was a slight problem. My car keys and shoes were in my bedroom where Mom was sleeping, and I didn't want to get them because I didn't want to have to explain to her where I was going in the middle of the night, again! Yet no shoes and no car didn't stop me from my downward spiral.

It's funny how I had money to buy drugs but none to put fuel in my car or even enough to take a bus. Taking a bus or cab would cost money, and that was money that I wouldn't be able to spend on drugs, so I decided to walk. Imagine walking five or six miles of city streets and alleyways in your bare feet just to buy drugs from street thugs! I knew the dangers, and I didn't even have a car in which to speed away if anything went wrong. Still, I went.

By the time I got home, all coked up, it was light. My feet were a mess. I had deep cuts from stepping on broken glass, and oozing blood blisters. I don't remember what excuse I came up with, but I'll never forget the look of disappointment on Mom's face and the deep sadness in her eyes. She said nothing. She didn't have to. My mother and I have always been very close, and the pain I was causing her was horrible. I was killing her son.

That look of sadness and letdown became very familiar to me. I saw it on the faces of my friends as well as my family. They knew what I was doing. I knew that they knew, and they knew that I knew that they knew, and still no one really said much about it because no one wanted to deal with all the drama that would ensue if I was confronted. No one wanted to deal with my wrath, excuses, or justifications.

Except for one night. Except for one of my very best friends, Kimo. And it went right to my core.

It was a Friday evening, and Kimo and I were driving home from work. We were crew members on some movie or other film project like a commercial or rock video. We'd done at least a hundred shows together, so it wasn't unusual for us to carpool once in a while. We were driving his car because I didn't have enough money to put gas in mine. Again!

Kimo is one of the best people I've ever met, a guy who can always be counted on one hundred percent in everything he does. He is a very well-respected lighting technician and grip in the movie industry, as well as a top professional photographer. He had also been good friends with Mike Graham and Don Marshall, who both died in the helicopter accident.

As we were driving home that night, I talked Kimo into lending me fifty dollars. It wasn't much of a talk because Kimo's the kind of guy who would give his friends the shirt off his back if they asked him. Then I convinced him to drive me to the neighborhood where I bought my drugs, making up a story about visiting some woman I was casually dating to throw him off the trail. I asked him to drop me off at a convenience store parking lot. I said I would walk the rest of the way there, using the excuse that there wasn't any parking by her house, and asked him to wait there in the store parking lot for me so that if she wasn't in he could drive me back home. Sure, it was a lame ploy, and, needless to say, Kimo wasn't buying it.

He pulled into the parking spot in front of the store. I was just about to shake his hand and get out when he spoke up. In all the years I'd known him, I'd never seen the look of anger and disappointment in his eyes that I saw then. He knew he'd been set up and used.

"Have you gotten me to drive you down here so that you can buy drugs, Kurek?"

His words cut right through me. Kimo has never touched a drug in his life, and here was someone he considered to be a lifelong friend putting him in a situation that went against everything he believed in. He stared at me, waiting for an answer to his question. Of course, I vehemently denied his insinuation.

"Kimo, I would never do that to you, I swear." I pulled a name out of thin air. "Her name is Linda Chavez." The lie came easily.

I got out of the car, walked across the street, and vanished into the darkness. I made my score and got back to Kimo's car in ten minutes.

"Linda wasn't in," I said.

I tried to make small talk, but Kimo didn't say a word. He didn't have to. The look on his face said it all. The lying devastated him. I had abused our friendship and the bond of trust. I had stepped way over the line of acceptable behavior. Worse still, I was treating him like an idiot, and he didn't appreciate that one bit.

For the whole drive home, Kimo was silent and fuming with anger. At my house I got out of the car, and, for the first time ever, he didn't say good-bye. He said nothing. He just stared straight ahead and sped away without even waiting for me to close the passenger door, the car's forward motion slamming it shut. The look in Kimo's eyes haunted me for weeks.

———

Those days are long behind me. Today I'm living an awesome dream. I am so lucky and blessed to be married to Marie. Not only is she my partner in life, she's also my friend, and my business partner. Together we have built a multimillion-dollar business which takes us all around the world teaching tens of thousands of people the strategies to take their lives to a much higher level, physically, emotionally, financially, and spiritually.

Every morning when I wake up at 4 A.M., I look around to see that everything is real and not just a dream. When I see Marie lying next to me, I know I am already a success and that everything else is ice cream on top of the cake. It's all a bonus.

People are always curious as to why I get up so early.

"Hey, Kurek," they say, "you've already got a great life, so why get up at four? Why don't you just sleep in?"

"*Sleep is for dreaming, and being awake is for living your dreams,*" I reply.

(Did you know that if you get up one hour earlier every day for a year, you get an extra nine and a half forty-hour weeks of life to enjoy? Just imagine if you applied those extra weeks toward your own personal development. Imagine how much further ahead you'd be toward achieving your dream goals. Now you know why I get up at 4 A.M. every day!)

Both Marie and I feel we are blessed to have each other, and to have a business that has rewarded us with financial freedom and a great quality of life. What I teach through my seminars, workshops, books, audios, DVDs, and coaching programs are the very strategies I was forced to learn myself to turn my life around in the years following the helicopter crash. I have since passed on these same strategies to thousands of people all over the world to help them create holistic success in their lives and businesses. Holistic success is success across the board, in all areas of your life.

The question I get asked more than any other is, "How did you turn your life around from those dark, depressing years to create the incredible life you have today?"

Well, there was one defining moment that created this radical shift and everything else that followed. I had just survived one more night of deep depression and yet another suicidal episode when . . . I had *a new thought*. It was as simple as that.

A New Thought, a New Beginning

Look at your life today. Is it what you planned, imagined, hoped, or dreamed it would be? What first came to mind when you considered this question—your finances, career, relationships, health, fitness, happiness, lifestyle, spirituality, fulfilling your purpose in the world, or something else? Is your life abundantly successful in all these areas? I imagine you are reading this book because you desire improvement in at least one of these, right?

Your current conditions and circumstances encompass all areas of your life, from the condition of your finances and health to that of your working environment and lifestyle. Look again at what Einstein says: "*All* conditions and *all* circumstances."

As a physicist, Einstein knew that everything was interconnected. Every area of your life is interconnected. What happens in one area affects what happens in another. No area is left untouched by another. No exceptions. So if you want your *whole* life to improve—if you want holistic success—you need to understand what is keeping the structure of your life in place and what you can you do to change it. Look at Einstein's quote again. What does he advise? Einstein says that absolutely everything in your life today is created by a level of thinking—by thought. When you think about it, you'll see he's correct. This book you're reading, the chair you're sitting in, the clothes you're wearing, the house or apartment you live in, the city or town where you reside, and the car you drive all started as someone's thought first. Someone had to have the idea before it could be built or created, right? Einstein is pointing out that everything that has ever been created by mankind began with someone's thought.

> "All conditions and all circumstances in our lives are the result of a certain level of thinking. When you want to change the conditions and the circumstances, we have to change the level of thinking that is responsible for it."
>
> ALBERT EINSTEIN

Even you, yourself, started as a thought. For all of us there was a time when we were just an embryo, a clump of cells with no real life. At the moment a baby starts thinking, life begins. Think about it. If you were born without any brain wave activity, you'd be dead. The only difference between a living person and a dead person is that one is thinking, and the other is not. Both the living person and the dead person have brains. They both have blood, muscles, and bones, so they both have the same physical attributes. Yet one person is thinking, and one isn't. The one thinking is alive, and the one not thinking is dead. If someone's heart stops while he's in the hospital getting medical attention, he's not considered to be dead immediately because often the heart can be started again and the person can go on to live a full and productive life. But if the person's brain activity stops, he is pronounced dead. Life is for the thinking.

So thought is the beginning seed of creation for everything and anything that we create in our lives. If you want to understand why your life is the way it is, examine your past thoughts. And when you want to have a different life tomorrow, start by having new thoughts today. *"Pull the negative weeds, and plant new positive seeds."*

"When you plant happiness, your happiness grows!"

Here's a warning. If you truly want to improve your life, if you truly want to grow in every area of your life, then, in addition to introducing new thoughts, you have to be willing to let go of some of your most cherished old thoughts and ideas.

I Already Know All This Stuff

If you're thinking, "Oh, I've already heard all of this before," or, "I already know this," the question I have for you is this: "Are you doing it?"

If your cup is so filled with what you think you already know, then there is nothing I or anyone else can do to help you make your life better. New thought is the seed needed to produce change.

> *"The usefulness of the cup is in its emptiness."*
>
> BRUCE LEE

What Bruce Lee means is that if your mind is already so filled up with what you think you know, there won't be room for anything new. So make room to take on something new. Even a single new distinction on what you know can make the difference to the quality of your life.

If your life isn't filled with the holistic success you desire, then it's safe to say that what you're currently doing isn't working to get you there. It's cause and effect. Whatever you're doing now is producing what you're getting now, and it won't ever be able to produce anything different from that. If you're not enjoying the rewards that you want right now, then whatever you're doing won't get you there. To get something different, you're going to have to do something different. That makes sense, right?

I'm not saying you haven't had some great results in your life already. That's not what we're talking about here. What we are talking about is how to make it better!

If there are any areas of your life you want to improve, it's clear that what you're doing in those areas is not completely working. If it were, you would already have the results. So something needs to change. That's what Bruce Lee is talking about. You need to pull some negative weeds to make room for you to be able to plant some new positive seeds. That's what will produce the rewards you desire.

Remember: I emerged from the depths of hell to the blissful life I now cherish. It started one morning when I woke up with that new thought.

So even if you think that your cup is already filled to the brim with all of the right stuff because you feel that you've heard this all before, the question to ask yourself is, "Am I doing it?" The world is full of educated derelicts. Most people know what to do, and most people aren't doing what they know. It's the person who is willing to *do* what the average person isn't willing to *do* that gets the rewards that the average people never get.

Imagine you have a table in the middle of the room but you want to put a couch there. What has to happen with the table before you can put the couch in its place? The answer is obvious, right? You'll have to move the table first before you can put the couch in that space. Why? Because there is a law of nature called the Law of Displacement that states that two things can't occupy the same space at the same time. This is also true with thoughts. If your cup is so full that you can't take any new thoughts in, and if you're not willing to empty some out to make space for the new ones, you will never be able to evolve from the place you are right now.

In life either you evolve or you dissolve; nothing stays the same. So if you're not evolving, then automatically, by default, you're going in the other direction and dissolving, because nothing stays the same. Think about it. If you stay the same while the world is changing around you, then how outdated are you going to be next year, or in ten years' time? How lost are you going to be if you haven't kept up with the changing world? Emptying out that cup from time to time is crucial in a fast-changing world if you want to take charge of your own life changes rather than have it changed for you!

It comes down to this: if you're not getting the results you want in your life, then it's obvious that what you're doing isn't working.

New Thoughts Lead to New Actions

Are the thoughts you've been having about your future the kind that empower you or disempower you? Do they get you excited about going after your grand dream goals, or do they get you to procrastinate and not take action toward reaching them?

Empowering new thoughts inspire you to act. That's the value of a new thought: it's the one and only thing that can produce a new action. A thought by itself is just a thought. It only becomes a tangible thing, a result, when you act on it. That's the value of having new empowering thoughts; they inspire you into taking action.

In this book, chapter by chapter, I'll give you the tools and strategies you'll need to ensure that those new thoughts are the very best they can be, the kind that lead to awesome actions and brilliant results—in short, the kinds of new thoughts that bring you holistic success.

So remember the empty cup, keep your mind open, and stay with me for the ride of a lifetime. Somewhere within these pages, in between all the things you already know, are the diamonds you have yet to discover.

To get something new, you're going to have to do something different. That makes sense, right? It's called the Law of Cause and Effect.

Remember: the way I turned my own life around and created the incredible life Marie and I now share began when I woke up with a new thought. One new thought was the first step to creating holistic success. And yes, I will share that thought with you soon. Are you curious about what that thought might be?

Your Body of Thought

Did you know that every new thought you have changes the biochemical composition of your body? For instance, when you're thinking negative thoughts, you start creating negative chemicals and negative reactions in your body. Negative, disempowering, or stressful thoughts cause your body to produce large amounts of free radicals. Free radicals are scavengers that steal the electrons from your molecules, changing their structure and causing a wide range of damage to your cells, which in turn speed up the aging process.

Stress is the by-product of having stressful thoughts, and when you're stressed, it means that your mind is not at ease. Another way of saying this is that your mind is at dis-ease. **It's the dis-ease of your mind that creates the disease of your body.**

Science has proven that when you're depressed, stressed, angry, negative, or thinking in any other disempowering way, it weakens your immune system, and this makes you more susceptible to sickness, disease, and even death. That's how destructive negative thoughts can be to your health and well-being.

One in three people develops cancer these days. Anti-depressants are the most prescribed drugs on the planet. Why are so many people taking anti-depressants? Because they're stressed out. Why are so many people getting cancer? Would you think it just might have something to do with how stressed they are?

Yet taking anti-depressants isn't the solution to your problem. When you take artificial anti-depressants, which means man made, your body recognizes that it has an abundance of those chemicals and because of that it stops producing its own. If your natural anti-depressant production system is dormant for too long, it can shut down altogether. If you don't use it, you lose it!

And now for the good news! You can change all of that because positive, empowering thoughts strengthen your immune system. Your mind already has its own well-being medicine cabinet built into to it, stocked up with everything that you need to be happy and healthy, including a full range of natural anti-depressants. The way you access your well-being medicine cabinet is through your use of consistent thoughts. When you want to be happy, you need to start with happy thoughts first. That's what Einstein is talking about. When you want to change the conditions of your life, you have to change the thoughts that are creating those conditions.

When you think happy, positive thoughts, your body starts producing happy, positive, health-inducing chemicals such as interleukins, which regulate inflammatory and immune responses by activating your lymphocytes (white blood cells). Interleukins are the most powerful cancer-fighting agents known to man. If you go to a medical facility for interleukin treatment, it may cost you hundreds of thousands of dollars. Yet by thinking consistently happy, positive thoughts, your body will produce millions and millions of dollars' worth of interleukins absolutely free of charge. And why wait for cancer or some other ailment to arrive when you can make it easy for your body to remain strong and free of disease?

Again, the beginning of all creation starts with thoughts. So look again at your life. Are there areas that are in a state of dis-ease? Your bank balance? Your relationship? Your health and fitness? What does this tell you about the dis-ease of your thinking about those areas of your life?

All it takes is that new thought, one that inspires you to make a new decision and take a new action. And what does that new action do? It creates a new result. This is the formula for all of creation. It's that easy.

Thoughts → Actions = Results
(Thoughts that get turned into actions produce results)

Every single thing mankind has ever created followed this formula. Everything that will ever be created in the future will follow this same formula, because this *is* the formula for all creation.

"The universe started with the Creator's first loving thought."

Everything you have in your life today is a direct result of the consistent thoughts you have been having. Everything you want to have in your life will come about through the process of putting carefully chosen consistent new thoughts in place.

The formula for creation goes hand in hand with the Law of Cause and Effect.

$$\text{Thoughts} = \text{Cause}$$
$$\text{Results} = \text{Effect}$$

Your thoughts cause the actions that create your results. So, very simply, when you want to change the results you have in your life, you're going to have to change your thoughts first. That makes sense, right?

If it feels like I'm going over this a few times, you're right. Have some faith; there is a method to my madness. The reason that I am sticking with this topic for a moment is because it's that importantly crucial in helping you transform the quality of your life. Without putting anything new in, there's no possible way to get anything new out.

Think about it this way: you can't walk up to an empty fireplace and expect it to give you heat before you give it a log. You have to start with the new thoughts first, and that's the only thing that can get you to take the new actions that produce the new results.

The new thought is the seed of creation. You have to plant the seed to get the result you desire. You reap what you sow. You don't get one without the other.

When you want health in your life, it makes sense that you're going to have to start with healthy thoughts first, right?

When you want happiness in your life, you're going to have to start with happy thoughts first.

When you want financial wealth in your life, you're going to have to start with wealthy thoughts first.

Whatever seeds you plant will determine what you'll to grow.

I *Do* Think Rich Thoughts, So Where Are My Rich Results?

If you're thinking, "I do have rich thoughts, so where are my rich results?" here's why.

Before you really paid attention to the formula for creation, you were in what I call "total blindness." Total blindness is where you don't know that you don't know about what you should know. Once you've learned about the formula for creation, you've moved up from total blindness to just being blind. That's a major jump in your level of awareness. The reason I'm saying you're still blind is because now you *do* know that you don't know what you're supposed to know.

I'll explain what I mean. Once you understand that all of the results you have or don't have in your life are a direct result of the consistent thoughts you have been having, your brain starts to figure out that in order for you to get the new results you want, you're going to have to start with having new consistent thoughts. We've already covered all of that, right?

So here's where the challenge comes in. From where you are right now, there is a good possibility that you don't know what those new thoughts that you are supposed to be having are. The reason that I can confidently say you don't know what the new thoughts are is that if you did know what the thoughts were, you would already be having them. And if you were already having those new thoughts, you would already be taking the new actions, which means that you would also already have the new results. That would mean that you were already living your ultimate dream life.

Make sure you understand what I'm saying. I'm not saying that you haven't already produced some great results in your life. I'm actually assuming that you have. What I'm saying is that the thoughts you've been having until now have produced the results that you have now. They have produced to their limit, and they won't be able to create the new results you want. Whatever you've been putting in has created what you have gotten out, and that's all it can create. In order to get something new out, you have to put something new in first. See where I'm going with this?

You may have noticed that saying things like, "I want more money, I want more money," doesn't actually produce the wealth you want. And the reason this doesn't work is because those aren't the thoughts that produce wealth. Those aren't wealthy thoughts; they're poor thoughts. Just saying, "I want to be healthy," or, "I should start exercising," won't get you physically fit either, because those aren't healthy thoughts; they're unhealthy thoughts.

It's like putting together one of those pieces of furniture you buy from stores like IKEA. If you don't have the proper instructions, it won't work. You'll never get your dresser drawers to work if you use the wrong pieces in the wrong places, and you'll discover that forcing them doesn't help either. It works the same way with your mind. Once you get the proper instructions and you actually follow them, you notice it's so much easier, and when it's complete, it works just like it's supposed to. That's what this book is helping you to master. By the time you finish reading it, you will know the specific new thoughts you need to start having in order to create the changes you desire.

I did it in my life using these same tools. You can do it too. And you don't have to start from the same dark, miserable hole I was in after the helicopter crash. Once you've mastered the formula for creation, you will have the power to transform your life from whatever shape it is in now into exactly what you want it to be.

When you properly use the formula for creation, your wildest dreams come true. Remember: everything we enjoy today started as someone's thought, a thought followed by taking the necessary action. This is the formula that can turn your dreams into a reality.

———

Think about the invention of TV. Just imagine how wild it must have sounded when the inventors tried to describe their thought. Using a bit of a theatrical license here, the description might have gone something like this:

"I am going to capture your image in color, along with your voice, with this special thing called a camera. Then the camera is going to change your image and voice into an electrical signal that will be transported wirelessly through the air to an object we'll call a satellite. The satellite, by the way, is in orbit around the Earth at 17,000 miles per hour. Then the satellite is going to beam that signal back down to Earth to anywhere we want, including everywhere at once. Yes, all of this will happen with no wires attached! It will be done through airwaves. Then anyone anywhere in the world who wants to see you in color and hear your voice will be able to do that.

Yes, they'll be able to watch and hear you at the same time as you're speaking."

How crazy would that have sounded to people back in those days? Why did it sound crazy? It sounded crazy only because no one had ever had those thoughts before. Yet this is not such a strange idea today because the majority of people on the planet have a TV. They have experienced the result of what those thoughts, backed by action, produced.

> *"Imagination is more important than knowledge."*
>
> ALBERT EINSTEIN

Now, what's the difference between the inventors of TV making their totally wild and crazy dream come true and you making your dream goals come true?

Do you think even the TV inventors themselves really knew *how* they were going to make their idea a reality when they first had the thought and when they first started trying to make it work? The truth is at first they didn't know how they were going to do it, and that didn't matter. They knew they had to start with a vision and then take the necessary action to make it come true.

Your knowledge is limited by your level of education and life experiences, either your own or experiences people have shared with you, yet your imagination is limitless. Every new thing that has ever been produced since the beginning of mankind began as a thought in someone's imagination. So this means all the things you desire in your own life also need to begin in your imagination.

Twenty-Five Thousand Thoughts a Day

The average person has about 25,000 thoughts a day. How powerfully creative is that! Unfortunately most people have the same 25,000 thoughts a day, every day. The majority of people live a life of habit. They're basically living the same day over and over again. They get up on the same side of the bed every morning, and that's probably because they sleep on the same side of the bed every night. They get in the shower and grab the soap in the same hand they always do. They wash their body in the same pattern as they do every day, day after day. They brush their teeth holding the tooth-brush with the same hand as they do every day. (God forbid you change hands—you could poke out an eye and kill yourself!)

The majority of people get to work the same way every day. It's so repetitive that some days they can't even remember the experi-ence of getting there. They've memorized the entire route. They know every traffic light, turn, stop sign, and detail along the way. They can drive without having to think much at all. (Until the day when they hear, "thump, thump, thump," and think, "Oh, no! Pedestrian crossing! I should have remembered that." No doubt the pedestrian would have been a lot happier had the driver remem-bered that too!)

And that's just the beginning of the average person's day. The rest of the day is pretty much more of the same. They go to lunch around the same time every day and eat at the same few restaurants day after day. They even have the same few things off the menus. They go home about the same time every day, driving the same route. They have dinner at about the same time every night, sitting in the same place they always do, only to retire to the same seat in front of their television to watch their same favorite shows. Does this sound like anyone you know?

You don't need any new thoughts to keep living your habitual life. It just takes the same consistent 25,000 habitual thoughts a day to create the same day over and over again.

How can you take any new actions if you're not having any new thoughts? Without new actions it's impossible to create any of the new results you desire.

I'm not saying all habits are bad, because the truth is we all have habits. It's not the habits that are keeping you from achieving your grand dream goals. It's the kinds of habits you practice.

The Best of Servants or the Worst of Masters

There are three types of habits: empowering, disempowering, and neutral. Examples of empowering habits include keeping a regular exercise routine, maintaining a healthy eating regime, and reading your goals and positive affirmations every day. All of those things empower you to have a better quality of life.

Disempowering habits include smoking, overeating, and procrastination. I don't think I need to go into why those activities are considered to be disempowering.

> "Habit is either the best of servants or the worst of masters."
>
> NATHANIEL EMMONS

Neutral habits include the things you do every day that neither hurt you nor help you. They're just things you do regularly. For example, you might drive the same way to work every day. It doesn't help you, and it doesn't hurt you either. It's just neutral!

And here's something most people don't know. Success itself is a habit. When you make taking successful actions your habit, you make becoming successful easy because you won't have to think about it anymore—you'll just automatically keep doing it. This applies to all areas of your life.

If you think being successful is hard work, then think again! By making a habit of taking consistent actions, success comes easily when it's habitual. There's one new thought you can adopt right away!

One of the quickest and most powerful ways to improve the quality of your life is to take some of your disempowering habits and exchange them with some new, empowering habits.

Take cigarette smoking, for example. Smoking is a hand-to-mouth habit. You have the cigarette in your hand, and you lift it up to your mouth in order to smoke it. Think about it, when most people quit smoking what do they go to next as their new habit to replace the smoking habit? That's right. They substitute one disempowering hand-to-mouth habit with another: overeating. Then, for many of them, once they see the results of their overeating, they often return to smoking, saying, "I'd rather be a thin smoker than a fat nonsmoker." So it's clear that replacing one disempowering habit with another disempowering habit isn't a good strategy to use to create the great results in your life that you desire.

Trading your old, disempowering habits with new, empowering habits is the winning strategy. Again, if we're using giving up smoking as the example, instead of habitually lifting the cigarette or a fork full of food to your mouth, you can create the habit of lifting a bottle of water to your mouth. This way you're making positive use of the hand-to-mouth habit that you already have. How easy is that?

I recommend that you always carry a bottle of water with you wherever you go. When you carry a bottle of water, you'll drink from it. Having the habit of drinking more water has benefits. Three-quarters of your body is made up of water. It is one component that your body is in constant need of replenishing. It helps your body to flush out toxins and is loaded with oxygen, which is the other key component for physical health. Quite a contrast to the effects of cigarette smoking, isn't it?

Oh, and by the way, for those people who try to tell you that having a cigarette relaxes them, they are incorrect. Ingesting the smoke constricts your capillaries, which raises your blood pressure, which creates the experience of being stressed. So, in reality, smoking creates more stress in your body, not less. What creates the feeling of relaxation is the deep breathing that smokers do when they are inhaling. All meditation practices are based in deep-breathing exercises. So if you continued to do the deep breathing without the cigarette in your mouth, you would feel relaxed without the bad breath.

Here's another great empowering habit to replace the disempowering smoking habit. Since the average smoker buys at least one packet of cigarettes a day and so has the habit of spending that money every day anyway, the new, empowering habit is to put that same money into an investment account. Make it a true investment account, one without a debit card or check facility. Soon you'll earn interest and then compound interest on your investment, and before you know it, that old habit of spending money on something that was costing you your life will have changed into an empowering habit that gives you a life of financial freedom! How's that for a great strategy?

It's important to know that when you drop an old habit, it leaves a void in your behavioral patterns, and that void creates a vacuum, forcing it to be refilled with another habit. If you don't replace your old habits with new, positive empowering habits that you choose, it will be very easy for the old habit to slip back in or for it to be replaced by another disempowering habit.

And here's another great strategy to use: start replacing some of your neutral habits with empowering ones. For example, take the neutral habit of driving the same way to work every day listening to music or the news on the radio, start listening to thought-provoking audio programs. Make it your empowering habit to consciously fill your mind with the kind of new thoughts that benefit your life.

Listen to programs that teach you things like personal development, wealth creation, vocabulary, or maybe even learn a foreign language. Anything that will stimulate your mind to have new, empowering thoughts, which in turn will give you new skills and tools to improve the quality of your life.

If you're not consciously and consistently putting the thoughts that you want into your mind, then other thoughts are going to seep in to fill that void. That's a very dangerous way to operate, because it means that you will be randomly accepting thoughts into your mind without deciding if they are the type that will help you or hurt you. Your mind will act on whatever thoughts are in it.

Oh, and by the way, there are no neutral thoughts. There are only empowering thoughts or disempowering thoughts. If they're not one, then they have to be the other. Empowering thoughts cause you to evolve. Disempowering thoughts cause you to go the other way, to dissolve. There's no middle ground. Remember that if you're not actively putting the thoughts that you want into your mind, the other kinds of thoughts can seep in and cause havoc.

We'll return to this in more depth in chapter 8. For now, just remember: *in life you either evolve or you dissolve; nothing stays the same*. It's your choice, and it depends on the types of thoughts or habits you choose.

Exercise your mind with consistent new, empowering thoughts every day, and you will strengthen your creation system. If you don't exercise your mind, it will grow weak and atrophy, just as your muscles do when you don't exercise them. If you don't use it, you lose it!

The same applies to your new success habits, or "success muscles," as I like to call them. The most successful habit, or success muscle, you can develop for yourself—the habit that will guarantee you the happy, healthy, wealthy, successful, fulfilled life you desire—is the habit of being consistent and relentless in making sure you're constantly filling your mind with only positive, empowering thoughts. Remember that your thoughts are seeds, and whatever you plant determines what you will grow.

One Drop of Poison

A word of caution! Negative energy, or negative thought, is a much heavier, denser energy than positive energy, or positive thought. A little bit of negativity can wipe out a heap of positives. Think about relationships, for instance. You can do a hundred good things for your partner followed by one messed-up thing, and then what happens? It's that one negative thing that gets remembered. And it wipes out all the good stuff you did.

Think about it this way: if you put ten spoonfuls of sugar in your cup of coffee, you will end up with very sweet-tasting coffee; if instead you put in one drop of poison, you're dead!

The point I'm making is that if you don't make a habit of stimulating your mind with positive, empowering thoughts, the chances of negative, disempowering thoughts getting in there and wreaking havoc dramatically increase. Negative, disempowering thoughts are weeds that can destroy your crop of happiness.

And that's why it's so important to stay conscious about whom you are spending your precious investment of time with. We become products of our environment. Whomever you spend the most amount of time around, you'll wind up starting to think like they do. And when you start to think like they do, you'll start to act like they do, and that will produce for you the same kinds of results that they have. That makes sense, right? So it becomes obvious that we need to make sure we are spending the majority of our time with the type of people who think the way we want to think. Take responsibility for making sure that you spend as much time as you can with the kind of people who have the results in their lives that you want in yours. Remember that birds of a feather flock together. It's who you're choosing to spend your time with that's a big determining factor in who you're going to be like. If you surround yourself with depressing, unhappy people long enough, eventually you will become one yourself, or when you choose to spend your time with happy, successful people, you will become one too. The choice is yours! (If you don't make the choice, it gets made for you.)

Understand that there are times when you may have to be around negative and disempowering people as part of your work or because they are members of your family. Making a habit of filling your mind with positive, empowering thoughts helps to protect you and carry you through these times. Make sure you take responsibility for not getting caught up in their way of life. If you must see these people, make sure you are fully charged up, and try to make the visit short. Does this sound mean? Think again. If you don't make the decision to keep yourself happy, then who are you giving your power away to? Do you think they are going to be as responsible with your power as you would be for yourself? Of course not! In fact, that sounds like the recipe for creating a lot of disappointment.

"Remember that the most expensive advice you can get is free advice from poor people."

———

Marie and I were in a second-hand bookstore when we found an original copy of a book titled *Self-Help* by Samuel Smiles written in 1859. The book sold so many copies that by 1909 it had been reprinted sixty times. This was so significant for us because this book is considered by many to be the first major personal development book ever written. You can imagine how excited we were to find this copy, and, to make it even better, it only cost ten dollars.

Marie and I happily strolled down the street relishing the beautiful day we were enjoying in Devonport, New Zealand. We both love it when miracles happen. We found a quaint little café looking out onto the bay facing Auckland. I pulled our newfound treasure from its wrapping and savored the moment before gently lifting the front cover. These were the first words I read:

I Woke Up to a New Thought

So, as I was saying at the start of this chapter, everything changed for me forever when I woke up one morning after surviving yet another night of deep depression and yet another attempt at suicide, and I had *a new thought*. What I didn't tell you was what that new thought was.

Are you curious about what that new thought might be, especially considering it was so powerful that it transformed my emotional state from deep depression into overwhelming joy and happiness? And it is a thought so powerful that it transformed my financial situation from living in poverty to being wealthy and financially free. Well, here it is.

I woke up that morning with the thought, *"Your life is not your own."*

> *"Might I give counsel to any young hearer, I would say to him, Try to frequent the company of your betters. In books and in life, that is the most wholesome society; learn to admire rightly; the great pleasure of life is that. Note what the great men admired; they admired great things: narrow spirits admire basely, and worship meanly."*
>
> WILLIAM MAKEPEACE
> THACKERAY

First there was my mother, who carried me in her womb for nine months and then went through all the pain and effort to give me the gift of life. I had witnessed all the disappointment, letdown, and pain on her face in recent years, and I realized that if I succeeded in committing suicide, she would be haunted for the rest of her life, wrestling with herself over why she couldn't save her son. For as long as she lived, she would be forced to endure the painful memory of her son who took his own life.

Then there is my father, who, when he first saw me on the day of my birth, held me in his hands with dreams about who I would grow up to become. His dreams would be shattered by my actions if I persisted in my disempowering habits any longer. He too would suffer for the rest of his life wondering where he went wrong in raising me.

I thought about Kimo, who would torture himself over why he couldn't help his friend. I thought about the rest of my family, my friends, and all the people I didn't yet know who might one day look up to me for hope and inspiration.

When the people who love and care about you see you down, they try to help you up, but since negative energy is heavier and denser than positive, it starts to drag them down too. The people who try to help you get caught up in the drama glue, and it pulls them down with you. Everyone around you begins to suffer.

I didn't even have to commit suicide to cause them pain. They were suffering just watching me in my dark, depressing world. I wasn't fooling any of them. They all knew I was hooked on drugs. They all could see me smoking cigarettes. For twenty-five years I had tried to get my parents to quit smoking because I knew it was such a nasty, unhealthy habit. I was the one who had always treated my body as a temple, and now I was the one smoking. They all tried to help me, and because I didn't respond, they suffered pain and self-doubt.

When you live in the loser loop and let your life go down the tubes, you don't take the ride alone; you take other people with you. They can't drag you to the winner's finish line. But you sure can drag them into the gutter. (In chapter 11, we will examine the loser loop and the winner's formula in greater detail, so you can learn the strategies to ensure you are a total winner.)

Once I absorbed the impact of that thought—that my life was not my own—I knew I had to change. I didn't want other people's pain to be my legacy. I didn't want my life to be just another story about someone who had so much promise and yet threw it all away.

I decided on that day that it didn't matter how many times in the past I had tried to change and failed, because today is the day I take responsibility for making the change and succeed.

This is what I did next. I went into the garage, unscrewed the handle from the broom, and took it to a sandy area in the backyard.

I held the broom handle over my head and assumed the pose of a samurai warrior with my blade pointed straight out in front of me. This is the samurai pose that means "death before dishonor." It signals to the warrior's opponent that he is going forward to his destination, and the only thing that could stop him from succeeding is death. The samurai knew that whatever didn't kill him would make him stronger.

So, with a powerful swipe of my makeshift sword, I sliced a line in the sand at my feet. I told myself that the moment I stepped over the line was the moment I decided I would never go back to my old ways.

After the thought comes the decision to take action on that thought. The decision point sets the change in motion. The moment you make a real decision, the change happens instantly.

For example, you might know some people who tried to quit smoking and it took them months or even years to finally do it. The truth is it didn't take them months or years to do it. What took them all that time was them finally getting to the place where they made the decision. Once you make the decision never to touch another cigarette, no matter what, you don't smoke anymore. You instantly become a nonsmoker. Think about it. If you don't ever touch a cigarette, how can you smoke it, right?

Understand that saying "I should do something" is not the same thing as making the decision to do it. You'll hear people say, "Oh, I should quit smoking," or, "I should lose some weight," or, "I should work on my personal development." I should, I should, I should. The truth is most people "should" all over themselves. Think about it. Has saying to yourself you *should* do something ever given you the power and commitment to actually go and do that thing? It never has for me. Has there ever been a time when you told yourself you should do something and yet you still didn't do it? Or has there ever been a situation in which you told yourself you shouldn't do something but you went ahead and did it anyway? See what I mean? A "should" just isn't powerful enough to get you to change. It has to be a "must."

It's when you make a real decision that your life instantly starts to change.

Once I cut that line in the sand with my broom handle sword and stepped over it, I instantly freed myself of all those old, disempowering habits forever. I decided right then and there that I would never use cocaine again, nor would I would ever smoke another cigarette. And I mean never! Even if I was offered a starring movie role that called for me to smoke, I would turn down the part.

I also got rid of all my guns by giving them away to friends who collected them because I didn't want them around me as reminders of all of those dark nights I had put myself through.

I realized that I needed some help to make the massive changes to my life that I wanted, so I went in search of anyone who could help me do it. I started going to seminars again, and I got back to consistently listening to audio programs and reading personal development books. I became a sponge for learning. I soaked up every strategy I could to help me to improve the quality of my life, and then I put those strategies into action.

We all start on a level playing field. We all have equal potential. What makes the difference is the decision to put the strategies into practice.

On that transformational day, I changed my life forever, and it all began when I chose to have a new thought. As I look back on it, I can clearly see a line between the moment of the new thought and the blessed life I now live. All the wealth, health, and happiness—and even the incredible relationship I am so lucky to have with my beautiful, wonderful wife Marie—all stems back to deciding to have that new, positive, empowering thought, "Your life is not your own."

"If I want things to change,
then I must change first."

P.S. Thanks, Kimo, for being my friend and for showing me some tough love. I promised you that I would make you proud and pay you back for all that you have done for me. It was that look in your eyes that one night that told me what I needed to know—if I want to change my life, I need to change first!

———

Don't you think it was a good move on my part that I mended my relationship with Kimo, considering he's the one who took the photograph that's on the cover of this book?

7

Transformation

The Big Win

Right from the start, the signs are there that this is going to be an awesome day. If you were up and out early enough you would have seen the beautiful red-orange sunrise, which in itself was an incredible event. This is the prelude to something amazing that's happening today. The birds are singing, the ocean seems the most beautiful shade of blue it has ever been, and the waves are simply perfect, softly rolling onto the shores like fields of wheat swaying in the breeze.

Can you feel it? There's electric energy in the air, and some lucky contestant is going to get a chance to win it all today. The game is set up for an easy win, so the biggest prize is already a certainty, and the odds are in the winner's favor to keep on winning everything they desire. If only the players in Las Vegas had these kinds of odds!

Wow, this must be really special, for two other lucky people will also be big winners today. They've been hoping for this for a long time, and now the payoff is finally about to happen. There are quite a few people in the room and they're all preparing for the big moment. For our three lucky winners, all of their patient waiting and expectations are about to be rewarded.

How many times have they tried to win the lottery without success? Who cares! Today all of that is going to change, because the game is set up so that as soon as the first person wins, the other two people win as well.

The game is filled with suspense and excitement. Everyone in the room can feel it. The outcome of the game that is about to begin is so momentous that the winners can change the world! Everyone who comes in contact with these winners will have their lives changed in some way. At this moment it's unclear just how they'll be changed; those exciting details will be revealed as the story unfolds.

For the other two big winners waiting in the room, every second feels like an eternity, because in order for them to win, the first winner must show up. The person standing in the middle of the room has signaled that the moment we've all been waiting for has arrived, and you can almost hear the game show announcer call, "Will the next contestant come on down!" It takes a little coaxing from the other two winning team members to get the third team member into the room. But they don't mind because that's what they are here to do.

And that's when it happens. You find out that you're the big winner. The doors open, and you come gliding into the room to collect your prize, looking wide-eyed and surprised as if someone has just woken you up from a peaceful sleep. All eyes are focused on you, and everyone is so excited to see you, already celebrating in your honor.

It's what happens next that really takes you by surprise because it lets you know that this game is just the start of something really big for you. If you had a choice you'd probably have chosen a different introduction, yet that's not the way it works out and so what? It's not what happens that counts. It's what you do with it.

The game show announcer grabs you by the legs, hangs you upside down, and for no apparent reason slaps you across your backside. You're thinking, "Only a few moments ago, I was comfortable and minding my own business, and then this happens. What kind of game is this?" And it's at that exact moment that your question is answered when the game show announcer blurts out, "Baby, this is your life!"

Congratulations! You've come into this world already a winner after surviving your birth, and your prize is life, with all its awesome possibilities laid ahead of you. For the other two winners, your parents, there were times during the winning event that weren't so comfortable, especially for your mom! And as you're first laid down on your mother's chest, cradled tenderly by her loving arms, you finally get to meet the planet's ultimate master of transformation.

Meet the Master of Transformation, Mom

Why is your mother a master of transformation? Because she has just had your head pass through an opening in her body that's the size of your eye socket. Ouch! We all owe a lot of gratitude and love to our mothers for going through that extreme level of pain to give us our ultimate gift—life. And the pain and discomfort began long before your birth: she carried you for nine months without being able to put you down, enduring uncomfortable sleepless nights and lower back pain as you kicked, punched, and stretched her beautiful body into a new shape. Yet Mom finds a way to instantaneously transform all the pain she suffers before and during childbirth into unconditional love for you, her newborn baby. And if you're her second, third, or fourth child, your mom loves you even more because she knew how bad it was going to hurt and yet she still willingly went through with having you!

As a man I will never truly comprehend the enormity of that. If men ever had something that big come out of our backsides, we would never eat solid food again. No way. We're just not that tough! That's probably why when you see a big, tough athlete being interviewed after winning the game, he always looks straight into the camera and says, "Hi, Mom," because he knows, no matter how big and strong he thinks he is, she's the toughest because she gave birth to him.

You have to really think about that for a moment to see the power in it. How often in life do we immediately give total, unconditional love to someone who has just caused us extreme pain?

It's in that very first experience that your mom teaches you the ultimate lesson of life, which is really an amazing gift, and when you really understand that lesson, everything else you want in life will start to reveal itself to you. It's amazing to think you are taught the most valuable lesson of your life first, at your birth. Your mom was able to transform all the pain you caused her with your entrance into this world by turning it into unconditional love. She was able to turn one extreme into another. In transforming pain into the ultimate power of all, the power of unconditional love, your mom teaches you the lesson of transformation. And the lesson is that you have the power to change anything, even extreme pain, into something better, something positive.

If your mother can transform all that pain into something positive, then anything you want to transform in your life must surely be easy by comparison. Which seems easier: first creating life from nothing, then transforming the extreme pain from childbirth into love; or making money and becoming wealthy? Or creating the relationship of your dreams? Or getting your body healthy and fit? All of a sudden, transforming your life and achieving your dreams doesn't seem that difficult, does it?

I finally understood this lesson that morning I woke up with my new thought. At that moment I understood the formula for being a master of transformation of my own life. I understood I had the power to transform absolutely anything in my life—even the pain of the years following the helicopter crash—into something great, something positive.

It started with the new thought, followed by the decision to take action. I saw all the darkness of those last years in a different way. My old life could be transformed into my new life. I left the drama behind me and became a new person.

Either You Evolve or You Dissolve

Whether you're already enjoying a life filled with success or you're down and out in desperate need of a better life, this book offers you gifts you can use to take your life to the next level and beyond, because this book is all about transformation.

What does transformation mean? "Trans" means to go beyond, "form" refers to what you currently have in your life right now, and "ation" means the experience of. So we could be talking about the "form" your life is in right now, or the form your health and fitness is in, the form your relationship is in, your wealth, or your spirit. So when we're talking about transformation, we're talking about "the experience of going beyond what you have now" in any or all of these areas of your life.

Let's take a closer look at how this actually works.

Take your health, for example. What is form is it in? Are you already in good health and want to make it better, or are you in poor health and desperate for improvement? Remember: if you are already in great health, that doesn't guarantee you will always be that way, because even though you may continue to do the same things, time is passing, and you are going to have to make adjustments as your body goes through different stages and forms. Many people in their thirties and forties have told me that when they were in their teens, they could eat five candy bars a day and not gain an ounce of fat on their lean and athletic bodies. Now, as soon as they look at a piece of chocolate, they gain weight. Do you know anyone like that?

And what form is your relationship in today? Do you even have a relationship? If you are in a relationship, is it the wonderful, passionate, loving relationship of your dreams, or is it headed for divorce, like 60% of the marriages in this country? If you are in a long-term relationship, you may have noticed the things you used to do in the early stages of your relationship don't get the same responses from your partner anymore. The form has changed over time.

Think about it. Even the rules of your relationship change the longer you're together. For example, when you were first dating and you saw each other's clothes all over the floor, it was a good thing. It meant you were having a good time, and afterward, one of you was going to put his or her clothes back on and leave. Then, after you moved in together, did the scenario change? When she sees his dirty underwear lying on the floor, she's thinking, "What does he think, that I'm the underwear fairy? I wasn't put on the planet to pick those up!" And when he sees her pantyhose hanging over the shower curtain rod, he's thinking, "Is there anywhere in this house I can call mine? She has taken over the entire kingdom!" Remember: At the beginning of the relationship, she thought getting his underwear off was sexy; now she considers them toxic waste. He couldn't wait to get her pantyhose off back then, and now he wishes they were made illegal.

Life is changing constantly and it always will. The form of your health, your relationship, your wealth, and your spirit are all in a constant state of change. So, no matter where you are right now in life, there is always a newer and different place to take it.

And it is your choice what that newer and different place is. You can consciously invest in yourself, which in turn will elevate your experience of life to a more joyful and fulfilling level, or you can let nature take its course, and, bit by bit, allow the winds of time to erode the quality of your life until there is very little happiness left.

Either you evolve or you dissolve. If you're not actively creating your life, compelling it to evolve, then, by default, it will dissolve . . . and get worse. The key to having a truly fulfilling and enjoyable life today and every day that follows is conscious transformation—making "the experience of going beyond what you have now" a good one.

Take business, for example. A successful business needs the application of regular conscious transformation. Have you noticed the world is changing these days? The truth is that it always has been and it always will be. The marketplace is changing, and customers are more educated and have more choice than ever before. Even the way business is conducted is changing with the explosion of the Internet. If you're doing business the same way you were three years ago, there is a very good chance that you are now on your way out of business. Your business is either growing or dying. Nothing stays the same.

The same applies to your relationship. If you're doing the same things in your relationship now that you were doing when you first got together, then these may be the exact things that end it. The average person doesn't even do that much! The majority of people become complacent in their relationships, and, little by little, they start doing less and less. Look at most couples who have been together for a long time. Instead of getting in better and better physical shape, both partners become comfortable and complacent and let their bodies go pear-shaped. Yet when they were dating, being well groomed was a must because they knew it would better their chances of finding a partner. Why does conscious personal transformation for most people get tossed out like yesterday's garbage as soon as people find a partner? And you wonder why so many people are getting divorced, or, if they stay in the relationship, why they are so unhappy with each other. If you don't evolve, you dissolve!

Transformation: The Experience of Going Beyond What You Have Now

When you think about it, isn't that what you really want in life—to go beyond what you have now? Life offers us the opportunity to transform ourselves, and not just once. Life is about continual transformation because in life nothing stays the same.

Have you ever noticed that when things begin to decay, they also start to smell bad? Have you ever wondered why that is? It's nature's way of warning us to stay away, because if living matter spends too much time around the energy of decay, it will start to decay more rapidly itself.

Remember that the natural order of the universe is for everything to seek to reach its highest potential, to evolve, to go beyond what it is now. Grow in harmony with the natural order of the universe. Move away from the stink of decay.

"In order to fly, you have to let go of the world that you're hanging on to."

When you think about it, how are you ever going to transform if you keep hanging on to what you have now?

The Miracle of Transformation

Two normal human beings with no training, no manual, and no prior experience are able to create a life from nothing. How amazing is that?

What happens over the next nine months following conception is truly a miracle. Think about it. How can it be that one single cell, with no brain, can have so much intelligence to know everything it needs to do to turn into a human being? We're talking about something so small it can only be seen with a powerful microscope. That first cell divides, multiplies into more cells, and then starts organizing different cells to form a nose, two eyes, two legs, two arms, hair, all your different bones, and all your organs that function in different capacities. As a matter a fact, that first intelligent microscopic speck of matter even creates the brain that will later take care of the body it created for the entire length of your life. And that's only the tip of the miraculous iceberg!

The moment you are fully formed, you automatically experience birth and learn the most important lesson you will ever need to know—that you have power to create miracles. You've done this magic once and easily, and that means you can do it easily again! Think about it. Did it actually take any hard work by you to be born? Of course not! In nature creation comes easy.

You started from nothing, and everything that followed has been a continuation of the creation process that got you here in the first place. From the moment of your first thought, you got to choose and participate in what you were creating. And that continues today. Think about it. Each and every day, you get the opportunity to participate in the natural process of creating your life, using the magical gifts that have been yours from the very beginning.

You may be wondering, "If that's all true, then why haven't I been able to create the results I want or the joy I desire in life?" The answer is because you haven't figured out how to appropriately use your magical gifts for creation and manifestation. And one of the reasons you may not have used your gifts is because you don't know which ones to use.

"The universe always gives you what you ask for, and it rarely comes in the package you expect it to show up in."

You were taught the most important lesson from the very start, yet it wasn't spelled out in black and white for you. You may have noticed that when you were born, there wasn't an owner's manual strapped to your leg. (Your mom was probably pretty happy about that. You were painful enough!)

Your potential to be a master of manifestation with the ability to create all of your grand dream goals is infused into every atom of your being since the first spark of life was given to you, and it will always be with you. The question is how can you tap into that ability?

To Create, or to Be Created? That Is the Question.

Change is nonstop, within you and all around you, from the moment of conception to the moment of death and beyond. Everything that happens following the moment the sperm meets the egg is part of a constant process of changing form.

We are changing all the time, whether we choose to or not. As a matter of fact, *everything* is changing all the time, and there's nothing we can do to stop it. What you *can* do is choose the direction of that change, because transformation happens in two ways—involuntarily and voluntarily. If you don't proactively choose your direction, then, by default, a direction will be forced upon you, and most likely it won't be the direction you would have chosen for yourself. Remember: there's no such thing as taking no action, because that too is an action, and it too produces results—just not the ones you really wanted.

Now, think again about your transformation from conception to birth. From the original act of manifestation when your first cell was on the scene, your journey of involuntary transformation was automatically activated. For the rest of your life, your body is continually changing form, and you don't have to do anything to make that happen. The system is on automatic and continues to be after your birth. Your body automatically grows and transforms through childhood, your teen years, adulthood, and beyond. It involuntarily transforms the food you eat and the air you breathe into fuel you need to grow and develop. You don't have to learn involuntary transformation. It just happens by itself.

Even after death, when your body is no longer needed by your soul, involuntary transformation continues as your body is recycled back into the earth. Just look at past photos of yourself, and you'll see how many times you've transformed from the person you were before into the person you are now. And by the way, aging doesn't happen once a year on your birthday. It's always happening. Like everything else in the universe, you are in a constant state of flux.

So why can't you sit back and let involuntary transformation do what it does so well and take you to higher and higher levels? The answer is that while involuntary transformation can work for you, it can also work against you. For example, if you don't exercise regularly, your muscles will get weak and atrophy, whether you like it or not. If you don't actively improve your mind, it too gets weaker and atrophies.

Here's the challenge. As you go through life, you experience the advantages and disadvantages of involuntary transformation, and the lesson to learn is that you do have choices. The experience of watching your muscles weaken teaches that you have a choice. The experience of watching what dissolves in your life teaches you that you have a choice. You can choose to evolve. If you don't evolve, you dissolve, because nothing stays the same. So the key to having an evolving life with all the good things that come with that is voluntary transformation. And it's either one or the other. There is no neutral.

What is voluntary transformation? It's what happens when you consciously choose to participate in personally developing yourself to be the best you can be.

Think again about that moment of your birth and that very first, powerful lesson offered to you by that master of transformation, your mother. Her act of transforming the pain of childbirth into total, unconditional love for you was the first voluntary transformation you witnessed. Until that moment, all you had experienced was the miracle of involuntary transformation that delivered you into her arms. And that moment was when all your choices and life-creating potential began. You had to experience that lesson in order to learn it. Your mother didn't simply tell you about the lesson so you could file it away and never use it again. Lessons don't really work that way. It's in the doing that we develop the most. That is why we learned the first lesson that way. Experience is the way that the soul grows.

Isn't that an awesome start to life? There you are, newly born, the living proof that you have creative magic in every cell of your being, experiencing the one lesson that gives you everything you need to know to use your magic to participate in life to the fullest and give your soul the experience of a lifetime. After all, that's what you're here for, right?

Most people quickly forget that first lesson in transformation. Fortunately for them, the universe has a backup plan.

The Universe Has a Backup Plan

Where do we come from? We come from the source of creation. It's that same source of creation you tap into every time you put a thought into action and create a result. It's that same source of creation from which all the big plans you have for your life will also come when you put into action the lessons of transformation that were taught to you at birth.

Let's call the source of creation the universe. Or you can call it God. Or any other name. Regardless of what you call it, it's the source that created this experience of life for you.

The source has a grand purpose for everything, including for you. *Everything that happens in the universe has a positive intent attached to it.* For example, no one starts smoking cigarettes wanting to get cancer or emphysema. People start because they think smoking will give them some positive benefit, like the feeling of being cool or part of the group.

So when you forget that first lesson of transformation, the universe automatically delivers the backup plan: it keeps teaching you the lesson every moment you're alive by showing you the results—some painful, some joyful—of your thoughts and actions and giving your soul the opportunity to learn the lesson by experience. Its positive intent is to guide you toward choosing the kinds of thoughts that create positive, joyful results in every area of your life.

The feeling of pleasure urges you forward, encouraging you with constant feedback, in the direction to a totally holistic successful and abundant life. You can use that abundance to experience the full creative power of love. On the other side of that, the universe provides you with the experience of pain to get you to move away from danger and other things that might harm you. Pleasure and pain give you a lifetime of experiencing changes that either evolve or dissolve your progress, which is a wonderful way to encourage you to get the picture and realize that you do have a choice in the way your life turns out. What a way to awaken your creative genius and to awaken you to the power you have to help change the world and the people in it! It urges you to participate fully in this life and use your creative powers to produce all the wealth, health, and happiness you need to help yourself and others to evolve.

If She Can Do It So Can I

When you finally understand that first awesome lesson delivered by your mother, the lesson that pain isn't always negative and that it can be voluntarily transformed into whatever you choose it to be, you can move your life to a higher level.

The Power to Change the World

Every child coming into the world has the opportunity to change the course of history with the actions he or she takes or doesn't take. From the moment life begins, we're given the power to create, make, generate, produce, fashion, form, craft, build, and construct, or we can obliterate, wipe out, annihilate, demolish, devastate, tear down, and destroy. All these actions are transformational because they change what we have into something else, delivering us the experience along the way. Some of these transformations will be voluntary, some involuntary. Remember: if you don't take action and participate, you're leaving your destiny in the hands of others who may not have the same intention for your life as you do. Think about it this way: if you don't take action and water your houseplants, they wither away and die. The same is true of your grand dream goals.

Even the universe, the source of creation itself, needs to constantly evolve or else it will decay and then no longer exist, because nothing stays the same. How does the universe evolve? One of the

ways it happens is every time we, as human beings, ch
sonally develop. No wonder the universe encourages u
No wonder it offers joy and fulfillment as rewards for d
because when we evolve, it evolves.

Sadly, the universe also suffers when people fail to participate in empowering, evolving ways. Wars, fighting, pollution, crime, racism, prejudice, poverty, starvation, and gluttony are all results of disempowering thoughts and actions and are all forms of decay. These things happen because people aren't making the choice to evolve and therefore are contributing to the dissolving of the world and the universe. Remember, too, that if you're not part of the solution, you're part of the problem. Instead of saying it's everyone else's fault these things are happening, contribute to the positive transformation of the world by participating in empowering ways.

When I say these things are happening because people are not choosing to evolve, understand that I'm not just talking about people whose lives are in the gutter, or people who are down and out. This is about all of us. We all need to evolve from where we currently are, because if we're not growing, we're decaying. Nothing stays the same. The Law of Vibration states that everything is in motion. So if you're not moving in one direction, you must be moving in the other. Remember: there is no neutral! We can choose to participate in making our lives the way we want them, or we can sit around, take our chances, and hope for the best. You may have already noticed that waiting around for your life to magically transform itself rarely gets you the life that you desire. So hoping for your life to get better, or hoping for your goals to be achieved, isn't going to get you there, right? Most people wish really big and expect very little, and in life you get what you expect.

If you're wondering why I keep going back and forth between talking about the state of the planet and talking about achieving your own grand dream goals, it's because they're connected. When you choose to change your life and start enjoying it at the highest level, you'll want to share your abundance of joy with others. When you do this, you begin to teach them how they can have it too. They, in turn, start teaching it to other people, and the number of joyful people grows exponentially. Yet it's impossible to teach others about being abundant and joyful when you don't have abundance and joy in your own life. How can you give away that which you don't have? That's like writing a check for a million dollars when you have an empty bank account, or being an overweight fitness instructor trying to teach others to exercise. The way to change the world is to start by changing yourself. The only way to experience going beyond what you have in your life now and getting the results you desire is to actively participate in your transformation, to choose to evolve.

The choice over which direction your life takes is entirely up to you. Right now your health is either getting better or it's getting worse. You're either in better shape or worse shape than yesterday. You're either improving your relationship with your partner, or it's getting worse. If you're not in a relationship, then you're either getting closer to having one or further away, because nothing in the universe stays the same. Remember: this applies to every aspect of your life. Either you're living life to the fullest or sliding deeper and deeper into a life you don't want. Whether your life evolves or dissolves depends on your level of participation in making change happen. It's your choice as long as you choose to make it. If you don't make the choice, the choice gets made on you.

Physics 101

The "evolve or dissolve" process is ruled by a law of nature called the Law of Vibration, which states that everything is in motion. Laws of nature are constants; they can't be broken, and they apply to everyone and everything in the universe. The laws are not good or bad; they just are. They can either work for you or they can work against you. It all comes down to how you utilize them.

The Law of Vibration states that everything in the universe is vibrating. It's simple physics! Everything in the universe is made up of atoms, and every atom is made up of 99.999999999999% empty space. The rest of the space is filled by a tiny bit of energy called a quark, which vibrates back and forth inside the atom. So every atom is vibrating or moving, and since everything in the universe is made up of atoms, then absolutely everything is in motion.

All that motion results in atoms continually bumping into each other, and that sets another law of nature into action. It's the Law of Cause and Effect: every cause creates an effect, and every effect is created by a cause.

So that means that everything in life is in motion, and nothing is standing still. That's why we call this place the universe. "Uni" means one, and "verse" means song. (It's the one song of Love that we all sing together.)

And in order for any song to be sung or any music to be played, something has to vibrate. When you sing, your vocal cords vibrate. And you'll notice within any musical instrument, something must vibrate for it to produce musical tones. So "universe" means the one vibration that runs through everything and everyone. We are all part of this one verse, this one vibration, so whatever you do affects everyone and everything else. So what's your contribution?

Remember: knowing something is not enough. Knowledge by itself has no transformational power. Most people know what to do, and most people aren't acting on what they know. It's taking the action that creates the results.

The only way to fail at life is failing to participate. When you don't participate and take the necessary action, you end up getting what's left over after everyone else has made their choice, and honestly, I don't think getting handed the leftovers is going to make you happy or bring much joy into your life, do you? Are you the person you dreamed you would grow up to be when you were a child?

When you look at what's happening in the world, it's pretty clear the majority of people on this planet aren't consciously making an attempt to have the quality of life they desire. They'll tell you they want a better life for themselves and the people they love, yet they still don't take the actions that produce those results.

Don't take my word for it; just look at the statistics to see the truth:

60% of all marriages end in divorce. It's pretty clear that instead of evolving, most relationships are dissolving.

65% of the population of most developed countries is over-weight and out of shape. Again, it's obvious these people aren't actively participating in evolving ways. Currently, one in three people will experience some form of cancer in their bodies. We've already discussed in chapter 6 how disempowering thoughts can contribute to cancer.

Studies show that out of every 100 people who work for the best forty-five years of their life, ninety-seven end up dead or just dead broke. They end up with nothing positive to show for their forty-five years of hard work. Of the remaining three people, two will manage to survive their retirement years without charity from their friends, family, or government. You may have noticed I use the word "survive," not "thrive," for these two, because that's what their condition becomes: survival. If something happens and they have a financial setback of some kind or a major health challenge during their retirement years, they're thrust into the group of ninety-seven people who are either dead or dead broke. Only 1 out of the 100 retires wealthy.

Here's something for you to think about. How many of those ninety-nine people do you think might have gotten different results if they had participated differently?

Imagine being in your retirement years, supposedly the golden years of your life, only to discover you're stuck feeling overwhelming remorse and regret for the quality of life you missed, and also feeling the day-to-day stress and fear about how you're going to make ends meet on a small pension. Sadly, this pain-filled destiny is what the majority of people on this planet have to look forward to, and what makes it even sadder is that it all could have been avoided and a different destiny created. Is that the life you want for yourself?

The most consumed drugs on the planet are anti-depressants. The reason so many people are depressed is because they aren't choosing to actively transform their lives, and therefore their lives are dissolving. The statistics show the majority of all people are leading unhappy, depressed, unfulfilled lives. What can you learn from this? It's common sense that the minority, those are the people with the great results, are obviously doing things differently than the majority, and that's why they're getting different results. Better results. It also makes sense that if you want your life to be different, it's not a good idea to keep doing what the majority does. That makes sense, right? So what's the solution? That's easy; join that other group, the minority group.

The minority are the people who don't conform to the mold. Instead of cutting back on their wants to fit their incomes as the majority of people do, they create their incomes to fit their desires. They take the necessary action to design their lives to fit their dreams. Those of the minority are the fortunate ones who get to enjoy life at a higher level. No matter what results you have already achieved in your life, wouldn't you still get value out of having more joy?

This book is dedicated to helping you cross that line from the majority way of life to the minority way of fulfillment. Remember that this book isn't just about learning how to make more money; it's about learning how to be rich. When I'm talking about being rich, I'm talking about being "enriched." Living an enriched life means you'll get more joy and fulfillment out of every facet of your life. Does living a life like that sound like something you might be interested in? And if you also want to make more money, then you can use the same strategies to do so. Once you master the strategies in this book you'll realize there is only one kind of real success in life, and that's holistic success. It's also called a balanced life. *If your life isn't in balance, then it's out of balance.* What's the point of being rich if you're sick? What's the point of being wealthy if you're lonely? Only holistic success is true success.

Transcending the Second-Biggest Lie

Have you ever been told that to be successful in life, you need to work hard? It's what the majority of people believe, and it's the second-biggest lie we are all told from childhood. Think about it. How hard do you work to get ahead in your life? If you are working hard, then you are not living the balanced life you dream of, unless you really do dream of a life spent working hard. Is that what you really want? I didn't think so! I've never heard of anyone on their deathbed saying, "Oh, I wish I had spent more time at work!" Why would you say that unless you wanted to have the company's name inscribed on your tombstone?

So if you're already working hard to get ahead and you're not there, then it's pretty clear that working hard isn't the strategy that's going to get you to the place you want to be.

Then when you don't have the results that you desire, even after you've already been working hard for it, the majority gives you the follow-up lie. And that being, "If you're not where you want to be, then you're going to have to work a little bit harder to get there." Does that sound like a good strategy to you? Are you really excited by the idea of working even harder than you already are? Does working harder sound like it's going to produce a higher level of joy in your life? Wouldn't you like more time to spend having fun with your family and friends instead? Remember that whatever you plant will determine what you will grow, so hard work can only produce a hard life.

One thing I want to make very clear is that the people who tell you these lies aren't doing it to be hurtful or mean. They're just doing the best they can with the skills and tools they have. If they had better skills and tools, they would use them. They'd also have great holistic success for themselves. That makes sense, right?

Remember: they didn't start the lie. They were told it by their parents, who learned it from their parents, who learned it from their parents. The lie is perpetuated by people who don't really know how to become holistically successful so they're guessing at what the strategy might be. Plus, they hear the other members of the majority saying the same thing. So don't be angry or upset at people who tell you this lie. Just don't buy into it.

My father, whom I loved very much and with whom I had a very close relationship, was my hero. He was also the hardest-working person I have ever known, and yet at the end of his life, he didn't have many economic rewards or great experiences to show for all his hard work. In one year, my wife Marie and I make more money than my father made in all seventy-six years of his life, combined.

Understand that I'm not telling you this to impress you. I'm telling you to impress upon you that my father didn't teach me great wealth-building strategies. He worked much harder than I ever have, and yet I've gotten far better results.

Have you ever noticed that the people who work the hardest are not the people who are the most successful? Think about it. Even if they're making a lot of money working hard every day, they don't have any quality time left to spend with their loved ones. Does that sound like a holistically successful life to you? And if you look at conditions in the world today, not only are the world's fathers working hard trying to keep a roof over the family's head, so are many of the mothers. So now both parents are working full-time jobs trying to make ends meet, which leaves no one at home spending quality time with the children. Did you want to have children in your life only to miss the experience of watching them grow up? Is that the life you dreamed of? If you're busy working hard trying to pay the bills, who's teaching your children good values for life and how to live it? Again, is that a holistically successful life?

I want to reiterate that this book isn't about learning how to make more money. What it *is* about is putting into place some different strategies so that you and everyone you love can enjoy life at a much higher level. And isn't that what you really want? Isn't that the reason you work so hard—because you think it will provide a better life for the people you love?

Think about this for a moment: how do your children learn? That's right: they learn from what you do and not necessarily from what you tell them to do. Have you noticed that your children don't always do what you tell them? And have you noticed that no matter how old you are right now, you still do some things just like your parents did, whether you try to or not? That's because we learn from what our parents do rather than from what they tell us to do, and your children are no different.

Do you really want to learn how to be happy from someone who is depressed? Would you really have faith in people teaching you about how to become wealthy when they are broke themselves? What are you teaching your kids by the way you're living your life right now? And what are you teaching your kids by the actions you're taking or not taking? Well guess what, your kids don't want to learn things from you that you're not demonstrating in your life either. The only way you can inspire your family, your friends, your community, your country, and the world to be happy, healthy, wealthy, and holistically successful is for you to become that way yourself first.

Are you ready to break the mold handed down through the generations, the mold perpetuating the second-biggest lie, the lie that says you need to work hard to be successful? The strategies and tools in this book will enable you to do this.

Transcending the Biggest Lie

In chapter 10, you'll have the opportunity to transcend the biggest lie of all.

That lie is when you grow up and become an adult, it's okay to give up on your dreams. Not only is it okay, it's also expected that you get real about putting a roof over your head and fulfill the expectations of the majority life.

As soon as I went out on my own to pursue my dream of becoming a Hollywood actor, my father started asking me when I was going to give up on this crazy dream and face reality. He kept reminding me about how many people dream of being actors and how many people never make it. Again, my father wasn't saying these things to be mean to me or to dash my hopes. He was just trying his best to be a great father. He didn't want to see me wasting my life chasing something that might never happen.

In his reality it was better to have a good, steady job than to chase your childhood dreams. Luckily, that isn't the reality I hold for myself. I know that when you give up on your dreams, you die. It's not your body that dies; it's your spirit. Each day you're not actively pursuing your dreams, your spirit dies a little bit more, until there is nothing left. That's why you see so many people walking around without any spark left inside. They have no sparkle in their eyes. They are just enduring their own day-to-day existence. Does that sound like a holistically successful life or a wonderful way to inspire others to evolve?

When I first moved to Australia, I used to sit in a coffee shop in Brisbane right at the time when people were walking through the city on their way to work. I was amazed at the body language the people displayed. Every step they took seemed slower and more painful than the last, as if they were walking through ankle-deep wet cement. Their heads hung low as they stared at the pavement in front of them. No one said good morning or talked to anyone. They just stayed in their own little worlds. The sad, disillusioned looks on their faces told the whole story of their inner child who gave up on their dreams in order to survive in the cold, cruel world.

The saddest part for me is the knowing that it doesn't have to be that way if only the people could see that the lies they bought into don't make sense. The truth is the people who work the hardest don't have the best rewards in life, and the people who have the best lives aren't the hardest workers.

I once heard Deepak Chopra say, "Do less and have more; do nothing and have it all." It sounded awesome, yet I just could not comprehend how it could possibly work. It took me quite a few years to figure out what it really meant and how to make it a reality in my life. In this book I'll show you how to transcend the biggest lie and discover the truth in Deepak's advice.

Almost There!

If you've already started running through some of your old stories about how the conditions of your life are different from everyone else's, and that you've already heard, read, and tried everything to make a positive difference in your life, yet nothing has worked for you in the long term, you need to challenge those beliefs. It's those beliefs that will continue to hold you back and stop you from ever creating the true happiness you desire in your life. In chapters 10 and 11, you'll learn what it really means to say that you've already tried everything, and you'll discover the things you haven't tried—the things that *do* work.

So have faith. You're so much closer to having your holistically successful life than you think. Stay with me on this. In chapter 10 you'll get a clearer picture of that new life, and throughout this book, you'll learn the consummate strategies and tools to get you there.

What's the difference between first and fourth place? If you're an Olympic athlete, the difference between the gold-medal winner who gets all the rewards and the fourth-place winner who gets nothing, not even a free T-shirt, can be $1/100^{th}$ of a second. That tiny fraction of time can mean the difference between being a lifelong legend and someone who is instantly forgotten, moments after the race is over. The gold medalist gets offered book deals, endorsement deals, high-paid speaking engagements, and ticker tape parades. The only thing the fourth-place winner gets is a pat on the back and, "Too bad! Better luck next time." (If he's lucky!)

The point I'm making is that you're not as far away from everything you want in life as you may think. Right here is where I usually hear someone tell me about how they are the exception to the rule because they feel that they aren't even close to achieving their grand dream goals. Those are the exact kind of thoughts that will keep you from achieving the success you desire. In order to undertake your transformational journey, you are going to need to keep an open and unprejudiced mind. You're going to have to be willing to let go of some of your old ways of thinking so you can adopt new, successful ones.

Make room for what you don't yet know, for what you will discover in the rest of this book. Make room to evolve and transform.

Remember, too, that there's a difference between knowing what to do and actually doing it. The world is full of educated derelicts. Are you willing to do what the average person isn't willing to do? Are you willing to evolve and transform?

When you are, you will instantly start to get results that average people don't. The best part is that when you get better results, you can teach others that they can have them too, and you can also show them how. Remember: no one wants to learn from those who haven't achieved results themselves.

I promise you the strategies in this book work because they are the same ones I used to transform my life from being so low that I was at the brink of extinction into being a life filled with all the many rewards I now enjoy. And because all the thousands of people I've taught who also consistently put these strategies into action have evolved and transformed their lives as well. The strategies work the same way for anyone who chooses to learn them and use them.

So, face the facts. The actions you're taking now are producing the results you currently have, so it's time to choose new actions to transform your life. If you already have an incredible life, what you're going to learn will make it even better. As soon as you put into action the simple and common-sense strategies in this book, you will instantly experience real, lasting, and measurable results. You will evolve and transform.

> *"Dreams come true when you make the decision to make them come true."*

I know holistic success is what you want. Why else would you be reading this book? You're almost there. You're only 1/100th of a second away from your dream life right now. You're so close!

Even though you're close, there will probably be times when you feel frustrated or confused by what you're reading in this book. When this happens, rejoice, because this signals a new time of learning, of transformation. It's a very exciting point to reach. It's the point at which you start to ask new questions. And what does this do? When you ask new questions, you get new answers.

When you keep an open mind and go in search of answers, you will find them. Whenever you feel frustrated or confused, ask yourself, "What's the best thing to do when I'm frustrated?" Then give yourself the answer: "Ask great questions!" Because when you ask good questions, you'll get good answers. So there's no need to get frustrated about being frustrated! In the next chapter, you will learn more about how to ask good questions—the kinds of questions that instantly supply the kinds of answers that will totally transform your life.

> *"Seek, and ye shall find."*
>
> MATTHEW 7:7

8

The Power Is in Your House

*I*magine a warm summer night. You're sitting on the front porch of a house in the countryside. The night air is filled with the sound of chirping crickets calling out to each other. The sky is a black satin carpet peppered from end to end with shimmering, sparkling stars. Next to the front door, the porch light is on.

Looking at the porch light, what do you notice? Do you see an array of bugs and moths flying and crawling around the light? Have you ever wondered why they do this? The answer is simple. They're attracted to the light.

In some places in the world, you will also see geckoes near the light. They're attracted to the light because the bugs are tasty treats for them to eat.

Let's say the porch light uses a 50-watt bulb. The lightbulb produces light when electricity passes through the filament inside it, causing it to glow, producing the light we see.

A 50-watt bulb has low wattage going through it, and that's why it produces a lower level of light than a higher-wattage bulb. You could say that a 50-watt lightbulb is dim, because it gives off such a low level of light.

What happens when you have a dim bulb in your porch light? Well, you'll see a small number of bugs and moths congregating around it. What happens when you exchange the 50-watt bulb for a 250-watt bulb? That's right. The light gets brighter, and the brighter light attracts a greater number of bugs and moths. And what makes the 250-watt light brighter than the 50-watt light? The power. The 250-watt lightbulb has more power going through it. The more power flowing to the source of the light, the brighter the light gets and the more life is attracted to it.

I spent over eighteen years living in Los Angeles, working in the motion picture industry, where we used many different sizes of lights to create the look and feel needed for various scenes.

Working at night outside on location, we sometimes used lights big enough to handle 24,000 kilowatts of power. These lights are so powerful, so super bright, they can light up a whole neighborhood. The power is so great that if you stand too close to them, they can melt a nylon baseball cap right off your head, and if you look into them, they can blind you.

As soon as you turn one of these 24,000-kilowatt lights on, bugs by the millions amass around it and swarm in its beam, soon joined by birds, bats, and other flying creatures, all attracted to the light. It becomes its own little ecosystem!

Almost everyone in Los Angeles has seen movies being shot, and most have been inconvenienced in one way or another by a film production, either by being caught in a traffic jam because a street has been blocked off or by being unable to park in front of his or her own home because the film company has commandeered all the street parking for cast and crew. Can you imagine how irritating that can be, considering the film company might be there for days, weeks, and sometimes even months?

What used to amaze me was that, despite people's negative associations with a movie being filmed near their home, whenever those big, bright 24,000-kilowatt lights were turned on, they would come out from all over the neighborhood, curious to see what was going on.

It's the same with people driving by. When they see the light, their curiosity takes over, and they too just have to find out, "What is going on in the light?"

Think about this. When you turn on your 50-watt porch light, do people driving by slow down or park their cars and come up on your porch to investigate what's going on? Do your neighbors from all the surrounding blocks come out of their houses and apartments to see what all the excitement is about at your house? Of course not!

Then why is it that when you turn on a 24,000-kilowatt light, they are attracted in droves? It's because the brighter the light, the more life is attracted to it. And the reason that the light is brighter is because more power is going to the source of the light.

When there's a big event—the opening of a shopping mall or a film premiere—have you ever noticed the big searchlights they shine into the sky? They sure do get your attention, and now you know why! The marketing people know that when people see the light, they are attracted to it. It works every time!

Ask yourself this: what's the biggest light of all, a light so powerful it is greeted and worshipped by billions of life forms every day? It's the sun, of course, and though it makes its appearance every day, we never tire of its magnetic attraction. Think about it. The whole planet gets up to meet it! Plants grow and stretch themselves in the direction of the sun. Most of the animals and birds wake up to enjoy their new day at the first powerful rays of sunlight. The majority of people get up in the morning to go to work, go to school, go shopping, go to the beach, participate in sporting activities, and do everything else—far more often than they do at night.

And it goes deeper than that. All life on this planet exists because of the sun, and it continues to thrive because of this bright light too. Why is it so bright? Because it is fueled by massive levels of power at its source. Without this power source, without the light, there would be no life. This is why life is automatically attracted to the light. It's instinctive to move toward it, because light is the giver of life. It's the source of life, and it affirms life.

What happens when you try to mix light and dark together? Close your eyes and do the experiment. How did you go? It's interesting, isn't it? Light and dark coexist with each other like night and day, yet they cannot occupy the same space at the same time. Nor can they mix together to create a neutral state. There is either light, or there isn't.

There's No Fence to Sit On

Imagine that sitting on a table in front of you is a brand-new, fully charged-up car battery. You'll notice it has two terminals—a positive and a negative. The positive is marked in green, and the negative is marked in red. Both are also marked with different symbols.

Do you know the symbol for the positive terminal? If you said "+" you are correct. In mathematics the "+" symbol is known as a plus sign, meaning addition, or to add to. Now, there is a method to my madness, so if you're thinking these questions are simple and wondering where I'm going with this and how any of this relates to improving the quality of your life, have faith.

What is the symbol for the negative terminal on the car battery? If you said "−" you are correct. In mathematics the "−" symbol is known as a minus sign, meaning subtraction, or to take away.

Now for the next question. Since the symbol for positive energy is the plus sign, and the symbol for negative energy is the minus sign, what is the symbol for the neutral energy terminal on a battery?

Not sure? Think about it some more. Have you ever seen the neutral energy terminal on your car battery? Right about now I can feel you racking your brain trying to come up with the correct answer, and your frustration in not being able to. Trust me when I say that that's okay because it's a trick question.

There are only two terminals on a battery—the positive and the negative. There's no such thing as a neutral terminal on a battery. There's only positive and negative.

Think of it this way. Positive (+) means add to, and negative (−) means take away, so either you are adding power to your battery or else you're taking power away. There's no in between. It's either getting stronger or getting weaker.

What happens when you leave a brand-new, charged-up car battery on a shelf for a long time? That's right. Even without use it loses its charge and eventually goes completely dead.

The reason the unused battery eventually goes dead is because *it takes energy to maintain energy*. Nothing stays the same. It's either getting stronger or getting weaker; it's growing or dying. It's the same for everything and everyone in the universe, including you.

Either you're adding power to your life, or you're taking power away. There's no neutral. Nothing stays the same. You're either growing or decaying, either evolving or dissolving.

When you add power to your life by applying positive energy, you're growing and evolving. When you take away power from your life by applying negative energy, you begin to decay, which can eventually lead to death. Remember: negative means to take away, so when you apply negative energy or negative thinking in your life, you're taking away from your own energy source and dimming your own light, which means you're attracting less life to you.

To make it worse, when negative energy takes power from your light, not only do you fail to attract good things into your life, you're also pushing all of the positive stuff away! Instead of powering a life-attracting positive light, you actually create a life-repelling negative force field around you. Think about it this way. Do you like hanging out with negative, angry, depressed people? No one does! Now you know why!

Another word for positive charge is "empower." When you apply positive energy in your life, you become empowered, and you also empower the other people who are attracted to your positive light.

Another word for negative charge is "disempower." When you apply negative energy in your life, or when you fail to recharge your life with positive energy, you become disempowered and you also disempower people who are affected by your negative force field.

To keep your life-attracting light bright, the main thing to remember is that you have to stay consistent in being empowering about everything you do. Simply by being empowering, you're generating more positive energy and adding more power to your light.

It's your responsibility to make sure that your batteries are always full of power so you can keep your light bright. If you don't, they will lose their charge and your light will go dim. And if you let it go too long with out a recharge, your light will eventually die. Always remember: it takes energy to maintain energy, so if you're not adding to your energy, it's automatically seeping away.

> *"With great power comes great responsibility."*

The Power Is in Your House. Take Responsibility for It.

In chapter 7 we explored the Law of Vibration. In short, we learned this: absolutely everything in the universe is made up of millions of atoms, and atoms are mostly made up of empty space, apart from an energy vibration known as a quark. What this means is everything in the universe, including you and me, is basically composed of vibrating energy. We are all about vibration and movement. Everything in the universe is always in motion.

So, here we are, you and I, each the source of millions of bits of constantly moving energy. Now, we know from physics that energy can't be created or destroyed, and that it can only be transformed into other forms of energy. Plainly stated, a tree will evolve and grow into a strong, healthy tree, or it will dissolve and die, turning into another form of energy, fertilizer, which will feed the other plants, trees, insects, and animals. It takes energy to maintain energy, so if you're not adding to your energy, it's automatically seeping away. Evolve or dissolve. Nothing stays the same. Physics proves it.

Empower Versus Disempower

You may notice that I use the words "empower" and "disempower" a lot in this book. When you truly understand their meaning, your life changes forever. That's powerful!

So what does it really mean to be empowering? An empowering person is someone who takes responsibility for his thoughts and actions, someone who is positive and fun to be around, someone who encourages others to be the best they can be. After spending time with a person who positively inspires you to evolve yourself, you might say, "Wow, that was great! He's so empowering to be around." Or you might refer to him as being inspiring. To be inspired means to be "in your spirit," and your spirit is a being of light.

And it's true, isn't it? After you've been with an empowering person, for the rest of the day you still feel fully charged and brimming with lots of energy. You're charged, and so is everyone else who spends time with him.

How do you feel when you spend time with negative people? Do you really enjoy being around people who are depressed, angry, or sad? Or those people who are constantly blaming everyone else for their problems, justifying why and complaining about how their life is such a downer? Or they're full of excuses as to why they didn't follow through with what they said they were going to do? Given the choice, wouldn't you rather avoid spending time with people like this? These are disempowering people.

Have you ever spent time with a disempowering person only to find later that you feel drained and out of energy and power?

Isn't it interesting that when we're around people who are empowering, we feel revitalized and charged, and when we're around people who are disempowering, we feel tapped out and drained? And isn't it also interesting that everyone likes being around and spending time with empowering people, and we all try to avoid spending time with disempowering people? It's as though disempowering people have this invisible force field around them that pushes positive people and things away from them, and this makes sense because positive energy naturally moves away from negative energy.

"I See the Light"

So let's start to put this all together and see how it relates to achieving your goals and dreams.

A person who consistently has a positive mental attitude and displays that attitude to everyone around him is an empowering person. The word empowering means "adds power to." All of a sudden, when you look at it like this, the connection between being positive and being empowering becomes very clear. They are one and the same thing.

When you're being empowering, you're adding power to the source. And remember that physics tells us everything in the universe is made up of energy, including us, meaning that we are the source of the light. So, in a nutshell, the more positive we are, the more power goes to our source, and the brighter our light becomes. Then, as our light grows brighter, more life is attracted to it.

We all naturally gravitate toward empowering people, and when you're being empowering, people want to be around you too. It's a law of nature called the Law of Attraction. Energy attracts like energy. Positive energy attracts more positive energy to it. See, there's that the "adding of power" we were talking about!

What we all really need to understand is that we are the source of the light. The more energy that goes to the source, the brighter the light becomes and the more life is attracted to it. Oh, and by the way, when I say that life is attracted to the light, that includes the nice car you want to drive, the beautiful house you want to live in, the trips you want to take, the loving relationship you desire, and even the money you want to make. Because cars, homes, money, trips, clothes, and everything else on this planet are all just different forms of life. When you're dead there are no homes, cars, furniture, money, or anything else. Because all of those things are different forms of life, and the more positive and empowering you are, the more those things are attracted to you.

Think about it. What first attracts you into a new relationship? Are you attracted to that other person when they are in their most positive and happy state? Or are you attracted to them when they're angry, negative, and upset? Of course not! No one sees a really depressed person and says, "Oh, I want that person in my life." We are attracted to people when they are in their most empowering mood. And it's when we are in our most positive empowering mood that people are attracted to us too.

At the moment when we are filled with empowering energy, our light is brighter. People then see our light and then they are naturally drawn to it. That's what charisma is—it's energy. Think about someone you know who is charismatic. He or she has lots of positive energy, right?

So the more positive and empowering you are, the more people are attracted to your light. These people can turn out to be romantic partners, friends, acquaintances, and even business customers, and with all these people come more opportunities.

Understand that we're not talking about being positive just for the sake of being happy, even though that in itself is a good thing. Being positive has far more powerful benefits than you may have recognized in the past. The more empowering you are, the more of a gravitational pull you create around yourself, and the more things in life are automatically attracted to you.

You only have two choices here. You're either a gravitational pull attracting positive rewards into your world, or by default you are a negative force field pushing everything away from you. You're either gaining more power and attracting more to you, or you're losing power and pushing things away. It's one or the other. Either you evolve or you dissolve. Nothing stays the same. There is no neutral.

The challenge with allowing your energy to drain out and get low is that *low levels of power promote ill health and even death.* There are scientific studies that show that being positive and happy actually strengthens your immune system.

Did you know that when a person performs a random act of kindness, it strengthens your immune system? This happens whether you are the receiver of the act of kindness, the giver of the act of kindness, or just the witness to an act of kindness performed for someone else. The opposite is also true. Negativity weakens the immune system.

For example, this scenario is not at all uncommon: there are two patients with the same condition in the same hospital, the same doctor, the same treatment, and the same medication, and, after a couple weeks in the hospital, one of the patients completely recovers, and the other patient dies. In many of these cases the doctor will tell you that the person who lived had a positive mental attitude, whereas the one who died didn't. It was the positive mental attitude that strengthened the survivor's immune system and made him stronger.

Remember: having a negative attitude doesn't just keep your immune system from being strong; it actually weakens it. Again, there is no neutral. Either you are making yourself stronger, or you're making yourself weaker.

And it's not just your physical body that's affected. Being empowering or being disempowering affects all areas of your life in the same way. You are either making them stronger, or you are promoting ill health in those areas too.

Look at it this way. In your car you have only one battery. If that battery goes dead, it doesn't matter how expensive your car is—it still won't run. The whole car shuts down. And it goes the same for you and every area of your life.

Think about your relationship. When you have two empowering people in the relationship, you will have a very strong relationship. And not only will it be strong, it will actually grow stronger. It will evolve because energy attracts more like energy. So the more positive you both are, the more positive things and people will come your way. That makes sense, right? Remember: this is all simple physics! This is how the entire universe works. It is all governed by laws of nature.

On the other side of the coin, if one person in a relationship is consistently disempowering, you'll notice they are a drain on the relationship. And the longer that person stays disempowering, the weaker the relationship gets. Can a disempowering person promote ill health in a relationship? Of course he can! Can the relationship get so sickly and weak that finally it dies? You bet! Whatever area of your life you empower will get stronger, and whatever area of your life you disempower will get weaker.

Let's look at your business or the place where you work for a moment. If someone at work is consistently negative and disempowering, can he or she make your entire work environment weak? Think about it. Have you ever been around someone at work who left you feeling totally drained long after you've left the premises? That's how damaging disempowering people can be. People who act in a disempowering way are known as "energy vampires" because they literally suck the life energy out of everything and everyone. Do you know anyone in your life who is an energy vampire? Energy vampires in the workplace can be deadly, promoting ill health in the business. And if there are enough disempowered people in a business, do you think it can eventually lead to the death of that business? Of course it can!

That's why we try to avoid people when they're being disempowering. It's instinctive. Our bodies naturally know that being around disempowering people can drain our own supplies of energy, and if we get too drained, we can be faced with the possibility of ill health as a result. The body knows that low levels of power promote ill health, and it also knows that if we get too drained, we may even die. Isn't it interesting that we are programmed with a natural defense system to keep us away from negative, disempowering people? It's a protective response to stop our energy from being stolen away. How awesome is that?

That's why positive people just don't like hanging out with negative people. It's why they try to avoid them.

And it goes both ways. Negative people don't like being around positive people. Now why do you think this might be? It's because it makes them feel they have to justify why they are the way they are. For example, when a positive person gives a book to a negative person to read, what usually happens? First the negative person doesn't read the book. Then they try to avoid the positive person so that they don't have to explain why they haven't read it.

What's the first thing you do after being stuck around negative people? As soon as you get away from them, you go looking for someone who is empowering to get a recharge, right? The body knows that low levels of power will promote ill health and can eventually lead to death, so it is naturally drawn to seek out other sources of power to get recharged. There's the gravitational pull that we were talking about. People are just naturally attracted to the light of positive, happy people.

Oh, and by the way, I've said it before and I want to remind you, those people who are attracted to you when you're being positive and empowering may be new friends, a new relationship, new acquaintances, new customers, and all of these bring you new opportunities. And that's where the cars, houses, boats, clothes and money also come in. All of those things are just other forms of life and they are all attracted to the light. The more power that goes to the source, the brighter the light gets, and the more life will then be attracted to it. Do you see how this is all connected?

———

I was helping a couple who were experiencing some challenges with their marriage. Let's call them Tom and Sue to protect their privacy. As I listened to them, I could instantly see the cause of their problems. Their story clearly shows the effects of empowerment and disempowerment in action.

The Story of Tom and Sue

Tom and Sue have been married for around twenty years. They married quite young, so even after twenty years of marriage, they're only in their forties and are both attractive. Tom was upset because Sue liked spending time with her male friends, and he didn't like the idea of her spending time with other men. This caused a lot of drama in their relationship and was the basis for most of their arguments. These had gotten so regular and out of hand that their friends and family members had been drawn into it, and they all wanted to avoid Tom and Sue like the plague. (There's the force field we were talking about.) No one enjoyed being around them when these blowups happened, and as they were known to happen at any time without warning, people were starting to make excuses as to why they couldn't make time to be with Tom and Sue. That became another thing to fight about. They became trapped in this circle and couldn't see their way out.

When they asked me for help, I knew I had to get to the cause of the problem and deal with it. I wanted to make sure I didn't get fooled into trying to work on the symptoms. What were the symptoms? The arguing and what they are arguing about. I had no desire to listen to their "he said/she said" stories, or to take sides in the matter. My task was to find out what was driving them to take certain actions that were getting them into trouble with each other.

I looked at what was happening. Sue knew that whenever she spent time with this one male friend, it drove Tom crazy, and she was guaranteed to get an earful from him as soon as she got home. (And, just for the record, there was absolutely no hanky-panky going on between Sue and her male friend. They were just good friends.) Sue disliked getting yelled at by Tom and really hated the arguments that followed. Yet there were times when Tom and Sue were out together at a social event also attended by the male friend, and Sue would go and spend time with him even though she knew she was going to pay the price for it with Tom later. Here's the real twist to the story. Neither one of them wanted a divorce. They both still loved each other and wanted to be together. They just hated the constant fighting and drama, and so did everyone else around them.

When I asked Sue about her friendship with her male friend, she said he was just a casual acquaintance, and not even a dear friend. What I wanted to know was why a person would go and do something that isn't even all that important to her, when she knows that she's going to have to endure loads of pain from her partner as a result. I knew this was the key to discovering the cause of their problems.

It turned out that as Tom was getting older, he was having challenges with his own self-confidence. He was a little down on himself and didn't feel he still exuded the same positive qualities he once had. He felt they had faded away with time. As a by-product of that, he became more and more disempowering with Sue and everyone else around him. He would constantly try to get everyone and anyone, whoever was around, to listen to his drama stories about how Sue was wrong and how he was a victim of it all.

So here's what I finally put together. Tom was being consistently disempowering when he blamed and accused Sue of inappropriate behavior. These accusations would leave Sue feeling drained from massive energy loss. So, she would go and spend time with her positive, empowering male friend to help recharge her internal batteries. This would give her enough energy to go back and be able to deal with Tom.

Here's the vicious circle we were talking about earlier. Sue had to go and spend time with her friend to get recharged, even though this was the exact catalyst that would make Tom become even more disempowering.

The body moves toward other people's positive energy when it has been disempowered. It's an automatic instinctive survival response because the body knows that energy drainage can be very damaging, so it needs to recharge to survive. People ask me what happens to the empowered person during the recharging process. Doesn't that person get drained? Not necessarily! Empowered people don't have to sacrifice any of their energy in order to help you recharge, and neither do you when you help others.

Another law of nature is the Law of Circulation. Everything in the universe circulates. The blood in your body is circulating. We breathe in oxygen and breathe out CO_2. The plants and trees breathe in CO_2 and breathe out oxygen. First things grow and then they die and to become the fertilizer for other things that are growing. What goes around comes around! The more empowered we are, the more power is attracted to us. The more empowering you are, the more positive energy you give, and the more you give, the more you get. As you sow, so shall you reap! Whatever you give out is what you get back. What you plant is what you will grow. Remember: it takes power to make your success magnet work, and you won't have any power to operate it if you have been disempowering to yourself or to others.

Understand there is a difference between being empowering and giving your power away. Giving it away will leave you feeling drained. That's why it's important to make sure you don't get sucked into a disempowering situation. That's why I didn't want to listen to Tom and Sue's "he said/she said" stories. What I focus on when working with people isn't the past. The strategy that I use is very simple and it's also very powerful. I simply ask myself the question, "How can we make it better?" That's empowering. And I don't need to listen to their disempowering stories about their past in order to do that.

So how did this apply to Tom and Sue? Sue was being pulled toward her empowering friend to get a recharge of positive energy, and Tom was actually pushing her to go there. He was so disempowering that his strong negative force field was pushing Sue away from him. This, in turn, made him even more disempowered and disempowering!

The more disempowering you are, the faster and farther you are pushing things away from you. That includes all of your goals and dreams as well. No one wants to be around that energy. And remember: there are only two choices. Either you're being empowering, or you're being disempowering. There is no neutral, which also means that you're either getting stronger and healthier, or you're heading in the other direction. Nothing stays the same!

You're either pulling your goals and dreams toward you, or else you're pushing them away. The more empowering you are, the more of a gravitational pull you create, and the faster things get pulled into your world. The more disempowering you are, the faster everything you want moves away from you. Remember, no one likes being around or spending time with angry, upset, depressed, negative, disempowering people, except for other negative, disempowering people. Misery loves company. The other thing to remember is that those people who are avoiding you when you're being disempowering are the positive, empowering people! What a waste! They could have been your new friends, or maybe a new romantic relationship, new acquaintances, new customers, or even new opportunities. You'll never know if you keep pushing them away with your negative energy force field. And remember that opportunities are like butterflies; once they fly away, you may never have the chance to catch them again. Think about it. Have there ever been opportunities you didn't act on that could have created something really great for your life, and later on you regretted not taking them?

You're either a gravitational pull attracting all of the wonderful things you want into your life, or you are a force field pushing those wonderful things away from you. There is no neutral. The choice is yours to make.

And remember that the Law of Attraction works both ways. Energy will always attract like energy, which includes negative energy. So when you're being negative and disempowering, not only are you draining your own energy, you're also attracting more negative, disempowering energy toward you. What effect do you think this has on your total energy? That's right. The energy drain you experience keeps on increasing. As they say, "When it rains it pours." The longer you allow yourself to stay disempowering, the more intense and greater your loss of energy will become, and it will only keep intensifying. It will keep attracting more and more negative situations and people into your life.

And there's more. The negative energy force field replaces the positive energy you lose, so the more positive energy you lose, the stronger the negative energy force field becomes. What you really need to remember about this is that the force field doesn't just keep the things you desire away from you. It actually pushes them farther and farther away! That means all of your goals and dreams become harder and harder for you to achieve. How do you feel about that?

Once I spelled this out for Tom and Sue, they really got it and made huge improvements in their relationship. The first step was for Tom to start taking responsibility for making sure he was happy, and to quit looking for other people to be responsible for making that happen, especially Sue. Blame, justification, and excuses are disempowering. They steal your personal power away from you, because when you blame others for your downfalls and justify why your life isn't working and have excuses for why things are not working, it shows that you're *reacting* to life instead of *proactively responding* to it.

If you're being reactive, you're in a very weak and disempowering position. When you're so busy reacting to everything that happens, you don't have time to proactively create what you really desire. Because it's so disempowering to be reactive that it quickly tires you out so that you don't feel you have the energy to put into creating the life you really want. What a vicious circle that one is!

That's what Tom was doing. Because he was feeling unhappy within himself and his self-confidence was so low, he was trying to make Sue responsible for making him happy. That doesn't work in a relationship. In life that doesn't work! When one person relies on another to make him happy, it's known as dependency.

The Dependant Relationship

By looking at the following drawing, the two lines representing the two people in the relationship, what do you think happens to the

Dependant

person who is constantly holding up the other person? This person discovers that he just doesn't have enough energy to hold the other person up because the dependant person is disempowering and is stealing his energy from him. Eventually, the person feels the need to move away or be with someone else who is empowering instead. That's why these kinds of relationships break up. Even a very strong person doesn't have enough energy to hold up the dependant person forever, because that dependency is taking power away from their relationship.

Tom was very dependant on Sue to make sure he was always happy. Yet Sue found it very tiring trying to hold Tom up all day long, every day of the week. When she wasn't doing what Tom was imposing on her, he became even more disempowering, which in turn took even more energy away from Sue and the relationship. Can you see how unattractive a situation like this can be? That's why Sue was drawn to want to spend time with her male friend who was light and fun to be with. That's how she got recharged so that she could deal with Tom and his disempowering ways.

What's the solution for those who want to stay together, like Sue and Tom? The first thing I did was work with Tom on some strategies that would help him take responsibility for making himself happy, which would in turn make him more empowering and a lot less dependant. All of those strategies are in this book.

The Co-Dependant Relationship

Now we know a dependant relationship is when one person places responsibility on the other person to fulfill their needs. What if both people in a relationship depend on the other person to make sure they are happy? This is a co-dependant relationship. The two sticks in the drawing represent people in a co-dependant relationship.

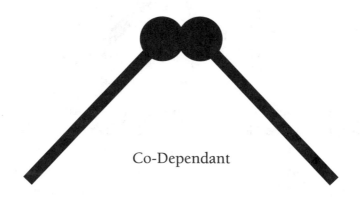

Co-Dependant

The challenge with being in a co-dependant relationship is that it doesn't stay in balance. The diagram looks balanced, with each person holding up the other, but that's not what actually happens. One person is usually needier during certain times of the relationship, and the other person is needier at different times. So both people are constantly drawing energy from the relationship, which is weakening it from both sides.

These are the type of people who feel that if they each give 50% to the relationship, then their relationship will have 100%. Here's the problem with that: there's still 100% missing. That's the recipe for a relationship headed for disaster. What it really means is that there are two disempowering people in the same relationship. If you have friends that are in a co-dependant relationship, you'll notice that after spending any time with them, you feel drained from the experience. It's such a disempowering environment that it takes energy away from everyone who is around it.

The Empowering Relationship

What makes a strong relationship work is when you have two empowering people who take responsibility to make sure that they are happy within themselves. A strong relationship is made up of two happy people sharing the experience of a happy life together. This is what an empowering relationship looks like.

What brings two empowering people together in a relationship is connection. People in a happy relationship are like two sticks floating down the stream of life together. They can each float on their own, and they choose to share the experience of the ride together. A

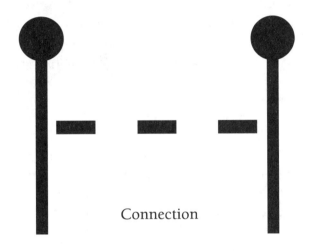

Connection

person who takes the responsibility to be consistently empowering is personally developed. And as the rewards you get in life are always in direct proportion to your level of personal development, a person who is empowering is also empowered.

Are You Giving Your Power Away?

Understand that there is a big difference between empowering someone else and giving your power away to them. When you give to others, it needs to be in a way that empowers both you and the other person. When you allow others to drain your energy for the sake of trying to help them out of their problems, you're displaying a victim mentality, or playing the victim, and that's not an empowering way to be. It's quite the opposite, in fact. Playing Joan of Arc, the martyr, is very disempowering. In actuality, when you play the victim, you do it for the ego ride, because you think it makes you look good. Instead of empowering others, you're giving your own energy away in an attempt to gain acknowledgment from others. No one really gets any joy from you sacrificing yourself for them because the person you helped ends up feeling there's an unpaid debt they owe you.

And where's the love in seeing someone else suffer just so you can get what you want? Isn't it much better when everyone wins? Isn't it better to know that no one has to lose in order for you to win? That is the abundant mind-set.

The easiest way to make sure what you're doing is empowering is to ask yourself if you feel empowered during all your interactions with other people. If you feel empowered, then you are being empowered. If you're not feeling empowered, then neither is anyone else.

The truth is that you are not really empowering anyone else when you are giving your power away, because the Law of Attraction is always in effect. So when you're being disempowering by giving your power away, then, in reality, you're disempowering the other person, too. Energy attracts like energy.

That's the great thing about empowerment. When you're in an empowering environment, everyone is empowered! There is no shortage. The more an empowered person gives, the more he receives. It is a self-perpetuating energy source. The more that is given, the bigger the energy source grows, and so more is attracted to it and it just keeps on evolving.

If you're with people you feel are stealing your energy away from you—the energy vampires—then it is your responsibility to make sure you re-empower yourself. No one has the power to disempower you unless you give them that power to do so. It's also disempowering when you blame others for taking your energy. That too is a form of victim mentality. And so is justifying why you allowed someone else to disempower you. To avoid playing the victim, or being the victim, start taking responsibility to make sure that you are always empowered and always empowering.

And what about allowing your power to be stolen from you? This too is disempowering. Take responsibility for maintaining your personal power. If someone tries to disempower you, you don't have to accept it. Turn it around, redirect it, and convert it into something empowering, or choose to walk away. Both strategies work. The way you turn it around is by asking empowering questions, one of the best being, "How can I look at this in an empowering way?" Another great empowering question is, "What's great about this?" You'll learn more about how to turn disempowering situations around in chapter 12.

Understand that this is not about gaining power over anyone else. Attempting to gain power over someone else isn't empowering at all. It's disempowering! It makes you the energy vampire! *With great power comes great responsibility.* Trying to take someone else's power away from him will only cause you to lose yours. As you sow, so shall you reap.

Empowering Lessons

You don't have to work hard to get what you desire in your life. All you have to do is be empowering in everything you do. As soon as you begin this, you'll notice you're not working hard anymore, because you're enjoying what you're doing. Since being empowering automatically attracts positive energies to you, there's far less effort involved. The more power you have, the brighter your light gets, and the more life is attracted to the light. How easy is that?

Two of our greatest teachers, Buddha and Jesus Christ, taught this lesson, and their light was so powerful that we still remember their teachings thousands of years later. Buddha taught about the path to enlightenment, and Jesus taught us how to live in the light.

Buddha taught us to live an enlightened life. Enlightened means "in your light." And whenever you see pictures of Jesus and Buddha, you'll notice they are surrounded by light, often around the head in the shape of a halo. A halo really should be called an "empower-ring," meaning a ring of light and power. The reason the empower-ring is shown around the head is because the empowerment they taught was generated by their empowering thoughts. They were empowering about everything. They had peaceful thoughts about everything. To be peaceful means to be surrounded by and immersed in the light. And that's what they told us to do.

Think about it. Isn't that what peaceful thoughts do? They make you feel lighter. As soon as you hold yourself to a higher standard, to being empowering about everything in your life, you too will have an empower-ring, or light, that others will see and be attracted to.

> *"As you think in your heart, so you are."*
>
> PROVERBS 23:7

The light cannot be seen with your eyes. It's perceived with your being. It's like ultraviolet light. Just because you can't see it with your eyes doesn't mean it's not there.

What's the easiest way to train yourself to be empowering about everything? It's this: consistently examine your thoughts and ask yourself, "Is the way I'm looking at this situation now empowering or disempowering?" If your answer is "disempowering," ask the next question, which is, "How can I look at this in an empowering way?"

Empower-Ring

When you start thinking in an empowering way, you'll start acting in an empowering way, because thoughts lead to actions. That's why both Jesus and Buddha taught empowerment throughout their lives. It's when you're being positive and empowering that you're enlightened, and when you're enlightened, you are in your light. You're in harmony with the natural order of the universe. That's why it feels so good to be positive and giving. And it's also why everyone and everything is attracted to you. That good feeling you get from being positive and empowering is the universe's way of letting you know you are on the path of light.

When you look into the teachings of these two masters, you'll notice that they taught not just by what they said, they also taught by how they lived. That in itself is a very important lesson. The only way to be truly empowering is to make sure you are always walking your talk, which is leading by example. Saying one thing and doing another isn't empowering; it's disempowering. And if you think it doesn't matter when no one is looking, you are incorrect. The universe is always watching. And so are you! When you know what you're doing is disempowering, even when no one is around to witness it, face the fact that it's still disempowering.

The lesson that flowed through everything that Buddha and Jesus did and said was this: to be able to live in the light you need to *be empowering about everything*. That's what they did. They were empowering about everything, and that's what made them so powerful. Think about the stories of their lives and you will see that they were positive and empowering to everyone and everything.

There was a period in Buddha's life when he was living in the forest and he went without food for forty straight days. Most people would say that going without food for over a month is a bad thing. If they were in that situation, they might see themselves as unfortunate or deprived. Many would be angry, and hate others for what they had. Yet that's not what Buddha did. Instead he said, "I found a way to laugh at my hunger." He found a way to be empowering about something as difficult as going without food for forty days. This was his way of teaching the path of enlightenment, the way to be in your light.

And think about the way Jesus lived his life. During the last few days of his life they were crucifying him. This had to be an extremely painful experience. First they drove big metal spikes through his wrists and ankles. Can you imagine how bad that must have hurt? When Jesus first felt the pain, he found it tough to be empowering. He asked, "My God, my God, why have you forsaken me?" Do you think that's an empowering question or a disempowering question? It's actually disempowering. It was a weak moment Jesus was having, a moment in which he started to doubt his beliefs. Imagine what would have happened if he had died right at that moment. Do you think anyone would have followed his teachings knowing that, at the moment when it was most needed, he too doubted his own faith? Probably not! He knew that too. He knew his question was disempowering, and, being the leader he was, he knew that if he was disempowering, he would disempower countless people if he left it that way. Think about it. Even though Jesus spent his life being positive and empowering, if he had died at the moment of disempowerment, it would have wiped out all his good work. That's how much damage being negative can do.

Negative Energy Versus Positive Energy

If you're in a relationship, you may have already noticed something like this. You do a bunch of nice things for your partner. Then you go and do one messed-up thing, and watch how fast it quickly wipes out all of the good you did before! Have you ever had that experience? Have you noticed your partner remembers the negative thing you did a lot more readily than all of the positive things you did before? That's because negative energy is a much heavier, denser energy than positive energy.

It's the same in business. Do a 98% great job with your customer but fall down on the last 2%, and it's that last 2% that the customer will remember. You can lose a lot of customers by not following through with that last 2%. After all, they paid for at least 100%, and that's what they deserve and expect. Remember what I said in chapter 6 about the cup of sweet tea? Fifteen spoonfuls of sugar makes a very sweet tea and just one drop of poison makes it deadly!

You can get a sense of just how dense and heavy negative energy feels by the words and phrases we use to describe negative feelings and experiences. For example:

> "I'm feeling down today!"
> "I feel like I have the weight of the world on my shoulders."
> "I'm depressed."
> "I hate you."
> "I want revenge."

And when people are really low on energy, they'll say things like:

> "I'm drained."
> "I'm tapped out."
> "I'm exhausted."
> "I need a vacation."

Now here are some examples of sentences that use positively charged words and meanings. Notice how they sound so much lighter:

> "I'm so happy today that I'm floating on air."
> "I'm light as a feather."
> "I'm skipping through life."
> "I love you."
> "I forgive you."

And when people are feeling empowered, they'll say things like:

> "I'm raring to go."
> "I'm charged up."
> "I'm feeling unstoppable."

Think about it. If you're in a boat in the middle of the ocean, does it matter where you drill a hole in your boat? It's going to sink regardless of where the hole is. It's the same with your energy. When you are being disempowering in one area of your life, it will take energy away from your whole life because, in reality, your life doesn't divide into separate areas. Every part of it is connected, and the weaker areas can drain the strong areas of their power.

You only have one energy containment system, and that's your body. So if you're being disempowering in your business, it can have a negative effect on your relationship. If you're being disempowering in your relationship, it can have a negative effect on your health. And so on. If you're being disempowering by treating people negatively, then you have drilled a hole in your lifeboat, and all your energy is draining out. When this happens, you'll notice it becomes exhausting just trying to keep your energy levels consistently up. And if you are being disempowering in more than one area of your life, just imagine how hard it is to maintain healthy energy levels at all, let alone have the extra energy you need to achieve your grand dream goals!

And there's more. Just by having that negative energy attached to you, you're automatically attracting more negative energy, which is like making the hole in your boat bigger and bigger. When that happens, your boat sinks faster and faster.

Jesus knew he couldn't leave this world on a disempowering note. He knew the poison it would spread would kill all the good work he had done, as well as kill the faith and hope of countless people. His death would have been in vain. And that's when he regained his power, saying, "Father, forgive them, for they know not what they do."

Look at what they had done: They had strung him up on a cross and left him hanging there for days in the hot sun and the cold of night without food or water. They beat and tortured him. Now imagine trying to be positive and empowering at a moment like that. And yet that's exactly what Jesus did. He found a way to be empowering even during the worst experience of his life. He knew the choice was his to make. He alone could make his experience an empowering one or a disempowering one.

He knew that the only way to the light was through peace, and the only way to have peace was to make an empowering choice, so he forgave his captors. To be able to forgive the people who were torturing him, even as they were doing it, is the empowering way of a transformational master. That's why there is no doubt that he knew the way to be in the light. Jesus also said, "Even the least among you can do all that I have done, and even greater things."

To be empowering about everything means just that. You need to start being empowering about everything that happens in your life, and toward everyone in your life. Not just when things are going your way, and not just toward the people you like or those who agree with you. It means you need to be empowering even when it feels as if things aren't going your way, and you need to be empowering even toward the people who don't agree with you or who aren't like you. Now that's true life mastery!

It's easy to be positive when things are going your way. When you feel that life has handed you a raw deal, or when you feel as if someone has wronged you, you still need to be empowering. When you do that, when you take control of your life and the results that you create in it, you truly stop being a victim of circumstance. When you take responsibility to always be empowering about everything, you instantly move above the line, and everything you desire in life is drawn to you without any effort at all.

Life Isn't Always Fair

If you want to make God laugh, tell him your plans. Face it: things won't always turn out the way you planned them or the way you think they should be. Think about this: everyone is unique. Not everyone on the planet follows the same rules for living as you think they should. There are even some people who are bent on making other people's lives a living hell, people who go out of their way to try to inflict pain on others. Things don't always turn out fairly. But guess what! Life isn't fair, and it never has been! Have you already noticed that? *Life doesn't turn out the way that it should. It turns out the way that it does. It's what you do with it that makes life what it is.*

When you choose to be empowering about everything, you'll see how light life can get, and how wonderful your life can be no matter what's happening around you. That's "being in your power." That's what both Buddha and Jesus taught us by the way they lived their lives—the way to the light, the way to be empowered. It is when we consistently act in an empowering way about everything that we are the best we can be, and that is when we are closest to our Creator.

Did you notice that when I talked about people who set out with the intention of hurting others, I never called them wrong? Why do you think this is? When you say that someone else is wrong, it implies you think you are right. Yet there is no real right or wrong. The words "right" and "wrong," or "good" and "bad," are judgmental terms. There is no right or wrong, or good or bad. It's only your own judgment speaking.

The problem with judgment is that once you get involved in judging, you are automatically being judged. When you judge someone else, you're doing it by comparing yourself to them. So you're judging yourself too. Making judgmental comparisons never gets you anywhere positive. Think about it. A judgment is an opinion— your opinion—one you're trying to disguise as a fact. It's not a fact. It's only your opinion.

When you judge someone to be stupid, ugly, or bad, your judgment of them doesn't make those things true. It does, however, make you a person who feels the need to judge. Judge not, lest ye be judged.

And think about this. The more you pass judgment, the more you cement your opinion and the more you determine your perceptions about how you think things are. When you pass judgment on people and their actions, you reveal your own personal rules for life. Just because they are your rules doesn't mean they are everyone else's rules!

Understand that all conflicts in life are created when different rules clash. When two people with polar opposite views both think they are right, what happens? The defenses are up and no one budges. This is how all conflicts are created. The conflict may involve two different people, two different groups, two different countries, or two different religions defending their positions, each arguing that their rules are the "right" rules, and that's where wars get started.

Yet there's a universal law of nature called the Law of Polarity, which states that there are opposite sides to everything. You can't have a right without a left, a top without a bottom, or an inside without an outside. According to this law, a thing cannot exist unless it has two sides. Everything has its opposite. The question is which is the right side? Is the top better than the bottom? Is the inside better than the outside? In a conflict, such as a war or argument, which side is right?

When you're involved in a conflict, your ego is pretty convinced about which side is right. Your side, of course! According to your ego, your rules are the right rules. It's only your judgment that says your side is the right side. Think about it. The other person's judgment says his side is the right side too, but if both sides are opposites, how can they both be right? Remember: what you are claiming to be right is governed by your rules for life. These are not necessarily the same rules that everyone else has for their life.

When you look at it in this way, you see that all conflicts in life are created by rules conflicts. So when you're fighting with someone about who is right and who is wrong, is that empowering or disempowering? It sure seems like a lot of wasted energy over something that may never be resolved. You may never get the other person to see your point of view, and why is this so important to you anyway? It's only your ego that says you have to prove your point. It's your ego that has the need to always be right. It's your ego that gets you out of balance and out of harmony with the rest of the universe, because the ego is about being separate, not about being connected.

You are a true master of life when you can turn your enemies into your allies and your foes into your friends. It takes a powerful person to do that. When you start living your life that way, you become a transformational master because you are making the decision to turn disempowering experiences into empowering ones.

Think about Nelson Mandela. He was locked up in prison for twenty-seven years because he spoke out against apartheid. When he was finally released from prison, he was elected president of his country. Do you know who he chose to become some of the members his cabinet? Some of his prison guards. That's right! Some of the guards who had kept him confined for twenty-seven years of his life later became his most loyal supporters because he was able to turn his enemies into his allies. Now how empowering is that?

Aikido Through Life

Meeting force with force is never the way to get ahead. It's disempowering! Too much energy is wasted for not enough result gained, if any. Imagine someone throwing a punch at you, whether it's physically, mentally, or emotionally. When you block the punch, your block is still a form of strike. It's still force meeting force, and it consumes a lot of your energy to execute a block maneuver. Sometimes it even hurts. Do you really want to spend the time you were given to live your life blocking the stuff that people throw at you? If you get caught up consuming your energy on things that aren't going to bring your life forward, then how much energy will that leave you to actually move forward?

Choose your battles wisely. Don't fight every fight that comes your way. You'll be so busy fighting all the time that you'll have no time left to enjoy your life.

The secret is to learn how to apply Aikido throughout life. Aikido is a style of martial arts created by Morihei Ueshiba. Master Ueshiba's intention wasn't to create another style of combat. It was to create a way for a spiritual warrior to purify his soul by redirecting the energy that comes at him into something positive he can use for himself and for the betterment of

> *"The finest weapons of a land are enlightened warriors who have linked themselves to heaven and earth and thus understand the true purpose of the Divine Plan."*
>
> *"The great spirit of Aiki enjoins all that is Divine and enlightened in every land. Unite yourself to the Divine, and you will be able to perceive gods wherever you are. . . ."*
>
> *"The cross (and path) of harmony (love) is an instrument of the gods."*
>
> MORIHEI UESHIBA

the world. He defined Aikido as "the way of the harmonious spirit." Master Ueshiba taught that a true master is a person who stops the fight before the fight begins. True masters transform their energy to be so peacefully powerful that people just don't need to fight them. In this way they turn their enemies into their allies.

Live in the Light!

It's your responsibility to make sure you are empowered. It's not your partner's job. It's not your parents' job. It's not your boss's job. It's not even your government's job.

When you want your body to be full of power, make sure the food you eat is empowering food. Think about it this way: junk food in = junk performance out. That makes sense, right? The easiest way to make sure your eating regime consists of loads of empowering foods is to ask yourself the magic question: "Is this food going to empower or disempower me?" Think for a moment about the animal kingdom. Which is the most powerful group of animals? It's the vegetarians—animals like the horse, rhino, ox, water buffalo, ape, and orangutan, for instance. So it's pretty easy to see which foods possess the most power.

And here's something else to think about. Have you ever noticed that plants are in direct sunlight all day long, yet they don't get cancer? This is because they contain photonutrients that protect them from the harsh rays of the sun. That being said, would you think that if you eat more foods with photonutrients in them, you too may be better protected against cancer?

> "A negative attitude toward others will never bring me success."
>
> NAPOLEON HILL

When talking to or talking about someone else, make sure you're always positive and empowering in what you say, because if you're not, then you're taking power away from not only the other person, but also from yourself. As you sow, so shall you reap. The Law of Circulation is always in effect. *If it doesn't serve, then don't say it!* When you're being disempowering about someone else, you transform yourself from being a magnet that attracts all the good things you desire into you being a force field pushing all of those good things away. And remember that low levels of power are always going to be the catalyst for ill health. Whether it is ill health in your body, your relationships, your business, or any other area of your life, negativity is a destructive energy that will wipe out all of your goals and dreams.

When you take responsibility for your life, you are being proactive instead of being reactive. Being proactive is empowering; being reactive is disempowering. To be proactive means you are consciously choosing to be positive and empowering about everything and everyone, even when some people are attempting to disempower you. Just because they are attempting to disempower you doesn't mean you have to capitulate. Think of it this way: Imagine someone wanted to give you a gift and you refused to accept the gift. Whom does the gift belong to? Who has to keep it? The gift belongs to the person who tried to give it to you, so they get to keep it. Similarly, if someone wants to give you grief and you refuse to take it, whom does the grief belong to? Who has to keep it?

When you get caught up in reacting to the negative way other people are acting, you get sucked into being negative yourself. You are allowing yourself to be disempowered, so you are allowing your power to be taken away from you. It renders you powerless. When you are reactive, you activate a law of nature to work against you. That law is the Law of Cause and Effect, and it states that every cause creates an effect, and every effect is created by a cause. When you are reacting to the way someone is acting, or to an event you find to be negative or disempowering, what you're really doing is seeing that person or event as the cause of your grief. What is happening to you is the effect. Here's the problem with that. We can't change something that is outside of ourselves. If someone chooses to be negative, that's up to him. There are events that happen in life over which we have no control. Some of these events may be perceived as negative events. We can't change those negative events or those negative people from being that way. Yet what we can do is take responsibility to not let them disempower us.

Remember, *responsibility means that you have the ability to choose how you respond.* If you're being reactive, you're not choosing how to respond. Instead you are allowing the choice to be made for you by someone, or something, outside yourself. How powerless does that sound? Blaming other people for your disempowerment is disempowering in itself. It's your responsibility to make sure you are always empowered, even when others around you are attempting to be disempowering. When you blame someone else for disempowering you, you are reacting to what he is doing. Instead you need to proactively make sure you are always empowered. Being proactive means taking responsibility for how you respond to whatever is going on around you in a way that is always empowering. When you respond in an empowering way, you gain power. It makes you powerful. That's what personal power is.

> *"When you empower others you are more empowered."*

My choice is to always work toward empowering a disempowering person before I consider distancing myself from him. Remember that the more power you give, the more power you get. There are rewards in helping others see their own light. The first reward is that the world becomes a better place to live. If you think the world we live in is in strife, and you would like it to be better and safer for us all, then we need to take personal responsibility for making it that way.

Understand that a master is not defined by the size of the crowd around him. Helping one person transform from a negative energy source into a positive one can have a great impact on the big picture. It's the ripple effect. When a pebble drops in the pond, it creates ripples that touch all the shores. That one person you help to transform into a happier and more positive person goes on to positively affect others he comes into contact with.

How do you help change negative people to be more empowered? You ask them empowering questions. For example, when people start to tell me how rotten their day has been, I honestly don't want to hear it. Would you? It's not that I don't care, and it's not that I don't have compassion for them, because I do care and I do have compassion. The truth is that I don't have pity for them.

> "You are searching for the magic key that will unlock the door to the source of power; and yet you have the key in your own hands, and you may make use of it the moment you learn to control your thoughts."
>
> NAPOLEON HILL

Pitying someone is a very disempowering way to treat him. Pity cripples people and keeps them living a life of pain. Pity is speaking when you say, "Oh poor you! Life really is cruel, and there is nothing you can do about it, so let's go get drunk together and wash away your sorrows." Are you really helping a person make his life any better when you sit and listen to him complain about how rotten his day has been and how pitiful his life is? The more he is allowed to repeat those stories, the more real and powerful those stories become in his life and the more powerless he becomes to change it.

Every time someone tells their disempowering stories, they relive the experience in their mind. Think about it. The word "relive" means they are living it all over again. Do you think allowing someone to go through the pain of that experience again is a loving thing to do? Doesn't it sound more loving to proactively help him improve his life, instead of listening to him complain about how bad his life is? Feeling sorry for a person because of his downfalls isn't helping him back up onto his feet. You're not helping him by letting him relive his painful experience. You're actually bringing him more pain by allowing him to go through it again and again.

When people start to tell me about their bad day I ask, "How can you make it better?" I know that empowering them to focus on strategies for making it better is much more caring and compassionate than pitying them.

When you really care about people, you'll be compassionate. The difference between a friend and an acquaintance is that you can always count on a friend to hold you to a higher standard. And for you to be a good friend, you have to hold your friends to a higher standard, and the best way to do that is by you holding yourself to that same high standard. Allowing people to keep swimming in their pity pool is not helping them to live at a higher standard. When you start by holding yourself to a higher standard and being empowering about everything, you'll automatically be helping everyone in your life to be more empowering too. And, just by doing that, you'll notice that all you desire will automatically be attracted to you. The brighter your light gets, the more life is attracted to it automatically. It's that easy!

Remember that the more empowering you are, the more positive energy will be attracted to you, because energy attracts like energy. Strive toward being empowering about everything, and you too will have your empower-ring, and everyone will begin to see your light.

To make sure you feel empowered every day, start every morning with some powerful questions like these:

"How can I best add value to my life and to other people's lives today?"

"What do I love more about my partner today than I did yesterday?"

"What am I grateful for today?"

You can use empowerment questions in so many areas of your life. Imagine how much better relationships would be if both partners asked themselves every day, "How can I be more loving to my partner today?"

Or try it at your workplace with this daily question: "How can I best empower the team today?"

Instead of asking people how their day is going, ask them, "What's great about your day today?"

If you just ask how their day is, you'll get many different answers, and some of them may not be all that positive. How often have you heard that common response, "Not so bad"? I always wonder what is "not so bad." It's closer to bad than it is to being good. Yet when you ask, "What's great about your day?" you'll notice that to be able to answer that question, they have to answer it positively. Remember that you reap what you sow. The more power you give to others, the more power you get. The more you empower yourself, the stronger the gravitational pull you create, and the faster the things and experiences you desire are attracted to you. It's that easy!

"The more power that goes to the source of the light, the brighter the light is, and the more life will is attracted to it."

9

The Formula for Re-Creation

To start this chapter we need to quickly recap the past few chapters to discover the real magic that connects them. In chapter 8, we talked about increasing your internal personal power because it increases the intensity of your light, and when your light is brighter, everything you desire is automatically attracted to you, cutting out the need for stress or struggle. The way to do this is to decide to be empowering about everything—not just when things are going your way, or when everyone is singing your praises, but all the time, and about everything. Anyone can do it when things are going your way. It's about being empowering even when it seems the world around you isn't. Remember that the people who get the biggest rewards in life are the ones willing to *do* what the average person isn't willing to *do*. Notice I emphasize the word "do" because it's not about knowing what to do; it's about doing it. Most people know what to do, and most people aren't doing what they

> *"We don't see things as they are; we see things as we are."*
>
> ANAIS NIN

know. Isn't it curious that even though most of us actually do know the steps we need to take to get the life we want, or at least to accomplish of some of our grand goals, there still seem to be times when something within us seems to be holding us back from taking those steps? Have you ever wondered why that is?

This is exactly what we are going to focus on in this chapter, because when you start doing what you know, just imagine how much more joy, fulfillment, and accomplishment your life will have. Think about how valuable that is!

In chapter 7, we discussed the fact that everything in life either evolves or dissolves. It's either growing or it's decaying and dying. What direction our lives will go is completely up to us and the choices we make. If you argue with that fact, it will automatically render you powerless. It means you're participating in a condition known as "learned helplessness."

A monkey is put into a room with only four straight walls with nothing to grab on to. The room has a metal floor divided into four squares. As the monkey sits down on a square and gets comfortable, a high voltage of electricity is sent through the square that he is sitting on, causing him a lot of pain. The monkey quickly jumps up, looking for a safe place to go. He is relieved to find the other squares aren't electrified. The researchers continue sending electricity through each square the monkey sits on until there is only one square left they didn't electrify. They just let the monkey sit on that one square without any pain attached to it.

Interestingly, every time the researchers let the monkey back into the room, where do you think he chose to sit? Right on the square with no pain attached. To him, it was the only square that was comfortable. For humans, this square we live in is called our "comfort zone."

So many people ask me, "What's wrong with the comfort zone? Isn't that what we're trying to achieve, a comfortable life?" Let's look at the rest of the monkey study, and you'll see that the comfort zone isn't really as comfortable as it is made out to be.

One day they let the monkey back into the room with the metal floor, and, of course, he goes right back to the familiar comfortable spot to sit down. That's when the researchers play a cruel trick on the monkey. They electrify all four grids at the same time. The monkey goes berserk, constantly jumping in the air, screaming, trying to avoid the pain. The monkey keeps this up for as long as he can until he just doesn't have the strength anymore. That's the point at which he surrenders to the idea that there is no way out of his pain; he just sits there and accepts the pain being inflicted on him. That's what learned helplessness is. It's reaching the point in your life at which you believe there's no way you'll be able to achieve your grand dream goals, so you just try to make the best out of whatever is handed to you.

The best part of this example is that we aren't monkeys being forced to go into to a room that we don't want to go into. We can choose where we go in our lives. Yet if we don't make a decision the decision gets made for us. Not taking action is the prescription for failure. If we don't choose to evolve, the world around us still is, and because of our lack of forward movement, by default we start to slide backward.

That's why the comfort zone isn't as comfortable as it seems to be. In the comfort zone there isn't anything new. It's living the same day over and over again, without any evolvement, without any growth.

Remember: whether or not you're evolving, the world around you still is. So if you're not moving forward, then, by default, you're moving backward. That's why learned helplessness is something you want to avoid at all costs. If you feel you're already there, now is the time to decide to get out. *Evolvement is our life's quest.*

It is the natural order of the universe for everything to continually try to seek to reach its highest potential, to evolve. Evolvement isn't something we ever reach. There isn't a day when we wake up to find that we are evolved. "Evolved" refers to the notion that you've reached the top, and there's nowhere else to go. The reason we never become evolved is because as soon as we stop evolving, we start moving in the other direction, because everything is always in motion. That's why I said that evolvement is our life's quest.

In chapter 6, we discussed the formula for creation, which is $T \rightarrow A = R$. It's your thoughts that allow you to take actions, and it's those actions that produce results. So this is where we need to look at what kind of new thoughts you need to have to start evolving, because as you evolve, you produce the biggest rewards for your life.

Since thoughts are the beginning of all that we create, let's look at the most powerful thought you can have. Remember, the more power that goes to the source (you are the source) the brighter your light gets, and the more life will automatically be attracted to you. The most powerful thought you can have is your identity. *Your identity is who you think you are.* Here's why it is so critical to change who you think you are in order to create the holistically successful life you desire. The person you think you are right now is doing the things you do right now, and since "doing" is another way to describe "acting," it's those actions you're taking right now that are producing the life you're living right now. Here's the challenge: the "you" that you are right now can only keep doing the same things you're doing right now. In order to really take your life to the next level and beyond, you are going to have to reinvent yourself.

I'll give you an example of what I mean. Do you know anyone who wants to get in better shape or lose some extra weight? I'm sure you know a few of these people, considering that 65% of people in most Western societies are overweight and out of shape. Do you know of any strategies that would help these people achieve better health and fitness? The ones most people recommend are to exercise regularly, eat less food, and eat healthier foods such as fruits and veggies, right? How does that sound to you as a strategy for losing weight? Do you think most people already know those strategies? Of course they do! The question is why aren't they using them? Everyone knows eating better quality food and less of it, combined with a regular exercise regime, will make them healthier and fitter, yet more and more people are getting fatter and unhealthier. Have you ever wondered why that is?

The reason is that most people say when they lose the extra weight, they'll be healthy. Here's the challenge with that way of thinking: what they're really saying is that right now they're unhealthy. The problem with that is that unhealthy people don't do healthy things; they do unhealthy things. When you say, "I am unhealthy," the words "I am" signal that you're making a statement about the way you identify yourself. Whatever follows the words "I am" is your identity.

It's your identity that creates your beliefs. Your beliefs become your behaviors. It's your behaviors that get displayed through your actions, and it's your actions that produce your results.

To have the results you want, you have to do what it takes to get those results, and in order to do those things, you first have to be the person who would do them. If you're not the person who would do them, you won't do them. Remember: the people who get the best rewards in life are the ones willing to *do* what other people aren't willing to *do*. The reason they do those things is because they identify themselves as the type of person who does those things.

Wherever Your Head Goes Your Body Follows

Your identity is determined by you. It's who you think you are, and the identity you choose for yourself determines the beliefs you hold.

Here's an example. One person says he's Christian, and another says he's Jewish. Do these two people have different beliefs? Of course they do. You may be thinking that being Jewish or Christian means they practice different religions, not different identities. If you ask these people about themselves, they will say, "I am Christian," or "I am Jewish." By saying, "I am," they are defining their identities as Christian or Jewish.

Ask different people about themselves, and they'll tell you, "I'm a father," or "I'm a mother," "I'm Australian," "I'm Japanese," "I'm black," "I'm Hispanic," "I'm Catholic," "I'm Baptist," or "I'm Muslim."

How do you describe yourself? Whatever follows the words "I am" represents the identity you hold for yourself. It's who you're saying you are. That determines the beliefs you have for yourself.

Do Muslim and Jewish people have different beliefs? Do African and Korean people have different beliefs? How about smokers and nonsmokers—do they have different beliefs? Even when a person says he's a smoker or a nonsmoker he's describing his identity, the way he thinks about himself. Do smokers and nonsmokers have different beliefs about smoking? Of course they do! And if smokers and nonsmokers have different beliefs about smoking, then would you say a person who says he's average and another who says he's an achiever have different beliefs about what they could achieve in their lives?

How about a person who says he's a procrastinator? Do you think he has certain beliefs about the way he participates in life? Absolutely! When a person says he's a procrastinator enough times that he finally believes it, the next time something comes up that looks a little difficult or challenging, he'll say to himself, "I'm just a procrastinator anyway, so I might as well procrastinate again."

Each time he says he's a procrastinator, he just reinforces that disempowering belief, making it easier and easier to procrastinate again and again in the future. The more this goes on, the more that disempowering belief steals his dreams, because he doesn't take the necessary action to create the positive results he desires. Instead of saying, "I am a procrastinator," wouldn't you think that saying, "I am a massive action taker" would be more conducive to producing the awesome results he wants?

Remember that to do the things that will produce the results you want, you first have to be the person who would do those things, and whatever you attach to the words "I am" you become!

The important thing to understand is that your identity isn't written in stone. It's not who you are forever. It's who you say you are *now*. As soon as you start saying "I am" something different, you'll actually start to become that different identity, and the more times you say it, the quicker you'll evolve into that new identity and all the results it brings into your life.

As soon as you change who you say you are, your beliefs have to fit in with your new identity. Think about the difference between a smoker and a nonsmoker. Do they have different identities? Of course. One says, "I am a smoker," and the other says, "I am a non-smoker." Do they have different beliefs? Yes again—one believes it's okay to smoke, and the other doesn't. Do they have different behaviors and take different actions? Obviously! Do they get different results?

Let's say the smoker decides to quit smoking, and he does for a while. One night he's out with friends in a bar and he's had a few drinks. Then someone offers him a cigarette. Since he has been drinking, his resistance is down and he reaches for that cigarette. Next thing he knows, he's smoking again. Sound familiar? It should. It's the number one reason people go back to smoking after quitting. Do you know anyone this has happened to?

The average person would say the reason he started again was that his resistance was down because he was drinking alcohol and it took away his willpower. Before we go any further, let's talk about willpower. What is willpower? Has anyone ever taught you where to find it, or how to get more of it? The answer is no, because it doesn't exist. There is no such thing as willpower.

Willpower (or the lack of having any) is just an excuse that people use when they fail to take responsibility for their actions. They say, "I guess I just didn't have enough willpower to follow through with it." So since willpower doesn't exist, stop blaming it for your problems. As soon as you take responsibility for your actions, you'll be able to change your life and make it anything you want it to be.

Now back to our smoker. The reason that person went back to smoking was because he said he quit smoking instead of declaring himself to be a nonsmoker.

Here's the problem with saying that you quit smoking. A person who quits smoking is still a smoker who is attempting to stay away from the behavior of a smoker. A smoker's behavior is smoking. The only thing quitting does is make you a quitter. The challenge with being a quitter is that when your resistance is down, like when you're drinking alcohol, it makes it easy for you to start smoking again.

When you identify yourself as a quitter, it makes it easier to quit at quitting, which means it's easy to go back doing the things you don't want to do anymore. Make sense?

The proof in all of this is with nonsmokers. You'll notice that no matter how many drinks a real nonsmoker has, he or she still won't have a cigarette. For them there is no temptation. Why? Because they don't smoke!

In those years after the helicopter crash, I became one of those people with bad breath, yellow teeth, and stinky clothes, who make other people around them end up with stinky clothes and who are killing everyone else with their secondhand smoke. I can say that now, because I was one of those people.

Back in those days I tried quitting numerous times. Each morning after telling myself that I was quitting, again, I would arrive at work and tell my great friend Kevin that I was quitting. Kevin was one of the people with whom I worked on numerous movie sets. He was one of the guys on my grip crew. Every morning after hearing me telling him the same old story about how I was quitting again he would just laugh and hand me the ceremonial first cigarette of the day, as he had done every other day we worked together. This scene had been going on for months. Each morning I would walk in and tell him I was quitting, and at some point in the day, I always broke down and wound up asking him for a cigarette.

The funny thing was that I didn't officially think I was a smoker, because I never bought my own. I figured if you got them from someone else, you were only a "social smoker." (A social smoker still has the identity of a smoker.) Kevin didn't share my view, since he was always the one buying extra cigarettes every day to make up for the ones he gave to me all day long.

The reason I didn't have the "willpower" to give up smoking was because I was telling myself I wanted to quit. And that's what I was doing. I was quitting at trying to quit smoking. Remember: that's what quitters do—they quit.

One morning I had a new thought. (Here's the creation formula again!) I remembered my life before I smoked and wondered, "What's different about me now and who I was then?" That's when the penny dropped. What was different was that back then I was a nonsmoker. I asked myself, "Do nonsmokers have different beliefs about smoking than smokers do?" I thought about it for a moment and came to the conclusion that they do. A nonsmoker wouldn't smoke because nonsmokers just don't smoke. They don't even have to think about it because they don't even consider it.

That's when the proverbial lightbulb inside my head came on. I knew that instead of trying to quit smoking, what I was going to focus on was how to become a nonsmoker again. I wondered how I was going to do that. When I came up with the answer, it was so easy it seemed there was no way it could work, yet it still made sense. I decided the strategy to use was "fake it until you make it!" I figured that if I said I was a nonsmoker enough times, I would start to believe it.

If you wrote down a lie on a piece of paper and carried it everywhere and took it out several times a day and read it with passion and commitment, after a while you would start to believe that lie.

The weekend before I returned to work, I decided to reinforce the idea that I was a nonsmoker. I repeated the phrases, "I am a nonsmoker," and, "I don't smoke!" over and over with conviction and certainty. It was that day that I went into my backyard and cut that line in the sand with my broom pole sword. By the time Monday rolled around, not only did I give up cigarettes, I also gave up cocaine, the idea of suicide, and a lot of other disempowering behaviors.

When I showed up on the set we were working on, the first person I saw was Kevin. When he offered me that first cigarette, I said, "No thanks. I don't smoke."

"You quit again?"

"I don't smoke!" I said more forcefully.

Kevin still didn't get the message. He said, "Here, man, just take it. I know you're going to ask me for one later anyway."

The intensity of my voice went up a few notches.

Clearly and sternly I let Kevin know, "I DON"T SMOKE! I AM A NONSMOKER!"

Then I said, "If you ever hand me another cigarette—!"

Kevin got my message. To this day, whenever I see Kevin, he still talks about that morning. He says when he saw the look in my eyes, he knew I would never touch another cigarette again.

He was right!

When you want to live the holistically successful life of your dreams, you're going to have to change who you think you are. You have to transform yourself into the person who already has the results you want. You have to do it now, before you actually have the results. It's the only way you'll ever get those results, because it's only those kinds of people who take the necessary actions. That's why most people know what to do and still aren't doing what they know. They don't believe they're a person who would do those things. That makes sense, right?

The only way you'll ever get the blissfully happy life you desire is by deciding to reinvent who you think you are. The current you does what you do because of the way you think right now. It's who you are now that's gotten you where you are right now, and that won't get you to where you want to be. Only the new, improved you can do that. The more personally developed you. That's where evolvement comes in. You have to evolve the way you think about yourself. It starts with a shift in your identity.

Are you now seeing how this is all connected?

Remember: your identity isn't written in stone. You can change it by changing who you say you are.

I'll share an example of this strategy with you so you can see just how powerful it can be.

In 1998 I was giving a corporate seminar in Brisbane, Australia. Unknown to me, Natalie Cook, a 1996 Australian Olympic bronze medal winner for women's beach volleyball, was in the audience. At one point in the seminar I said, "Who remembers the person who stands on the third box at the Olympics?" I asked, "Does anyone remember any bronze medalists' names? Have you ever rushed out to buy a bronze medalist's book thinking, 'Oh gee, how did you come in third?"

At the end of the seminar, a very fit, very powerful-looking young woman walked up to me and asked, "How are you?"

I replied, "Excellent, thank you. How are you?"

Her demeanor instantly changed. So did the tone in her voice. "I'm Natalie Cook, and I was on the third box at the Olympics!" It was at that moment I thought there was a good possibility I just might have to eat some crow very soon.

Natalie's voice changed again. She said, "I know you have the skills and tools I need to get me where I want to go in life. Will you take me to the gold?"

Without a moment's hesitation I said, "Absolutely!"

About thirty minutes later, I was struck by a huge wave of self-doubt. I thought, "Who are you to think you can help this woman win an Olympic gold medal? You've never done anything like this in your life!"

Instantly an alarm went off in my head. I wasn't happy with the questions I had just asked. I asked myself, "Were those empowering or disempowering questions?"

The answer was clear: disempowering.

That's when I took the next step and declared my new identity. "I am the person who is doing this. I am the person who always finds a way."

The second those thoughts entered my mind, I immediately felt empowered.

A giant grin came across my face. "Go for it!"

For the next two and a half years, I worked with Natalie Cook and her partner, beach volleyball legend Kerri-Ann Pottharst. And on September 25, 2000, in front of 10,000 pumped-up fans on the sands at the Bondi Beach stadium in Sydney, Australia, Natalie and Kerri-Ann beat the Brazilian team in two straight sets, winning the gold medal. They had faced the Brazilians twelve times leading up to the 2000 Olympics and only beat them once. The Brazilians won the gold medal in the 1996 Olympics and were considered to be the best beach volleyball team in the world.

Not anymore! We got the gold in Sydney!

During the time I spent working with Nat and Kerri, we focused on many different strategies to tap into their peak performance. All of them were very beneficial in getting them to their grand dream goal, yet there was one strategy that stood out above the rest—one I was more insistent on their using above all the others. It even got them to perform at a higher standard at their practice sessions and in their strength training. The results they obtained by putting it into action stand for themselves. Nat and Kerri's performance at the Sydney 2000 Olympics made them legends in Australia and created a positive impact on the sport of beach volleyball worldwide.

Would you like to know what this amazing strategy is, so you can make your life golden too?

During the time leading up to the Olympics, I instructed Nat and Kerri to identify themselves as "the gold medalists from the Sydney 2000 Olympics." That's right. For two and a half years, Nat and Kerri were already saying they were gold medalists. They didn't just say it to each other; they said it to everyone. They said it when they were being interviewed in the media, and when they were asked to sign autographs, they signed them as gold medal winners.

You should have seen the looks on the faces of some of the reporters as they listened to the girls talk about their gold medals. Some of them looked at their watches to check the date, trying to figure out what was going on. That's how much conviction and certainty the girls had in their voices!

There's another part of the strategy I need to reveal. I told them I would fine them $5,000 each if ever I heard them say they'd settle for anything less than the gold. I wanted Nat and Kerri to hold themselves to a higher standard. When you hold yourself to a higher standard and expect more out of yourself, you'll live up to those expectations. And that's called peak performance.

By the way, because Nat and Kerri have always been shining examples of real professionals, they never had to pay a single fine. They lived my instructions to the letter, and that's why they got and deserve their gold medals. They were willing to do what no other athlete in their sport at the 2000 Olympics was willing to do and they got the result no other athlete in their sport would get.

Your body is limited by the space it occupies. It can only get so big, strong, or fast. Your mind, on the other hand, is limitless. For athletes, and in life, that's where the competitive edge is. You have to think the most powerful thoughts you can to perform at your peak. When you see someone doing that, you get to witness greatness at work. That's when a human being can take themselves to higher levels in whatever they're doing. The best part is that when it comes to this ability, we all have the same potential. We are all on the same level playing field.

Do you recognize the strategy I used with the volleyball team? I got the girls to reinvent themselves, and I did it with the use of the most powerful two words in the English language: "I am."

Nat and Kerri changed their identity from "I am an Olympic bronze medalist" to "I am an Olympic gold medalist." I got them to rehearse this over and over, day in and day out. Natalie went so far as to tape green ribbons to a gold tinfoil medal on her mirror so that every time she looked in the mirror, she would see herself wearing her gold medal.

They used the formula for re-creation by starting with a new thought about their identity. When you say, "I am a gold medalist," enough times, after a while you start to believe it. You may not believe it consciously, and that doesn't really matter. It's the subconscious mind that believes it. It doesn't know the difference. It just acts on whatever you are telling it to be true. And it's your subconscious that has access to your entire nervous system and has control over the movements of your body. That's why I say, "Fake it until you make it."

Keep putting those new thoughts into your mind with passion and certainty, and eventually your mind will start to believe it. When that happens, you'll start to behave like you are who you say you are.

Kerri and Nat said they were gold medalists for so long, they really started to believe it. Once they started to believe they were gold medalists, they started to behave and act like gold medalists. And once you start taking the actions that a gold medalist takes, that will produce what? That's right, gold medals. Every action creates an equal and opposite reaction—also known as a result! Take gold medal actions, and that will produce gold medal results. It's cause and effect. Makes sense, right?

The process of getting Kerri and Nat to identify themselves as gold medalists began with putting them in front of 450 people at one of my seminars. I convinced them to get onstage and declare they were the Sydney 2000 Olympic gold medalists.

They didn't just stand there and say it once. They had to say it in such a way that everyone in the audience believed them. They had to stay up there until they could convince themselves that they were gold medalists.

A public declaration is a very powerful strategy for achieving your grand dream goals, because everyone you say it to will help hold you to a higher standard. This book is a by-product of that strategy. During the year and a half it took me to write it, I told every audience I was in front of that I was writing this book and that I am a best-selling author. I've told that to thousands of people.

When I bump into some of them, they ask, "Hey, how's your book coming along? When is it coming out?" That's them keeping me accountable.

Whenever I got Nat and Kerri up onstage to make their public declaration of their new identities, it really angered a lot of people in the audience. They would say things like, "How dare you set those girls up for failure? What are you going to do if they lose?"

Think about this for a moment. Are those the kind of thoughts that will help you achieve your grand dream goals? Do you think those are empowering or disempowering thoughts? Would you think that having the identity of a loser is a good thing? Remember: your thoughts produce your actions, and those actions create the results you get.

Is "loser" an empowering identity or a disempowering identity? Or would you prefer the identity of "gold medalist"? Me too!

Remember that it's your **identity** that creates your **beliefs**.

It's your **beliefs** that become your **behaviors and actions**.

It's your **behaviors and actions** that produce your **results**!

It has been six years since the Sydney Olympics. During that time I have had the honor of being able to spend a lot of quality time with Nat and Kerri. Both of them now enjoy happy, successful lives. We even still do some media appearances together. Just recently Kerri and I were invited to be on a morning TV talk show in Sydney. One of the hosts asked her, "What do you think was the team's secret weapon to winning your gold medals?"

Kerri looked at him for a moment and then looked at me. Looking the host right in the eye, she said, "Without Kurek there would be no gold for us. The strategies he taught us not only changed the way we played the game, they changed my whole life."

I just about fell off the couch! I was blown away by Kerri's compliment, and what makes it so rewarding is that Kerri now has everything she ever wanted in her life. Two and a half years before the games, she told me about everything she wanted to achieve, and here we are, six years later, and she has all of that and so much more.

Nat and Kerri, I love you both, and I am supremely grateful for the opportunity you gave me to experience the adventure of going to Olympic gold. You are truly legends!

If you would like to see some pictures of the Nat and Kerri and their gold medals, go to www.howwouldloverespond.com.

"The me I see is the me I'll be."

———

When you decide to reinvent yourself, you'll make your life more holistically successful. You'll fill it with the achievements of your biggest grand dream goals and enjoy a much higher level of joy and fulfillment. The person you are right now can only do what you're currently doing. And because of the Law of Cause and Effect, that can only produce the same kinds of results you've been getting. Insanity is to keep doing the same thing over and over again and expecting a different result. What you plant determines what you will grow.

The strategy is simple. You're going to have to re-create your life by re-creating your identity. Start describing yourself as the person you want to become. When you decide not to smoke anymore, begin by saying, "I am a nonsmoker."

If you want to lose weight and get in better shape, start describing yourself as the healthy and fit person you want to become by saying, "I am a healthy and fit person who is getting healthier and fitter all the time." The best part is when you think you're a healthy person, healthy people naturally do healthy things, and when you start to do healthy things, it's those actions that will always produce the result of being healthy.

One powerful distinction to remember is that you must identify yourself as the person you want to become, the person who has the results in life that you desire, as if you already have those results right now. So you're phrasing it in the present tense. When you use the words "I am," you're stating who you are right now. When you use the words "I want to be," you're expressing a hope for the future. The problem is that the future never comes. You'll never wake up to "tomorrow" or "someday." Whenever you wake up, it's always "today." It's always here, and it's always right now.

When you identify yourself as the person you are right now, that identity will keep you participating in life exactly the same way you do right now. Again, that can only produce the same results that you're getting right now. It's impossible for them to produce anything different. The key is to identify yourself right now as the person you want to be as if it is who you are right now.

Remember that the people who achieve the most in life are visionaries, and one of the things that make them visionaries is that they define themselves as already being the people they want to become.

"I am a bestselling author!"
"I am young and powerful!"
"I am a successful entrepreneur!"
"I am healthy and in the best shape of my life so far!"

Whoever you consistently say you are you will become. Remember the formula that presides over all creation. Your thoughts produce your actions, and your actions create results.

That's why the most powerful thought you can have is the thought of who you think you are—your identity.

So right now come up with eight new identities for yourself. Make them the identities of the "you" you want to become, and make it sound as if it's who you already are, making sure to use the words "I am," and not "I want to be."

Some more examples are:

"I am happy and always loving life!"
"I am calm and peaceful!"
"I am a great dad/mom!"
"I am grateful!"
"I am blessed!"
"I am always living my dream!"
"I am constantly evolving mentally, physically, and spiritually!"
One of my favorites is, "I am one with the source!"

We've looked at how a disempowering identity like "I am a pro-crastinator" can steal your dreams, because it paralyzes and cripples you, preventing you from taking the action you need to create your dream result. Other examples of some disempowering dream-stealer identities are:

"I'm not good enough!"
"I'm not smart enough!"
"I'm too old!"
"I'm too young!"
"I'm lazy!"
"I'm scared!"
"I'm depressed!"
"I'm lonely!"

I'm guessing that there's a certain disempowering identity by which you may have already defined yourself in the past. It probably happened when one of your friends or family members said, "Hey, let's go on a trip somewhere, or go shopping and spend some money." And you said, "I can't, because I'm broke!"

Have you ever used "I'm broke" before?

When a person says, "I'm broke," he's not really talking about the status of his bank account. What he's talking about is his financial identity.

When you say, "I'm broke," you actually believe you're broke, right?

When you believe you're broke, you start behaving like you're broke.

When you behave like you're broke, you're acting like you're broke, and it's those actions that produce the condition of you being financially broke. See how this works?

Instead, you might want to start referring to yourself as, "I am an inspired multimillionaire!"

"Inspired" means you are in your spirit and your spirit is a being of the light, so when you're an *inspired* multimillionaire, in addition to having financial freedom, you're also healthy, happy, and you add value to others' lives. Doesn't that sound like something a being of the light would do? Remember that life is attracted to the light!

———

When your children do something you think is inappropriate, don't call them a bad boy or a bad girl. When you say, "You're a bad boy/girl," what you're really saying is that's who they are as people. In reality, there is no such thing as a bad person. No babies come out of the womb bad. All babies come out perfect.

That's not to say that some people don't behave inappropriately. Of course there are times when you may have to counsel or discipline your children. Instead of identifying them as being a bad boy or a bad girl, let them know you love them unconditionally and that it was their behavior that was inappropriate, and that's what you are disciplining.

If you keep telling your children they're "bad" enough times, there is a chance they might really start to believe it. The problem is that when people think they are bad, bad people do bad things and that can only create bad results.

It's our identity that creates our beliefs. Our beliefs create our behaviors. Our behaviors create our results.

So right now, on the next page of this book, write down eight new empowering identities for yourself. You'll notice there are actually ten spaces and I asked you to come up with only eight new identities. That's because I have two more for you to add later.

Remember: the people who are getting the best results in life are the ones who take the immediate actions the average person doesn't take. You don't want to identify yourself as average, do you? Of course not! So, right now, take the action and do the exercise so you can reap the rewards.

"The only person I have to get better than is who I am!"

I Am's

You did take the time to take the action and do the "I Am" process, right? You didn't just skip over it and keep reading, did you? Make sure you take the action!

We've discovered the most powerful thought you can have is your identity, or who you think you are. Now let's talk about the next way we can dramatically increase the levels of our own empowerment.

This is done by utilizing the most powerful force in the universe: love!

When you study the lives of the world's most successful and influential people, you'll notice that their most powerful source of inspiration is love. *Love is the most powerful force in the universe.*

> *"Love is the only reality and it is not a mere sentiment. It is the ultimate truth that lies at the heart of creation."*
>
> RABINDRANATH TAGORE

It might be the love they have for their partner, their wife, or their husband. Maybe it is the love for their, family, their team, or their cause. Or perhaps it is their love for their community or country, or for the human race and Mother Earth. The force of love has empowered people from all walks of life to achieve beyond what previously seemed completely impossible.

I know it was my love for Mike that protected me from the flames in that burning helicopter as I was getting him out. It was the love I had for Gadi that gave me the strength to lift the helicopter off his body so I could free him. And it was the love I finally got for myself that gave me the power to turn my life around and create the wonderful life I have now.

"The universe began as God's first loving thought."

I now know what the feeling was when I was with Mike in the light. I now know what the light is. It's pure, unconditional love.

When Mary Magdalene talked about Jesus Christ, she referred to him as "The Love." She identifies Jesus by calling him "The Love."

I personally don't have a religion. I don't identify myself as a Christian, or a Jew, or with any other religious identity, yet when I look at all of the wonderful and amazing things Jesus did in his life, I can see why his light was so bright.

Jesus said, "Even the least among you can do all that I have done and even greater things." He made a connection using the seed for creation: thoughts. The most powerful thought you can have is about who you think you are, your identity. And he connected that with the most powerful force in the universe: love. "I am Love!"

"I am Love!"

"I am Love!"

Take a moment and really process just how truly powerful having that identity is.

Imagine identifying yourself as Love. How would you respond differently to everything that happens in your life when you identify yourself as Love?

The most empowering question you can ever ask yourself in any situation is, "How would Love respond to this?"

Being Love, how would you respond to the person you're in a relationship with when he or she is having a challenging day?

As Love, would you respond differently to people who may have a different opinion from yours? Is it more important to be right or kind? How would Love respond?

When you have two people who both think that their opinion is right and they start defending their point of view, you now have a conflict on your hands. When I finally decided I wanted to enjoy a much more peaceful life, I started choosing "kind" as my response every time.

Throughout the rest of this book, you are going to see so many places that this all-powerful question applies and the results that asking it can produce in your life.

————

When I was a teenager, my father and I didn't see eye to eye with each other. We were two strong-willed people who used to dig our heels in and argue for what we felt was right. The only result that ever produced was disagreements or arguments.

Later in my life, I finally understood that life is too short to waste on negativity. Choose your battles wisely, because if you don't, you'll end up spending your time fighting about things that don't really matter.

Think about it. In your rules for life, does someone have to lose in order for you to win? In order for you to succeed in business, does someone else have to receive less than they are worth? Are you playing win/win or win/lose? How would Love respond?

Imagine how powerful you feel when, before any potential argument starts, you actually think to yourself, "How would I feel if I was the receiver of what I was about to say?"

Do you still say it after that?

Once I finally understood this powerful concept, I decided it was okay to let my dad feel that he was right. I no longer felt the need to have to be right. It is so freeing to just say, "You know what, Dad? You're right about that." Because of that I got to enjoy many wonderful, fulfilling years of having a great relationship with my dad. For my whole life he had been my hero, and I finally got the opportunity to let him experience the love and respect I had for him because we weren't caught up in the drama of trying to prove our own "rightness" to each other. Instead we could spend our time enjoying each other's company.

"Kind" is always the more empowering choice. Don't you think that's how Love would respond?

The great relationship I had with my dad lasted up to the very last moment of his life. I was one week away from flying back to Chicago to visit him because his health was starting to fail when I was awoken at 2 A.M. by the sound of the phone ringing.

It was my stepmother, Pauline. It was hard to understand what she was saying because she was sobbing. She handed the phone to the nurse who was helping care for my father. The nurse informed me that my father's health had taken a turn for the worse, and it was likely he would not live through the night. She told me my dad was conscious and very weak. I asked if I could talk with him. She said he was too weak to speak. I asked if she could put the phone next to his ear so I could talk to him. The nurse said yes and confirmed that he would be able to hear me.

I knew I had no time to waste, so I quickly spoke up. "Dad, it's me, Kurek. I love you. I will always make you proud, and it's okay for you to now surrender and go to peace."

The nurse got back on the phone. She said my dad smiled and knew it was me. Then he closed his eyes and went to sleep.

Five minutes later I got another call. My dad had passed away. I was so grateful that I got to have that last good-bye with my father.

As I hung up the phone, I felt an overwhelming sense of joy, brought on by the first question I asked myself, "What's great about all of this?"

The answers started flowing into my mind immediately.

What's great is that I got to have my father until I was forty-four years old. I know so many people who lost theirs when they were in their twenties, teens, or even younger. Some never got to meet their fathers at all because they died before they were born.

> "Darkness cannot drive out the darkness; only light can do that. Hate cannot drive out hate; only love can do that."
>
> MARTIN LUTHER KING, JR.

It was also great that I had a great relationship and friendship with my dad.

I thought about how great it was that he didn't have to suffer anymore because he died peacefully in his sleep.

And I will always be grateful that I got to say those last words and have that last moment with my dad.

You can focus on what you've lost or be grateful for what you gained. Which one of those two choices brings you the most peace and joy? Which one would Love choose?

Being grateful for everything and being empowering about everything—isn't that how Love would respond?

———

Go back now to your "I Am" list and add a new one, "I am Love." Remember that I had you use eight out of the ten spaces. "I am Love" is number nine. Make sure you add it to your list right now. In a later chapter you'll find out what the last one is.

———

"Everything in this life is borrowed. You have to give it all back. The only thing you get to keep is the love you gave, the love you received, and the experiences your soul got to have."

As I wrote in chapter 5, it took me a few years to truly understand the full message and what I was supposed to do with it. Finally it all made sense: it is a gift so powerful I am obliged to share it.

Throughout this book I am sharing this gift, bit by bit, so that you will understand it *and* be able to apply it in your life.

Love is the only thing your soul gets to keep after this lifetime passes. It's the currency of all that is. In the beginning, and in the end, it's all about love and it's only about love. The rest—the money, the things—are just there for borrowing. Those things are the props we use to gain our personal and spiritual experiences. You could think of them as toys on a playground—the equipment the kids get to play on and have fun with while they're learning about life. That's why we *can* have it all while we're here. The Creator placed it all here for us to use as tools for our learning experiences. In the Creator's eyes, all life experiences are ultimately experiences of love. Love is what we're here to learn about.

When you have love and gratitude for everything in your life, you do get to take it all with you. That's the meaning of the gift I was given. No, you don't get to take the physical stuff with you to a place where the physical is no longer needed. What you get to take is the positive essence of everything and everyone you experience in your lifetime, as long as they are all bathed in the love you have for them. Pure, unconditional love! That's how you and everything in your life all become one with the source.

Think about how much different the result will be when you can respond to even the "button pushers" of your life in a loving way!

Do you have any button pushers in your life? You know who they are—the people who know exactly how to get under your skin and push your buttons.

Who's the number one button pusher in the world? What is that person's name? Mom! Have you ever noticed that no one is better at pushing your buttons than your mom?

I'm not speaking badly about moms in any way. I don't want to do that. I have one myself.

The reason moms are such good button pushers is because Mom is the one who gave you your buttons. She created them. She knows where every one of your buttons is. The reason she pushes your buttons is because by maternal instinct she knows that pushing your buttons will allow you to clearly see the areas of your life in which you still need to evolve.

> "Thousands of candles can be lighted from a single candle, and the life of the candle will not be shortened. Happiness never decreases by being shared."
>
> BUDDHA

Think about it. If you were truly evolved in the area of your life in which your buttons are being pushed, it wouldn't bother you anymore, would it? There wouldn't be any button to push. The fact that it does bother you shows you still need to work on that area of your life. You still need to evolve. That's why I say we need to show gratitude for all the button pushers in our lives because, in reality, they're our spiritual guides. They're showing us where we still need to grow.

Once we evolve in that area, the button will no longer work. The button disconnects.

Remember that blaming someone else and being upset because you think they pushed your buttons is disempowering.

Being grateful for everything is empowering because gratitude is the way you show your love to the Creator for what you have been given.

So, Love, from now on, how are you going to respond?

10

GDGs—Grand Dream Goals

What do you really want? This book gives you all the strategies you need to help create everything you want in your life, but they only work if you've figured out what you really want. Let me ask you a question: Have you already written down your goals for this year?

When I asked that question in the hundreds of seminars and workshops I give all over the world every year, about the same percentage always answer yes—about 3%. On average, only 3% of people who come to my seminars have written down their goals for the year.

> "The future belongs to those who believe in the beauty of their dreams."
>
> ELEANOR ROOSEVELT

The same question was asked of a Yale University class in the 1950s. Then, too, about 3% of the class said they had written down their goals for that year. That class was followed for the next twenty years as a case study to see if writing down goals each year had any significant results in the long run. The results were amazing! What the researchers found was that the 3% who had written down their goals each year were worth more, financially, than the rest of the 97% combined. Why do you think that is?

Confucius said, "The person who aims at nothing is sure to hit it." If you don't know where you're going, how are you supposed to get there?

Imagine going to the airport and boarding a big commercial jet. As you're waiting to take off, the pilot's voice comes over the PA system. "Good morning, ladies and gentlemen. My name is Captain Bob. You'll be happy to know I've got a plane full of fuel, but I'm not really sure where we're going. Oh well, who cares? Let's fire up the engines and roar down the runway, and hopefully we'll find somewhere to land before we run out of fuel. Enjoy your meal and the movie, and fly with us again, if you live past the end of this flight."

If you heard that from the pilot, would you be looking for the exit? Would you trust a pilot who didn't know where he was going? Why trust yourself with your own life if you don't know where you're going with it?

> *"Repetition is the mother of all skill."*
>
> JIM ROHN

We're going to address this issue before we go any further. If you're one of the 97% who hasn't already written down their goals this year, you need to do this exercise. And if you're one of the other 3% who did, do this exercise anyway!

By doing this exercise there's a good chance you'll learn something new; it might just be a new distinction to what you think you already know, and that alone can be powerful.

It's a process I like to call "the magic two minutes." To participate in the magic two minutes, you're going to need some blank paper and something to write with. If you don't do this, you're already joining the 97% who don't take the necessary action. Is that really the identity you want?

Just do it. You're going to love it.

The best thing about the magic two minutes is that whatever you write down on the paper you are going to be able to have. I'm showing you how to do that. The sad thing is that if you don't write it down or don't do the exercise, you're not going to be able have it. Think about it. If you don't take the action, then how are you going to get the result, right?

Before we get started, there are some rules to discuss first.

> Rule #1: Make sure you actually do this exercise. Remember: the people who get the best results in life are the people who take action and do what the average person isn't willing to do. So take action!

> Rule #2: Do not write down your goals. Yes, you did read that right! Do *not* write down your goals!

If you're a bit confused and thinking, "Wait a minute! You've just told me that to achieve my goals, I need to do what the successful 3% do and write them down. Now you're saying, 'Don't write them down.' I don't get it!" The reason I don't want you to write down your goals is because adults write down their goals. When you ask adults to write down their goals, they don't say what they really want; they say what they think they can accomplish. There's a big difference between those two things.

When you ask most adults about the house they want to live in, they say things like, "I'd like a big house, but I don't want to be greedy. Something adequate will be okay. Something where the mortgage isn't too big would be good. And I don't want to have to clean a big house either. Something comfortable will do!"

When you ask them about the car they want, they say, "I'd like a nice car, but I'd be happy with something dependable and with good gas mileage, since gas is so expensive these days."

Then they start justifying their goals by saying there's no difference between an economy car and a luxury car because they both get you from point A to point B, and they both get caught in traffic just the same. They'll say things like, "The BMW doesn't have a helicopter attachment to fly over traffic, you know. Only people with big egos need to drive expensive cars." Honestly, the only people who think there's no difference between an economy car and a luxury car are people who drive economy cars! It's true that a BMW can get caught in traffic just like any other car, but when you're caught in traffic in a BMW, at least you're caught in style!

Be very clear about what I'm saying. I'm not saying there is anything wrong with owning an economy car, and in all the years I've been working with people to help them achieve their ultimate grand dream goals, I've never ever seen anyone put a Daewoo on their dream list. (Note: For everyone who works at Daewoo, or who sells them, and for anyone who owns one, please know that I'm only using Daewoo as an example of an economy car, and this is not meant to be a personal attack on the company.)

The point is that when the majority of people become adults and set goals, they have a tendency to only go after the things they think they can get instead of going after things they truly want.

Most people wish really big and expect very little, and in life you get what you expect.

> "A life spent making mistakes is not only more honorable, but more useful than a life spent doing nothing."
>
> GEORGE BERNARD SHAW

Most people think if they pursue smaller goals, they'll have a better chance of reaching them. They avoid going after their grand dream goals because they fear feeling like a failure or feeling let down if they don't achieve them.

This book isn't just about goal setting or achieving your goals. It's about identifying and living your dreams.

If you ask children to write down what they want, they won't start listing their goals. Instead they'll tell you about their dreams. Kids' dreams don't have limitations. When you ask children what kind of house they want, their responses are different from those of adults. They'll say, "I'm going to have a house with fifteen bedrooms, and they're all mine. I'm going to have ten swimming pools, all connected with waterslides, and I'll have pet dolphins swimming in all of the pools. And I'm going to have a different color Ferrari for every day of the week."

If they don't get their dream on the first attempt, they get up and try again. Think back to when you were a child. Did you ever try jumping off somewhere high using an umbrella as your parachute? Did it work? Of course not! It folded inside out, and you come crashing to the ground. Did you quit? No, you went looking for a bigger umbrella instead. The patio version perhaps! Or maybe you tried holding a bedsheet over your head like they do in cartoons. Whatever it was, you didn't quit.

One of the things I love most about what children teach us is that they dream big and they still believe that magic exists. Because they still believe in magic, for them, it still exists!

In chapter 7, we discussed the biggest lie we're expected to buy into as an adult: when you become an adult, it's okay to give up on your dreams. So many people surrender to the notion that working to pay bills is what's important and that going for your dreams is something only children do.

In 1977, when I was fifteen years old, I went to see one of my biggest rock idols perform live, the late great Rick Nelson. I was fortunate enough to be invited by Rick after the concert to come backstage to meet him and the band. I was over the moon with excitement. I spent two hours with him and the band just hanging out. When I decided it was time for me to leave, I said my good-byes to the members of his band and then went to say good-bye to Rick himself. While shaking my hand, he looked me in the eyes and said something so powerful that it has been with me the rest of my life.

He said, "Follow your dreams, because when you give up on your dreams, you die!"

I knew right then and there that he was right. When people give up on their dreams, they become zombies. The spark of life is missing from their eyes. Your body might still be walking around, but your spirit is dead because your soul is trapped in a vehicle that has thrown away the best part of human experience.

Do you believe it's okay to give up on your dreams? If you do, you should know that it's that kind of thinking that's trapping you in your current circumstances. Reality is only as real as you think it is. Reality is an electronic impulse interpreted by your brain. What's real for some people is not always real for others.

The proof lies in the difference between the results the majority of people get, and the results the minority get. There are two distinct groups of people in the world: the majority and the minority. The majority are the people who shrink their wants to fit their incomes. The minority are the people who increase their incomes to fit their desires. The majority of people don't take the time to set their goals. Remember: the average number of people who do this is only 3%. And if any of the majority does set goals, they go for what they think they can get, instead of what they really want.

The minority goes after their grand dream goals because they would rather have what they really want instead of only what they think they can get. Where the majority wish really big and expect very little, the minority not only wish big, they also expect big—and that's why they get big results.

Remember the statistics we explored in chapter 7:

60% of all marriages end in divorce.

65% of the population of most developed countries are overweight and out of shape.

Out of every 100 people who work forty-five years of their life, 97 will end up dead or dead broke. Only one out of every 100 people retires wealthy.

The most consumed drugs on the planet are anti-depressants.

Since all these figures are so large, they describe what's happening for the majority. Let's put that another way. The members of the majority are getting divorced, they're overweight, they're out of shape, they're taking anti-depressants, and they end up dead or dead broke after working forty-five years of their life. This is the reality the majority of people are living.

Look at the drawing. The people at the bottom of the pyramid experience a lot of unhappiness and lack of fulfillment because they're not living the dream life they desire. It's no wonder so many of them are using anti-depressants. Since the majority of people are at the bottom of the pyramid, it's a lot more crowded there than it is at the top.

Do you know what most people use as an excuse for not being at the top? They say, "It's lonely at the top." The truth is that it's not lonely at the top when you help your family and friends become happy, healthy, and wealthy too. And the only way to inspire your family, your friends, your community, your country, and the world to be happy, healthy, wealthy, and successful is by making yourself

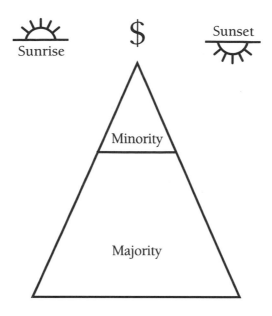

Sunrise

$

Sunset

Minority

Majority

happy, healthy, wealthy, and successful *first*. It's called leading by example.

If you're not leading by example, you're like an overweight fitness trainer telling people how to exercise. Is that the type of person you want to follow?

The majority accepts the status quo and settles for whatever their current conditions have to offer. The minority changes the world, while the majority waits for the world to be changed. That's called victim mentality, and it creates learned helplessness.

When you live in the consciousness of the masses, you'll wind up with the destiny of the masses. In other words, when you think like everyone else, you'll act like everyone else, and that means you'll get the same kind of results they're getting. That's why the statistics represent so much pain and unhappiness. As soon as you choose to think differently, you'll start to act differently, and that will create new results for you.

The majority say, "I can't afford it." The minority ask, "How can I afford it?"

The majority say, "I can't do it." The minority say, "I don't know how I'm going to do it, and I am going to do it anyway."

The majority tell you that something is impossible. The minority look at the so-called impossible and know that if there's a big enough "Why" for wanting something, the "How" to get it will present itself.

So you'll notice that at the bottom of the pyramid, it's much more crowded and sweaty. At the top, the minority gets to see the sunrise and enjoy the cleaner, fresher air. The reason the air is cleaner at the top and it smells bad on the bottom is because . . . well, we all know what rolls downhill.

> "While the difficult takes time, the impossible just takes a little longer."
>
> ART BERG

Think about it. If you really want to add enjoyment and fulfillment to your life and the lives of everyone you care about, you're going to have to make the decision to open your mind and allow some new thoughts in. Remember that your mind is like a parachute. It works much better when it is open.

Grand Dream Goals

If you had no limitations—if you could have everything and anything you wanted—what would you choose? These are what I call your GDGs—your **G**rand **D**ream **G**oals.

In the magic two minutes, instead of writing down your goals, you're going to capture your grand dream goals. To do this you need to tap back into the child still inside you and allow yourself to dream again.

When you were a child and imagined yourself as an adult, how did you see yourself? What did you dream you would become? Are you that person now? If not, it's not too late! No matter how old you are right now, it's never too late to have the kind of life you really want.

I believe the Creator made us children first so we could master it, not surrender it. It doesn't make sense to go through all that life training we get as a child, at the beginning of our lives, only to surrender it when we grow up.

Instead of joining the walking dead, become a Wise Child. A Wise Child is a person who still looks at life with awe and wonder, a person who still has a fresh and exciting view of the world and of life, a person who is still playful and has fun as he or she experiences new growth and evolvement throughout their entire life.

Here's a tip to help you when writing down your grand dream goals in the magic two minutes. It's a tip that will make all the difference. Instead of asking yourself, "What do I want?" ask yourself, "What do I want to *experience*?" Here's why:

One of the reasons so many people find it challenging to figure out what they really want is because they think that going after material things is too egotistical or materialistic. We've all seen people who have all the "stuff" and still aren't happy, fulfilled, or empowered. Why? Because wanting to own something is an activity of the ego, and the ego is all about being separate from the rest of the universe. Your ego wants you to separate your stuff from everyone else's stuff. It **E**dges the **G**od force **O**ut of you.

Remember the message I received from the light: *Everything in this life is borrowed. You have to give it all back. The only thing you get to keep is the love you gave, the love you received, and the experiences your soul got to have.*

The reason it seems so difficult to say what material things you really want is that you're acting from your ego by thinking you want to possess something, and it doesn't feel appropriate to your spirit because your true spirit understands there's nothing you can possess in the universe. Possession is an activity only the ego attempts.

Earlier, when I was talking about having a luxury car, I wasn't talking about *owning* a luxury car. I was talking about having *the experience of* a luxury car.

People are surprised when they ask me what I want, because I always say there's nothing I want. I have everything I want, and if there's ever anything I want to experience, I will either go get it or find a way to go get it while also enjoying the process of working out how I am going to create it in my life.

As I've said before, I don't personally have a religion, and I am very spiritual. I do know there has to be a wonderful, loving source from which this beautiful, magical, perfectly working universe came. It's just too perfect for me to think it's all just a by-product of a random chaotic event. I believe the Creator put all the wonderful things on our planet for us to experience and enjoy. After all, when we enjoy them, we're showing our appreciation for the Creator's creations. It doesn't make any sense if it was all put in front of us not to enjoy. Why would the Creator give us desire for these gifts but not allow us to enjoy them? Regardless of your religious beliefs, wouldn't you think the Creator loves to see us all enjoying His beautiful creations?

Even Jesus felt the same way when he said, *"You need not hesitate about asking largely. It is your Father's good pleasure to give you the kingdom."*

It took me a long time to accept the idea that I too was deserving of having wonderful things in my life. I felt that maybe I wasn't being spiritual if I had nice things when so many other people didn't have them. I spent most of my life having the experience of being financially poor. I was still happy back then because I decided to be happy no matter what my financial situation was.

We've all heard stories about wealthy people who were miserable in spite of their financial wealth, right? These stories are told by members of the majority. After they finish telling the story about the miserable wealthy people, they inject their personal views on what it means: "See, money doesn't buy you happiness!"

It is true that money *itself* can't buy you happiness, and it is true that some extremely financially wealthy people aren't happy. Yet what people who tell stories about miserable wealthy people forget to mention is that there are far more stories about the countless numbers of poor people whose lives are also miserable. Of course they just happen to overlook that important fact. It's because there are so many poor and miserable people in the world that it doesn't even seem newsworthy. Why would those people telling those stories pick on their own group? After all, they're loyal to their own, and the only people who listen to their stories are also in the majority! Misery loves company!

They also forget to mention that there are also a lot of wealthy people who have great lives and who are very happy. The reason the members of the majority don't tell you about those people is because there's no drama in it. The majority love their drama and drama glue! They're stuck in it!

Only people in the majority talk about the scarcity and pain of others. They're also the only ones who listen to those stories. They're the ones focusing on problems.

The minority would rather spend their time talking about abundance and solutions to the challenges of the world. They're also the ones who actually do something about it. Remember: we can't even get the majority of people to write down their goals. If they can't even make a decision as to where they are going, why would you think they're going to take the necessary action to get there?

It's true that money by itself won't buy you happiness, and it's also true that not having wealth is a guaranteed way to buy you and everyone you love a lot of pain.

I'm not talking about price tags here. It's not the cost of something that determines happiness or pain. Your grand dream goals don't have a financial value to them. They're about what you want to *experience*

> "When you cease to dream, you cease to live."
>
> MALCOLM FORBES

the most, and what will give you the most joy. The value of a thing is not measured by how much it costs; it's about how much enjoyment are you getting through the experience of it.

When Marie and I first got married and were just starting to build our business, something was bothering her that she wanted to talk to me about. She said that after hearing me talk at one of my seminars about adding value to everyone you meet and not getting attached to the activities of the ego, she wondered if having nice things was spiritually inappropriate. I was a bit surprised by her question and asked her to clarify it for me.

She said, "You know I'm not a materialistic person, and I love helping people improve the quality of their lives." I agreed with her wholeheartedly. She is one of the most loving and generous people I have ever met. "Since there are so many people struggling to get by," she continued, "is it wrong for me to want nice things? What if I really do want to experience something nice like a designer bag? Is it bad for me to want to experience those kinds of things?"

"Why would you think that?" I asked, still not quite understanding. "That's why we're creating a successful business—so you can experience all the nice things you want to experience in your life. Why would you think that's bad or wrong?"

"Because you said wanting things is an activity of the ego," Marie said, and she described how she felt torn between the desire to be spiritually connected and the desire to experience nice things. To Marie these felt like two separate paths. Now I understood Marie's confusion and upset

"Marie, why do you think God isn't in Gucci?" I asked. "The Creator is everywhere and in everything, and that includes Gucci. Just because some of the things that you want to experience are material things doesn't make the desire to experience them materialistic."

If you want to experience a designer bag and feel you're going to experience joy from that, then that's what you need to do. If it's driving a nice car that brings you joy, then that's what you need to be driving. If wearing cheap clothes or driving an old, beat-up automobile doesn't make you feel good, then by all means don't wear those clothes and don't drive that car. It's about which *experiences* will bring you the most joy.

Remember: experience has nothing to do with price. Just because something costs more doesn't make it better or better able to give you joy.

For example, I can afford to buy a Ferrari if I wanted to, except I have no desire to buy one. It's not my kind of car. I think they're nice cars and they look pretty cool, but I still have no desire to have one. I personally like driving a BMW. I get a lot of joy from experiencing our BMWs. Here's my point: a Ferrari costs about four times as much as a BMW, but since having a Ferrari isn't something I desire, it would be egotistical for me to get one. If I bought one even though I don't want to have one, I would be buying it to show it off to everyone else. That's an activity of the ego.

I'm not saying that buying a Ferrari is an egotistical activity if you want to drive a Ferrari. For me, even though it costs less than the Ferrari, the BMW brings me more joy when I'm driving it. That's what it's all about. When you have joy in your life, you'll notice how much easier it is to help others lead joyful lives as well. If you don't have it in your life, how are you supposed to give away that which you don't have?

I spent the majority of my life having the experience of being poor. Yes, I was still happy back then, and I have to admit that I'm enjoying the experience of a wealthy life even more, because worrying about paying bills back then wasn't enjoyable at all. Struggling to get by wasn't fun or enjoyable either.

The stress that comes with worrying about how you're going to pay rent every month isn't fun. It's painful! I had also spent months at a time living in my car because I couldn't pay rent. I made the best I could out of the situation and was grateful that at least I had a car to sleep in. Yet if I had a choice in those days, I would have chosen something else. Because I was poor, I had fewer choices, and fewer choices mean less freedom. Back in those days, I certainly didn't feel very free.

The experience of having a nice car beats the experience of having a car that you're always panicked about in traffic situations, thinking it's going to overheat or break down.

The best part about experiencing driving a luxury car every day is that when you're driving it, you feel wealthy. The reason that's so important comes back to the formula for creation we explored in chapter 9: when you feel wealthy, you start to think like a wealthy person. Once you start thinking like a wealthy person, and you take the actions a wealthy person takes, you get wealthy results.

For example, whenever I go to a business meeting with a prospective client, I feel incredible pulling up to that meeting in a beautiful automobile. I know that when I'm feeling that way, I do a better job of representing myself, because I feel more confident and stress free. When you feel better, you perform better, and when you perform better, you get better results than when you are stressed or feeling poorly.

Things are different for me now. Since Marie and I have been together, I have a much bigger purpose in life. I no longer do it just for myself. We do it for us. Because Marie is in my life, I have a much higher standard for what is acceptable. I would never let our situation reach the point at which Marie would be forced to live in a car like I had to.

As humans, we do more for others than we do for ourselves. When you expect more from yourself, you live up to those expectations, and that's called peak performance.

I love Marie so much that I want her to have the best life possible. At the end of my life, I want her to be able to say she got to live every dream she ever had and that her life was better because I was in it with her. Marie and I are committed to making sure we have as many experiences as we want to have during this lifetime, before it's all over for us.

And here's the best part. Because Marie and I live a happy, joyful, and abundant life, we also have the freedom and resources to help other people experience the same thing. You'd be amazed how many people are willing to take your guidance and act on it when you've proven yourself first. They're more hesitant to listen to someone who doesn't yet have the results and is still trying to tell them what to do. No one gets inspired by the "do as I say and not as I do" formula. Do you?

The challenge most people create for themselves is that they live their lives as if they have an unlimited amount of time. They don't. Our time here having our human experience is very limited. No matter what your spiritual or religious beliefs—even if you believe in an afterlife or reincarnation—this life that you are living right now is a one-time ride. You'll only be who you are now this one time. When it's over, it's over forever! Eternity! And whatever you have while you are alive—all your money, your house(s), your car(s), all your possessions, your family, your friends, everything you have or will ever have—is all borrowed, because at the end of your life, you have to give it all back.

Imagine you want to buy your dream house and it costs $1 million. Would you go to the bank and borrow $500,000 to pay for your new home? No, of course not! Why? Because if you did this, you would be in debt for the $500,000 you owe and have to pay back with interest, and you still wouldn't be able to buy your $1 million home. What's the point of working toward something if it doesn't deliver you the experience you want?

Having a worthwhile experience is about going for what you really want in life. $500,000 may seem like a lot of money, but in truth there is no such thing as "a lot." Like everything else on the planet, money is just atoms and energy. In the Creator's eyes, there's no difference between Gucci and Kmart. What matters is what is going to bring you the most joy from experiencing it.

After you die it's all worth nothing to you, because everything in this life is borrowed, so if you want a $1 million home, don't borrow $500,000. And don't borrow $1 million either because that just gets you the house and nothing more. Don't you want furniture, a pool, someone to clean your big house, and a nice car to park in the driveway?

The scarce mind thinks, "I want this *or* that." The abundant mind says, "I want to experience this *and* that." Would you like to have the nice house to live in or the ability to spend more quality time with the people you love? Wouldn't it be better to have the house *and* spend more time with the people you love?

Think about this for a moment. Since the formula for creation is Thoughts → Actions = Results, how can abundance come into your life if you keep allowing the scarcity mentality to occupy your mind?

Someone said, "If you owe the bank $1 million, you're in trouble. If you owe the bank $100 million, the bank is in trouble."

Understand that it's not only money we're talking about here. I'm just using money as an example. People who have a problem talking about money also have a problem creating money, because they don't know what money really is. Once you know what money really is, not only are you able to talk about it, you also see how spiritually connected it is to make it.

Our ultimate goal is happiness. The reason people want to live in a big house is because they think it will make them happy. The reason they want a nice car to drive is because they think driving it will make them happy. It's the same for the rest of your goals as well. It's not money that we're talking about here—it's joy and happiness!

Think about it. If you were investing in the stock market or in real estate as a financial strategy, wouldn't you want the biggest return on your investment? Isn't that the reason for investing in the first place—to get a good return? It doesn't make any sense to invest a lot to get a little a little return, right? Of course not!

Just by having this book and reading this paragraph you've already made a major investment. And because you've made that investment, the same criteria should apply—you should get the biggest returns for your investment. The investment we're talking about isn't necessarily the money you spent to buy this book. You may not have had to pay for it. Maybe someone who really cares about you and wants to add value to your life bought it for you so you can turn your dreams into reality. So if it isn't money we're talking about, what do you think the investment is? It's your time. Our investment of time is the biggest investment any of us ever makes in life because it's the one commodity in short supply for all of us. No matter how much time you invest in something, you'll never get that time back. It's gone forever. That's why the way you utilize your time is so important. You're constantly investing your time, whether you're conscious of it or not. You can invest your time on things that give you the biggest return, or you can squander it away on things that aren't valuable to you or your life's journey.

We're all going to die. There's nothing we can do to change that. None of us know when our last moment is going to be. There's no guarantee we'll make it to be 100. As a matter of fact, a lot of people on the planet who are the exact same age as you are right now lost their lives today, and most of them didn't think they were going to die today either. Whoever promises us tomorrow lies to us, because that promise cannot be kept.

The one thing we'll all have in common at the end of our life is that, at the moment of our death, we will have recently completed one of our goals and be in the process of going for the next one. Some people will have reached their last goal a long time ago; others will have reached it just the other day. Either way, the fact remains the same; we will all die sometime after achieving one of our goals and be in pursuit of the next one. Remember that when your time is up, it's up, and you may be surprised that it when it happens, it may not be convenient for you. It might even be up just before you achieve your next goal. Imagine: you've faced the challenges, you've overcome the obstacles, and tomorrow is the day this goal is supposed to be achieved, or so you thought. Surprise! Death comes a-knocking at your door. The point I'm making here is that since there will always be a goal waiting to be achieved at the time of our death, each of the goals we go for needs to be a goal worth dying for.

Since time is your most valuable investment, and it takes as much time to achieve a Grand Dream Goal as it does a small goal, wouldn't you want the biggest return for the time you invest? That makes sense, right? And since you don't know which goal it is going to be that you'll be unable to finish before you die, wouldn't it make sense to make all your goals **Grand Dream Goals**? Do you really want to gamble your time on going for a small goal when it could wind up being your final one?

The great thing is that when people are really inspired about their mission in life, their drive to accomplish that mission often results in a longer life. Why? The inspired mission gives them the will to go on.

If you discovered you were going to die tomorrow, what would you really want to do or experience that you haven't had the chance to experience before now? Whatever it is, that's the type of GDGs you need to be going for.

It's actually a lot easier to achieve **Grand Dream Goals** than small goals because GDGs *inspire* you, they put you in your spirit, and small goals don't. The passion GDGs give you creates the extra power you need to face adversity and launch yourself forward. Instead of going for what you think you can accomplish, go for the things you really want. There's a big difference.

> "Dream no small dreams. They have no power to stir the souls of men."
>
> VICTOR HUGO

When you want to experience something, you should. If you find out afterward that you don't want to do it anymore, that's fine. At least you tried it. I wanted to be an actor from the time I was ten. I worked professionally as an actor for twenty-three years, and then one day I decided I didn't want to do it anymore. The point that I'm making is this: at least I got to experience what it was to be a professional actor and then decide I didn't want to do it anymore instead of never trying it and spending the rest of my life wondering "what if?"

If you want to do something and don't even try to experience it, don't use the excuse that you didn't want to do it to cover up your fear of attempting it. Acknowledge the fear and know that fear, if left unchecked, can steal the quality of your life away from you. It's when we face our fear that we grow the most.

Remember: the only things you get to keep from this life after you leave are *the love you gave, the love you received, and the experiences your soul got to have.* Everything else is borrowed. It's like the loan we were talking about before. Whatever you borrowed you're going to have to pay back. And since you're going to have to give back everything you borrowed when you die, it only makes sense to borrow it all. Instead of borrowing the small stuff that doesn't even excite you, go for the grand experiences that passionately inspire you. Go for the experiences that bring you the most joy and fun. Don't sell yourself short. *Chase your passion, not your pension!*

When you get what you really want in your life, you automatically show everyone else that they can have what they want too. Furthermore, when you have the dream life you want, it's because you discovered the path to get there, so now you can show it to others. That's why I think of the word "goal" the acronym for **G**ive **O**thers **A**bundance & **L**ove.

Tap into the child still inside you, the one you've been trying not to listen to ever since you grew up. That child keeps telling you to live your dreams, while you keep listening to the "adult" lie that says it's okay to give up your dreams. It's not okay to give up on them. When you give up on your dreams, you die. Look at all the unhappy people taking anti-depressants, excessively drinking alcohol, and abusing drugs—all for the sole purpose of trying to avoid admitting they gave up their dreams. Make the decision to leave that majority group and choose to be in the minority group, the group that chooses to live life to the fullest. That's not to say you must leave the people of the majority behind. Instead you'll inspire them to do it too, because the only way you can inspire anyone else to be happy, healthy, wealthy, and successful is for you to be that way first.

No amount of suffering on your part will ever make anyone else happy. Would you want to learn how to be happy from someone who is miserable? Of course not! Then why would you think your suffering would inspire anyone to be happy? You can never be poor enough to bring abundance to other poor people, yet when you have wealth, you can help others and teach them how to be wealthy too. Your being sick won't ever teach others how to be healthy. It never has and it never will. In order to help other people get healthy you have to start by first being healthy yourself. Remember, feed a person a fish, and he eats once; teach him how to fish, and he eats for a lifetime.

Joy and happiness are universal experiences. They cross all boundaries and all cultures. The more you travel around this beautiful planet, the more you see that everyone in every corner of the world is the same, and we all want the same thing. We all want joy in our lives. We all want to spend quality time with our families and the people we love. We all want our children to evolve and have a better life than we had ourselves. All those things are difficult to do when you're slaving away at work and unhappy within yourself.

When you experience joy, you are closer to the force that created us all, and when you live in joy, you become one with that source. Go and do everything you want to experience so you can help others do everything they want to experience too by showing them the way. You won't know the way unless you have been there first.

Remember: our children learn from what we do and not necessarily from what they are told to do. Have you ever noticed your kids don't always do what you tell them to do? Why would they? They're only doing the same thing you did with your parents! You didn't always listen to them either, did you?

Do you remember when you were a child living with your parents? There were things they could do that you weren't allowed to do—things like staying up late or using swear words. How unfair was that! They had rights you didn't have. When you asked them why they could do things you weren't allowed to do, you were told, "Because I'm an adult!" Sound familiar? (If you have kids of your own, there's no way you've ever said anything like that, is there?) When you are a child, what's the first thing you want to be? An adult—because adults make the rules. As children we didn't like being told what to do, and as adults we like it even less.

The point I'm making is that telling your children how to be happy, healthy, and wealthy when you're not happy, healthy, and wealthy yourself won't work. If you're like the rest of the majority—lonely, unhappy, unhealthy, and/or financially broke—then just by being these things, you're teaching your children to live the same way. They're doing as you do, not as you tell them to do, just like you did as a child. Remember the overweight fitness trainer teaching others to exercise? The poor person trying to teach others to be wealthy? It doesn't work. Nobody wants to listen to someone who isn't doing it themselves.

If you don't take responsibility for actively transforming yourself into a happy, healthy, wealthy person, then that's what you are passing down to your kids too. If you don't take responsibility for making your life better, then neither will they. Your children will be destined to live out the same fate as you, because you taught them how to do it.

Oh, but it doesn't stop there. They're also going to teach the same painful lessons to your grandchildren, and they too will be forced to suffer unhealthy, unhappy, and unfulfilled lives. The chain of pain just keeps going on and on. Is that the lesson you want to teach your kids? Do you want them to buy into the lie that when you become an adult, the right thing to do is surrender all your dreams and spend the rest of your life working like a slave, trying to get by and pay the bills?

The whole "no pain, no gain" thing doesn't work. It never has, and it never will. The majority of people in the world are already working hard and still don't have the big payoff for all their efforts. I watched my father work hard his whole life and he never achieved an easy life in return. When you think about this, it's simple logic. How can an easy life come from hard work? After all, what you plant is exactly what you will grow. My dad planted years and years of hard work, and all he got out of it was a hard life and a lot of aches and pains. I'm not knocking my dad or talking badly about him. I loved my father, and he is and always will be my ultimate hero. I wish I had gotten to spend more quality time with him. I know he felt the same way. It was just hard for him to do because he was so busy trying to keep a roof over our heads. I completely respect him for everything he did for me, and I'm still disappointed that we never really had much time to spend together.

The point I'm making here is that, in spite of all his hard work and affection for me, my father wasn't able to teach me any appropriate wealth creation strategies because he didn't have any. He only knew what his father had taught him: if you want to succeed in life, you have to work hard to achieve it. Both my father and grandfather worked very hard, and neither one of them got the rewards they were promised by the lie. Both died way too young, and neither got to enjoy the feeling of being financially free. They both had to keep a tight watch on everything they spent, right up to the very end. They never got to experience thriving because they had to stay focused on how to survive.

When my father kept trying to teach me how to get ahead in life, I kept questioning his strategies. They made no sense to me. He was teaching me the same thing he was doing, but it wasn't working for him. I had to choose other skills and tools if I wanted to be financially successful. Long before that happened, I went through decades of my life working really hard, just like my dad, and I just wasn't seeing the great rewards either. The only prize I was getting from working hard was a hard life.

My father also died with his body riddled with disease, so he didn't teach me great health strategies either. I had to find my own strategies for that area of life too. My mom was married four times, so she wasn't teaching me successful relationship strategies. Most of my brothers and my sister have also been married more than once. By no means am I blaming my parents. I'm simply pointing out that we learn from watching our biggest heroes—our parents. They're the people we emulate the most. The truth is if I had continued to follow in their footsteps, I would have gotten the same results they got. I consciously made a choice to find another way.

Remember what I said before, "the concept of 'no pain: no gain' doesn't work." Imagine if someone you knew walked up to you every day, looked you in the eye, smiled at you, and then kicked you in the shins. Would you go out and buy that person gifts for his actions? Of course not! If you were the one doing the kicking, would you expect to be rewarded by the person you're injuring? If your answer is no, then why do the majority of people believe that stress and exhaustion is going to get them the results they want?

Do you work hard trying to keep ahead of the bills you owe, getting your body in shape, making sure you stay healthy, maintaining a good relationship with your partner, raising your kids, and, at the same time, trying to create a better quality of life for yourself? If you look around, you'll see that most people are so busy working hard to keep themselves afloat that they don't really have the time or energy to move their lives forward. Yet if you're not achieving your goals even though you're working hard, the strategy most people will suggest is to work harder. They say, "You're almost there. All you have to do is work a little harder."

Are you really inspired to want to work any harder? Don't you feel you're already working hard enough? Honestly, do you really want to work harder and longer hours than you are working right now? Think about it. Have you ever heard of anyone on their deathbed saying, "I really regret that I didn't spend more time at the office working"?

Let's take a little test. Have you ever worked hard? Are you still working hard? Are you where you want to be? Do you already spend the amount of quality time with your partner that you really want? How about your family? Are they getting the quality time with you they need and want? Are you putting aside time to exercise every day so you can be as healthy and fit as you want, or do you say you just don't have the time? In a nutshell, do you have the abundant life and holistic success you really want?

This is where those deadly dream-stealing phrases "someday," "one day," and "maybe tomorrow" enter the picture. Why are these phrases so destructive? Because they never happen. Do those days ever show up on the calendar? Have you ever scheduled one of them in your appointment book? Have you ever woken up and actually found yourself living a day called "tomorrow" or "someday"?

Why, then, do people say these things? It's because the majority of people's days are already consumed putting in long hours working hard at their jobs, and all that work still isn't getting them the results they hope for. They're just too busy to do the things they really want to do.

If you work hard and still don't have the dream life you want, it's pretty clear that working hard may not be the best strategy to use, right? If hard work hasn't worked for you so far, and you've already said you're not inspired to work even harder, this doesn't seem like the strategy you're looking for, does it?

Would Love want you to have all the pleasurable experiences you want to have, or would it want you to suffer without them? How would Love respond?

Would Love want you to keep beating up on your body, stressing it out, and causing it more aches and pains? Is that how Love would respond?

Would love teach others they have to shrink their desires to fit their incomes too? Because if that's how you're living, that's the example you're setting!

You've already said you're working hard and that it isn't working. Have you considered that you're actually getting further and further away from achieving what you want? Have you felt or noticed this in your life? If you have, then it's a clear signal that the strategies you're using aren't working. "No pain, no gain" isn't an appropriate strategy to use to achieve the life of your dreams.

Since we have already agreed that none of us are really all that excited about working any harder or working longer hours, then how about this as an alternative strategy to achieve the rewards in life you desire: have fun and enjoy yourself, and get everything you want! Doesn't that sound a more appealing strategy to you?

Does it sound too good to be true? If it does, then you need to open your mind to new possibilities and thoughts you may not know about yet. If, instead of someone coming up to you and kicking you in the shins every day, that person was always kind and generous and fun to be with, would you be more inclined to give him gifts in return? Of course you would! That makes sense, right? Since that makes sense, doesn't it also hold true that when it comes to your health, you have a much better chance of getting the positive results you want when you treat yourself in a kind and loving way?

> "The problems of the world cannot possibly be solved by skeptics or cynics whose horizons are limited by the obvious realities. We need men who can dream of things that never were."
>
> JOHN F. KENNEDY

This same strategy can create incredible results in all areas of your life, creating wealth, having an awesome relationship, or anything else you desire. The truth is that it doesn't matter what you want in your life—the strategies are the same. You have to open up your mind to accept some concepts that may be new to you, because it's the only way your life is going to transform to the next level.

———

It's time for you to experience the magic two minutes! Are you ready to start making your grand dream goals come true?

Here's what you'll do: for two solid minutes, write down everything and anything you want to *experience*. Don't sit there contemplating; just keep writing for the full two minutes. Make sure you capture what you really want, not just what you think you can accomplish. The best way to capture those things is by asking, "If I had no limitations and could experience everything and anything I wanted, what is it I really want to experience?" Then just let your hand go crazy. Don't judge anything. Just write it all down. Don't worry about *how* you're going to make it happen—that's what you're learning in this book. Just make sure you write for the entire two minutes.

If you're done in thirty seconds, then it's obvious that you don't want enough. Remember: you can have anything you want! If someone gave *me* a magic two minutes, I'd be writing up to the very last second trying to squeeze in as much as I could.

If you get stuck and can't think of anything else, just keep asking yourself, "If I could experience anything I wanted, what else do I want to experience?" Remember that everything you write down you can have, because I'm teaching you how you can have it. Better write it all down, because if you don't, you won't have it. If you're not willing to make the effort to write it down, why would you think you're going to take any of the rest of the actions it takes to make it all happen? Isn't it worth two minutes to have the life you've always dreamed of? Remember: it's the people who are willing to do the most in life who get the most in life. *It's in the doing that we develop the most.*

If you're thinking this all sounds too easy and too good to be true, then this is where you need to empty out some of your old thoughts to let some new ones in. Have some faith and play it full out. What do you have to lose? The only way to fail at life is to fail to participate. So ask yourself the magic question, "If I had no limitations and could experience anything I wanted, what is it I really want to experience?"

Take two magic minutes and write it all down. Go!

Welcome back. I hope you really did do the exercise. You already took the action to pick up and read this book, so I'm going to assume you're an action taker and you did do the exercise. (If you didn't, stop reading and go back right now and do the exercise.)

Now that you've now got a wonderful list of all your real GDGs, what's the next step?

In order to get anywhere in life there are two pieces of information you need: knowing where you are, and knowing where you want to be. By doing the magic two minutes you captured where you want to go. Now you know what the next part of the exercise is. We need to discover exactly where you are right now relative to achieving your GDGs. When you know where you're starting from and where you want to go, all that's left to do is chart your course. It's easy when you have those first two things in place. So right now we have to create the second half of the treasure map and figure out where are you right now.

The way to discover this is to answer a few simple questions, again writing down your answers. Take a couple of minutes to answer these questions: "Why is it that all the grand dream goals I captured during the magic two-minute exercise aren't already in my life today?" "What happened?" "What took me off my path?" "What got in my way?"

Make sure you take the time to write down your answers. Don't just skip over them. If you really want to improve the quality of your life and the lives of everyone you love, you need to take the actions that will produce results. Have faith that there is a method to all my madness. When you invest in yourself, you will always get the biggest returns on your investment. *The more you develop yourself as a person, the more personally developed you become.* So right now take those two minutes and invest in yourself.

> *"Act yourself into a new way of thinking."*
>
> UNKNOWN

Living Above the Line

Let's start to put this together so it all makes sense. Look at the line I've drawn below.

$

_____

In order for you to have all the results and rewards you want in your life, you're going to have to start living your life above that line, because, as you can see in the drawing, above the line is where all those beautiful, wonderful, lovely, rich rewards are.

Are you looking at that dollar sign right now and thinking, "Oh no—not more stuff about money"? Just to clarify, when I talk about being rich, I'm really talking about being *en*riched. Having an enriched life means having the wonderful relationship you want with the person who brings joy and fulfillment to your life on a whole new level, a level you couldn't achieve by yourself. Life is much better as a shared experience than going it alone. We were not designed to be islands. We're at our best when we interact with others. Not only is it unnatural to be alone, it's the worst punishment you can give a person. It's called solitary confinement!

When prisoners get punished for doing something wrong, they're put into solitary confinement. If prison is supposed to be punishment for committing a crime, then solitary confinement is the punishment of all punishments. Even hardened criminals fear being placed there. To be locked away alone without human contact is severe punishment even to them. It's obvious we're not supposed to be alone.

If you look throughout history at people who made the greatest personal achievements, you'll see their greatest inspiration was the love they had for others. It was the love of their partners, their family, their country, or the human race that inspired them to achieve excellence. It's in our genetic makeup to want to do more for others than we do for ourselves. The love I have for Marie, the angel of my dreams, has inspired me to my greatest personal achievements.

To be enriched in a relationship—to enjoy all the rewards of that wonderful, passionate relationship of your dreams—that's above the line.

Having a healthy, fit body to ensure you're physically able to enjoy your life and all the rewards you've earned is also above the line.

Remember back to the last time you felt really sick. Would having lots of money in the bank have made you feel better? What's the point of being rich if you're sick? Would you really enjoy traveling around the world, seeing all the sights, if your body was riddled with disease? You don't actually have to feel that bad to be robbed of some quality of life. Just being constantly tired and low on energy limits what you can do and enjoy.

Did you know that for every extra pound of fat on your body, your heart has to pump blood through an extra five miles of veins and arteries? No wonder so many people are becoming couch potatoes! They just don't have the energy to get them through the day, let alone the extra energy needed to do the other fun activities they dream about doing.

When you feel healthy and energized, life truly does get more enjoyable and more rewarding. The only way to have great health and fitness is to live your life above the line, where all the rewards are.

Being happy, having a quality relationship with your partner, having great friendships, and having a healthy body are all part of an enriched life. And let's not forget one other important part of an enriched life—financial wealth.

Did you know the number one reason marriages and relationships break up is because of money challenges? Two people who love each other very much and want to spend the rest of their lives together can feel stress trying to pay their bills and making ends meet. This creates tension and frustration, which manifests itself in all kinds of disempowering behavioral patterns. Gradually the couple realizes that with every passing day they're getting further and further away from making their dream life together a reality, and this is where arguments begin. As frustration and anxiety continue, more friction builds until the relationship just can't handle the strain and buckles under the pressure.

Money issues are also the number one cause of stress for people. Concerns about money, or lack of money, stress people more than any other issue, and stress is the number one killer on the planet. Remember: when you're experiencing stress, it means your mind is turbulent or at dis-ease. *It's the dis-ease of your mind that creates the disease of your body.*

When we're talking about having a holistically enriched life, we're talking about having financial freedom as well. The only way you can ever enjoy the holistically successful life you desire is by making the decision to live your life above the line, because it's above the line where all the positive results you want are to be found.

Result$

Living Below the Line

Below the line is where you find blame, justification, and excuses. The reason they belong below the line is because when you use any of them, it renders you powerless. They drain all your personal power out of you and get you stuck in a condition of learned helplessness.

As soon as you start giving excuses for why you haven't accomplished your grand dream goals, like, "It's my parents' fault," or, "It's my teacher's fault," or, "It's the government's fault," or, "I'm from the wrong country, and there are no opportunities here," or, "I'm not in a relationship because all the good people are already taken," you become powerless. Any time you use these excuses, it automatically robs you of your power. The reason it happens is easy to see. When you start blaming something outside of yourself for being the cause of your problems, you won't have any control in solving those problems because you can't control anything outside of yourself. That's what renders you powerless.

In the two-minute exercise, I instructed you to list all your answers to the question, "Why is it that all the grand dream goals I captured during the magic two-minute exercise aren't already in my life?" Do your answers to that question fall into the categories of blame, justification, or excuses? If they do, you need to go back and scratch those off your list. Stop giving your power away to things over which you have no control.

There's a good chance that the real reason you haven't accomplished your grand dream goals is because you've been giving your power away by living your life below the line.

Result$

Excuses
Blame
Justification

Did you know that only unsuccessful people make excuses? Truly holistically successful people don't have a place for excuses in their lives. You may be thinking, "Why would successful people need excuses? They're successful! Why would you need an excuse for that?" Think again! The people who have the best results in life are the same ones who've had the most failures simply because they've tried more things. The people who win big in life understand that every time they try something, it might not work out the first time, and they don't care about that. They know each time they face their fear of trying something new, they grow the most and learn the most amount about themselves. They learn new strategies and tools. They gain more experience and education. It's the experiences themselves that are valuable, not just the end result.

In life it doesn't matter how many times you get knocked down. What counts is how many times you get up. As long as you get up one more time than you have been knocked down, you're a complete and total success. The problem is most people quit just before they were about to succeed. If they had taken just one more step, one more action, or made one more phone call, they would have succeeded. Instead they quit the race an inch before reaching the finish line. And we all know there aren't any medals given out for almost finishing. Fortune is in the follow-through. Excellence is a commitment to completion.

> "I know fear is an obstacle for some people, but it is an illusion to me. . . . Failure always made me try harder next time."
>
> MICHAEL JORDAN

To make matters worse, many people come up with excuses to explain why they quit. They say things like, "I've tried everything and nothing worked." I love that one. How many times have you heard that one? Whenever I hear that, I ask, "You've tried *everything*?"

"Yes, everything!" they say.

Then I ask them, "Are you telling me you have tried 100,000 different ways to succeed?" I'm not surprised when they reply, "No, not 100,000."

> "Many of life's failures are people who did not realize how close they were to success when they gave up."
>
> THOMAS EDISON

I ask them, "How many ways have you tried?"

Then comes the real answer. "Well, maybe a couple."

The challenge with saying you've tried everything is that it stops your brain from continuing to search for the strategy that will get you what you want, because it thinks there are no ways left untried. Remember: your brain is always listening. And the truth is that if you really had tried *every-*

thing, then you would have also taken the action that worked because "everything" is all-inclusive. That means you would have come up with the winning strategy.

The excuse that you've already tried everything robs you of the ability to create the rewards you desire, and that's why excuses are below the line. When you live below the line with excuses, you deny yourself the ability to create the rewards you desire. To get those rewards, you need to move up and live your life above the line. It's just like the pyramid we looked at earlier. Where do the majority of people live—on the top or the bottom?

Blame and justification are also below the line.

We've all heard stories about people who were wealthy and/or famous, who seemed to have it all yet lived painful, lonely, miserable lives, or died tragically at a young age. When the people of the majority hear those stories about rich people with miserable lives, they view it as "proof" that the wealthy are unhappy and use it to justify the fact that they're not more financially successful them-selves. It provides them with the reason for why they're not even striving to be. The excuse they tell is delivered in the form of a story told to their peers, or even to themselves, goes something like this:

"Look how many rich people's lives are messed up. They have no real friends. People only want them for their money. It's lonely at the top. Rich people have miserable lives." And then comes the line that will forever keep the majority where they are: "I would rather stay poor and happy instead of being rich and miserable."

Have you heard that line before? Have you ever said it yourself? The truth is there *are* people who are rich and lonely and live painful, miserable lives. This tells us two things about them: first, that they learned how to make money (good for them!), and second, that they obviously aren't very enriched or personally developed. If they were, they would behave differently and wouldn't be so lonely and miserable. They would live enriched lives as well as be finan-cially wealthy.

The problem with the story told by the majority about "poor and happy versus rich and miserable" is that it's only presenting two choices, as if there are *only* two choices. From this fact alone, we can see that those types of stories are being started by people with a scarcity mentality. An abundant mind would realize those aren't the only two choices available.

There may be some true stories about famous people who were financially rich who lived miserable lives, but what many people fail to acknowledge are the other realities about the financially wealthy people who have incredible lives. Those stories aren't being told by the people of the majority, probably because they don't support the excuses they're using for why they're not more holistically successful.

Just look at the TV news reports or the newspapers. How many positive stories do you see about people who are happy, with great relationships, living their dream lives? They neglect to tell you about those people because there's no drama in talking about happy people enjoying their happy lives.

It is true that money by itself won't buy you happiness, and being poor is a guaranteed way to buy you a lot of pain. Yes, there are stories about people who are wealthy who have miserable lives, and the fact is that there are countless poor people who survive a painful existence every day of their lives. The reason those stories don't make the news is because they're so common. After all, it is the majority's story.

Playing below the line is very disempowering. The solution is to live above the line, to live where there are no excuses, no justification, and no blame, to live where all the rewards are. How can you achieve this? The answer is simple: take responsibility. As soon as you take responsibility for your life, you instantly empower yourself. And with more power, your light is brighter, and more life is attracted to you. Responsibility is above the line.

Responsibility
Result$

———————————

Excuses
Blame
Justification

Having responsibility means you have the ability to choose how you respond. To respond is to act, and when you take different actions, you get different results.

I'll give you an example of what I mean. Imagine you're in your car and you're driving through town. As you approach an intersection, you notice you have the green light so you proceed to drive through it. Right the middle of the intersection, someone else blows through the red light and T-bones into the side of your car.

Is what just happened your responsibility?

The answer is yes, it is. It is your responsibility. You decided to drive that day. You decided to be on that street at that time. You could have left five minutes earlier and chosen a different street to drive on, but you didn't. Therefore it is your responsibility.

You may notice that I said it was "your responsibility" and didn't say it was "your fault." The two things are different, and are not connected.

The truth is whenever you're in a situation like the accident I just described, you have the ability to choose how you respond to what happens next. That's taking responsibility. Even though we all have the ability to choose how we respond, most people don't act like they have that choice.

Have you ever experienced people getting all riled up and bent out of shape over the smallest fender bender that they're involved in? They get out of their car and instantly start calling the other person from the other car names like "stupid" and "idiot." They feel it's appropriate behavior to display their temper. Do you know anyone like that?

A couple of years ago, I was in a woman's car and she was very slowly pulling out of a parking space. Not seeing that a man had pulled up his car behind us and stopped, she accidentally backed into his car. The two cars gently bumped each other, and there wasn't a dent or a scratch on either car. The woman put her car in park and went to apologize to the other driver. She was calm and polite the entire time. He, on the other hand, used a completely different tactic and immediately began yelling out things like, "What are you, some kind of an idiot? Didn't you see me? Are you stupid?"

I could see my friend was getting very uncomfortable with the way the man was acting, so I decided to see if I could calm down the situation. As soon as this man saw me step out of the car, he became even more aggressive than before. He looked like he was getting ready for a fight. He was yelling, "Hey, you want a piece of me? Why don't you stay out of this and mind your own business?"

I calmly replied, "Sir, I'm just checking to see—are you hurt?"

My question stunned him. It took him a second or two to answer it. "No, I'm not hurt!"

I said, "Well neither are we. And that's why they call this experience an accident. It's obvious that none of us was actually aiming to hit the other, so why don't we just exchange insurance details and let them deal with it? That's what they get paid for, right? Instead we can go have a most incredible day. How does that sound?"

His whole demeanor calmed down, and he politely said, "That sounds a lot better than what I was planning to do."

He looked and saw there wasn't any damage and suggested we all just forget it and move on. We all walked away from the experience feeling positive and energized because we all chose to be empowering about it and take responsibility for our actions. We chose the response we wanted, and we got the result we wanted.

Instead of proactively choosing the best response, most people just react to what happens. Then, to make matters worse, having a big blowup with someone isn't enough. They have to keep bringing up the event with anyone else who is willing to listen to the story.

Have you ever noticed that when you're having a bad day, you don't actually have a bad day by yourself? Instead you get in your little group and start telling them about the bad day you're having. That's when the other people start talking about their bad day too. Then you get into competition with each other. "You think your life's bad? You should live mine!" It's as if you want to be famous for having the worst life of the group. Do you know any one like that?

> "You will not be punished for your anger, you will be punished by your anger."
>
> BUDDHA

You may also notice that when someone recounts the traffic accident he or she was in, they make sure to tell you that it was the other person's fault. Isn't it funny how it's always the other person's fault and never yours? Interesting! Proactive behavior is above the line, and reactive behavior is below the line.

When you want to start living the holistically successful life of your dreams, a life filled with happiness, joy, and fulfillment, you have to decide to live your life above the line. When you take responsibility for your life, you have the ability to choose how you respond, and when you respond differently, you get different results.

Three things have to happen for you to start living your life above the line.

First you have to make a **decision** to do so. Thinking, "I should do this," is not making a decision; thinking, "I must do this," is making a decision. The reason this is so important is because most people are poor decision makers. Think about it. You have five people in a room together and one person asks, "Who's hungry?" They all say they are.

Then that person asks, "Where do you want to go to eat?"

The first person asked replies, "I don't know. Where do you want to eat?"

Then the next person, "I don't know. Where do you want to eat?"

And the next, "I don't know. Where do you want to eat?"

And finally the last person, "I don't know. Where do you want to eat?"

This scenario goes on for twenty minutes. Finally someone makes a decision and suggests that they go for Chinese food. The rest of the group is relieved because someone finally made a decision—until one guy says, "I don't like Chinese food. Can we go somewhere else?"

So the person who suggested the Chinese food says, "Of course we can. Where do you want to go instead?"

That's when the guy looks you straight in the eye and says, "I don't know. Where do you want to eat?"

A decision is the starting point for all real change. When you make a decision, it means you are now going to engage and move forward. It's when the analyzing stops and the action begins.

For example, once you decide to never touch another cigarette, you instantly become a nonsmoker. If you have a tendency to procrastinate, the moment you decide now is the time to take action, you instantly become an action taker. This is how you can see the proof of just how powerful making a decision can be. *All real change happens at the moment the decision to change is made.*

After the decision comes the **commitment**. When you're fully committed, it means you are going to do whatever it takes to make sure the change will take place. When I say, "Do whatever it takes," of course that means with integrity. Remember the Law of Circulation: you reap what you sow.

Making a commitment is making the decision to follow through. People who get the best rewards in life are people who do what average people aren't willing to do. Most people quit just before they were about to succeed. The winners in life don't quit. They go past the finish line, because they know that *the fortune is in the follow-through* and that excellence is the commitment to completion.

The last thing you need to put in place to start living your life above the line is **investment**. Invest in yourself by taking the time to check that you're not using blame, justification, and excuses. Instead, choose to be responsible by asking yourself, "How can I deal with this in an empowering way?" Another version of that same question is, "How would Love respond to this?"

Your investment of time is the biggest investment you will ever make. No matter how much time you invest, you will never get any more time back from your investment. So make sure you get the best return for your investment. Look at the word "investment" broken down into parts, and you can clearly see what will be the best thing for you to invest your time in.

> Investment
> **Invest**ment
> Invest**me**nt
> Investment = *I invest in me*

The only thing in this universe that we have control over changing is ourselves. Once we change ourselves, the way we will participate in life also changes, setting into motion the catalyst for a whole new direction of cause and effect. The only way for us to change the world to a better place to live in is for us to make the choice to change ourselves. When we change, the world around us instantly changes too.

The best investment you can ever make is in your own personal development, because when you develop yourself into being a bigger, better, and more educated person, that new, improved version of you will automatically start to do things you didn't do before. And these new actions that you'll be taking will produce all of those new, great results that you're going to be enjoying. Makes sense, right?

The only thing I might add to what Lao Tzu said is, "Does it matter, as long as you're living the dream?" Live your life above the line, and start filling your life with the experiences of your grand dream goals. Imagine how happy and fulfilled you and everyone around you will feel when you start doing that.

> *"I went to sleep and dreamed that I was the butterfly. I flew around and did all the things that a butterfly does. Then, as I woke up from the dream, I was posed with a question. 'Am I the man who dreamed of being the butterfly, or am I the butterfly who is now dreaming of being a man?'"*
>
> LAO TZU

You have the choice between going for some small, uninspiring goals or taking the journey to achieve your grand dream goals. Which do you choose to do? How would Love respond?

Go to www.kurekashley.com and sign up for my free monthly newsletter, "Power Up Your Month." Always included in every issue are a lot of new strategies to help you achieve your grand dream goals and enjoy your journey of personal development.

> *"Even the longest of journeys starts with the first small step."*
>
> CONFUCIUS

11

The Fortune-Teller

he mystical silken tent billows slightly in the breeze as you wait your turn in the queue, enjoying the morning sun warming your shoulders and the playful mood of the weekend markets. You catch a glimpse of the fortune-teller or, at least, her bejeweled hand, as she sweeps the curtain aside enough to bid farewell to another satisfied customer. "Another happy future," you think to yourself, somewhat cynically. "They can't all be good."

She's obviously popular, and all the newspaper stories you've read attest to her 100% accurate skills. That's why you're here, after all. You've been dealing with mounting debts, a broken relationship, and whispers of cutbacks at work, so you're ready for some good news. Or are you? "Maybe I want to know the truth," you think to yourself, "like will I still have a job at the end of the month, and will I ever find my perfect partner?" Suddenly you get cold feet. "This is dumb," you mumble. "What am I doing here? A fortune-teller! Am I losing my mind? What can a stranger tell me about my future?"

You want to turn and go, eager to disappear into the crowds, hoping no one you know spotted you waiting to see a fortune-teller, but it's too late. The bejeweled hand beckons you inside, and your curiosity leads you in. Inside the tent you settle on a velvet cushion while the fortune-teller bends her elderly head and peers into the milky depths of a large crystal ball.

"You have a very bright future," she begins.

You wince. Clearly she's a fake. The job, the credit cards, the relationship—deep down you know disaster is imminent. Surely she can pick that up!

"Yes. It's quite clear," the crone continues. "The dream life you desire is here for you. It is going to happen."

A flicker of excitement passes through you. You'd love to believe this! And then she delivers the punch line.

"Come here and look into the crystal ball," she invites, "because you have extraordinary powers of your own. You can see your own future. If you don't believe me, have a look!"

Feeling totally weird now, you look into the crystal ball. The milky clouds part, and there, in stunning vibrant color, you see your whole future. The visions flow from one to another, as you see your dream life unfold. Deep down inside, something tells you this is real. This truly is going to happen for you, and you really do have the power to tell your own fortune, to see your holistically success- ful future.

Right now I know you're thinking, "Okay, Kurek, now you've really gone off the deep end! But you do have me curious as to where you're going with all of this!"

Trust me, there's a method to my madness. Think about it. If someone really could see your future, and she promised you that the dream life you desire is going to happen for you, how excited would you be?

Still curious as to where I'm going with this? Being curious is a good place to be right now because it means your mind is open to taking on some different thoughts and learning something new. That's exactly where it needs to be, because you're definitely going to need an open mind for what I'm going to tell you next.

All great achievers are excellent fortune-tellers. That's right! They all have the ability to see their futures. As a matter of fact, it is that ability to see their futures that makes it possible for them to create them. And for you to be able to create the happy, healthy, and fulfilled life you desire, you're going to have to become a fortune-teller too.

Real fortune-tellers don't have to wear rainbow-colored turbans, burn incense, do palm reading, and gaze into crystal balls. And neither do you! What I'm saying is the people who achieve their dream goals are visionaries. And you can be one too.

So what is a visionary? Visionaries are the people who focus their attention on where they want to go in life. Visionaries are people who don't see the world as it is now. They see it as they want it to be in the future. By looking toward the future and seeing where they want to be, they make magic happen, because they can see what they need to do to make that vision a reality. This book shows you how to do exactly this, so that you too will soon find yourself living the holistically successful life you desire.

You've probably noticed by now that almost every chapter mentions the formula for creation. There's a simple reason for that. It's because it reminds you that thoughts are the beginning of all creation. Like everything else in life, your future also starts with the formula for creation: $T \rightarrow A = R$. It's your new thoughts, followed by you taking new actions that will produce your new results. So it's pretty simple. Whatever you focus your thoughts on is going to create the results you get in life.

Focusing on the Past Equals Pain

When you focus on past experiences that didn't work out the way you wanted, that can only lead to one thing: creating more pain in your life today. When you keep bringing up stories from your past— the sad times, the hard times, the traumas, and the dramas—that too can only lead to experiencing more pain in your life today.

The majority of people on the planet are storytellers, and that's one of the most disempowering habits a person can have, because telling stories steals your power. It renders you powerless to make changes in your life because it keeps you stuck in the past.

Whether you're telling disempowering stories or listening to other people's disempowering stories, the result is disempowering for you. Why do you think most people's stories are disempowering? Because rarely do you hear people tell positive stories about how great everything is and how everything they want in their life is going to happen for them. They rarely talk about how excited they are about their lives and about how all their dreams are going to come true. Instead, they're quick to tell you all about the people they don't like. They'll tell you about how painful their childhood was, or about how they were raped, abused, molested, unloved, or uncared for, and how life has always been against them. They'll go on and on about how they hate their jobs, their boss, their lives, and anything else they can add to the list.

Anytime you talk about your past in a negative way, you're telling a disempowering story. Stop giving meaning to things that steal your power away from you, that keep you from taking the necessary action needed to move forward. Anytime you say things like, "They turned down someone else, and that means they will reject me too," or, "They didn't call, which means they're not interested in me," or, "No one has ever been able to do that, so that means I won't either," you're telling stories. They're stories because what you're saying isn't the complete truth. It's only your perception. And if you choose a disempowering perception, then you're going to be disempowered, which will rob you of the energy you need to achieve your grand dream goals.

Think about it. When you hear people telling stories about their pasts, aren't nine out of ten of those stories about painful or distressing times in their lives? They're usually stories about times when someone stole from them, did something dishonest to them, or was

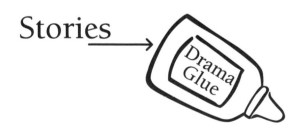

Stories

hurtful to them. They're stories about the partner who cheated on them, or the boss who mistreated them. Most people just love getting stuck in the drama glue of telling their disempowering stories or listening to other people's disempowering stories. The reason I call it "drama glue" is because once they get involved in telling drama stories they get stuck in the drama of it all.

Rarely do you hear people talk about the good times in their past. Even if they start off talking about something positive, it somehow always seems to lead back to some other painful stuff that happened, which is really what they wanted to talk about in the first place. You'll hear these people going on and on about their drama stories. For many people, that's all they talk about. Do you know anyone like that? Now you know why I call it drama glue. Not only does the person telling the story get stuck in his drama, so does anyone listening to it. The drama glue gets everyone in the area stuck.

Worse still, many people even identify themselves by their past experience. They refer to themselves as rape victims, incest survivors, or recovering alcoholics, for instance. The challenge with thinking about negative experiences from your past is that it gets your mind to relive those experiences all over again! They replay in your mind like you're watching a DVD. The problem with this is that your subconscious mind cannot tell the difference between an event that is happening right now and an event that you're imagining to be happening. In your subconscious mind, it's all the same thing.

More than likely there are some painful emotions attached to those past experiences. So as your brain is replaying the DVD of the painful experience, you're forced to relive that painful experience and feel those emotions again and again. When you relive an event, your body, as well as your mind, reacts to that experience as if it's really happening today. When you react, you're taking action, and those actions are automatically creating the results you're getting. See how this works? You're taking actions based on past pain because your body thinks it's today's pain, and the only thing those thoughts and actions can produce is more painful results, just like in the past.

That's why I say when you think about the past, it's going to equal pain. When you focus your thoughts on the past, you act like you did back then, and those same past actions can only produce the same kind of results as they did back then, if not worse results than they did back then.

Think about it. If you've already endured the pain once, why would you want to go back and live through that painful experience again? That makes no sense at all, does it? It's like driving your car while you're looking out the back window the entire time. It's the perfect prescription for creating a lot of future pain. When you keep looking backward, it cuts off your ability to see what's coming up in front of you, and that's a good recipe for creating a lot of crashes in your life.

———

Is focusing on your past successes instead of your past pain any better? Actually, that's not going to help you much either, because when you think about the past, you take the same actions you took in the past, and that's only going to create the results you had back then. You might be thinking, "What's bad about that? Why wouldn't I want those good results that I had back then in my life today?" The answer is because the world has evolved since then. Just because they were good results for you back then doesn't mean they will be great results today. Things have changed and moved on. You can't live by yesterday's standards and expect great results today.

Yesterday's Standards

On May 6, 1954, Roger Bannister became the first person in history ever to run a sub-four-minute mile. People had tried for hundreds of years to break that speed barrier, without success. At the time doctors and scientists said it was impossible for a human being to run that fast because the heart and lungs would burst or the legs would tear off.

Interestingly enough, after centuries of no one being able to do it, the year after Roger Bannister broke the record, thirty-five other people were suddenly able to run a sub-four-minute mile. Why do you think this was? Because Roger Bannister's achievement changed the way other people thought about the sub-four-minute mile. The old thought that it was impossible had become a new thought that it was possible. Once people had the new thought, they too could produce the new result.

Today there are young people in high school who can run a sub-four-minute mile. It's not even considered that fast a running time anymore. It's certainly not a fast enough time to qualify for the Olympics.

Imagine if Roger Bannister wanted to break the record again today. If he tried to do it by focusing on what he did in back in 1954, those thoughts would only produce the same results he got back then. They can't produce new, faster results because old thoughts can only produce old actions, not new ones. Running a four-minute mile today isn't going to break any records, so focusing on past successes can actually result in significantly less successful results in today's world.

When you constantly think about your past, you'll keep taking the same kinds of actions you did back then, and that can only produce the same old results. But who wants the old stuff? We were talking about how we can produce the new life we desire! Remember that in life, either we evolve or we dissolve. If you keep steering your life by constantly looking through your back windshield, all you're going to see is where you've already been, and if you keep doing that long enough eventually you'll crash. And that's painful!

Focusing on the Present Equals More of the Same

We've just discovered that focusing on your past isn't the winning strategy for creating the fulfilled life you desire. Neither is focusing on the present.

If you keep thinking about what you have or don't have right now, you'll just create more of what you already have—or don't have—right now. When you think about the results you have now, you'll only continue to take the same actions you're already taking right now, and those actions can only produce the same results you're currently getting. There's no growth in that. It's like running on a treadmill. You're expending a lot of energy to go nowhere fast! Not a great strategy for success, is it?

The Loser Loop

Let's talk about the loser loop, because it helps explain the problem with living in the past. One quick note: when I use the word "loser," I'm not name-calling or being judgmental.

The loser loop is a cycle, and when you live your life in the loser loop, you lose the ability to achieve your goals and dreams. The

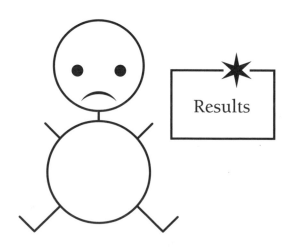

chances are also high that you'll lose a lot of the quality of life you have already created for yourself.

Sadly, this is how the majority of people live their lives, and it's the reason they're not living the abundant life they desire.

Everything you do creates a result. Even if you don't take any action, that too will produce a result, but it probably won't be the result you were looking for. It's like going into a shooting range where someone blindfolds you, spins you around, then hands you a pistol and tells you to shoot. You will definitely hit something, and it probably won't be what you were aiming for. (It could be the person who just told you to shoot. Now that would be ugly!)

People in the loser loop try to achieve their goals by focusing on their past results. They look at what they've achieved in the past, and especially the things they've failed to accomplish. They look at how starting up a business ended in failure, or about how getting married

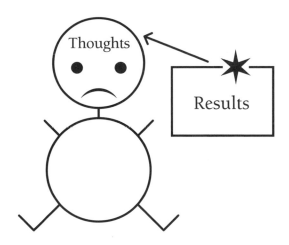

ended in divorce. They look at the diets they started that didn't work, or the times they tried to quit smoking, only to later go back to it again. The loser looks at his past results and lets those results dictate his thoughts about what's possible to achieve now and in the future.

Some examples of loser loop thoughts are:

> "I can't do it."
> "I'm not smart enough."
> "I'm too old."
> "I'm too young."
> "I've tried something like this before, but it failed."
> "Other people have tried to succeed at something like this before, and they failed, so there's no way I'll be able to do it."

Are these empowering or disempowering thoughts? The losers let their past results determine what they think is possible or impossible to achieve.

"Wherever your head goes,
your body follows !"

Remember: what you think about determines what actions you take.

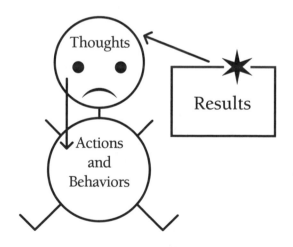

And it's those actions that determine the results you get, or don't get. As the Law of Cause and Effect clearly states, every cause creates an effect. Your thoughts are the cause and your results are the effect.

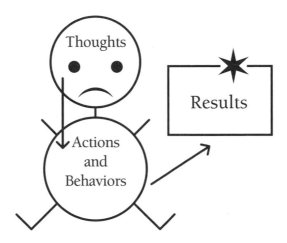

Think about this for a moment. If you knew there was no way you could succeed in creating the life you wanted, and you were convinced there was no way to achieve your grand dream goals, would you still get up and take the necessary action to make it happen anyway? The answer is no, you wouldn't! You wouldn't take the action because you already know you're not going to get the result you want! Why waste your time doing something that isn't going to produce the result you want, right?

Even if you did decide to go for it, in spite of knowing that you're not going to succeed, what kinds of actions do you think you would take? You've already told yourself there's no way you're going to succeed, and with those kinds of thoughts running around in your head, do you think you would really take the consistent necessary actions needed to succeed? Doubtful! With negative, disempowering thoughts flowing through your mind, are you really going to hang in there and follow through if there are any setbacks or delays? Probably not! Now you can see why this is called the loser loop. Every time you go around this circuit, you get less and less inspired to do it. You believe less and less that it can be done. Your enthusiasm dwindles away. Your actions become lackluster, and that can only produce mediocre results.

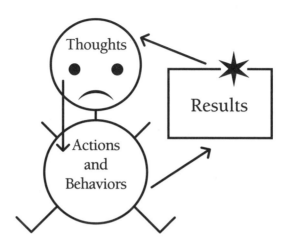

Those negative, disempowering thoughts about how it didn't pan out for you in the past are stopping you from even attempting to take the necessary action and follow through until you finally have what you desire. This is a guaranteed way to always lose every time.

> "When you want to keep your limitations, keep defending them!"
>
> WAYNE DYER

Some people find it hard to relate to the loser loop scenario even when they're in the middle of it. They challenge the formula by saying that their personal situation cannot be summed up so simply. They tell you how it's different from anything anyone else has ever been through. This is where their drama glue story starts. They go on to tell you all the reasons why having a happy, healthy, holistically successful life isn't a reality. They justify their story, saying they've read all the books, been to all the seminars, and know all "the stuff." Finally, they say they've already tried everything and still nothing worked, and that's why they're giving up. As you now know, it's that story about how they have tried everything that's preventing them from moving forward. Drama glue!

They defend their position and challenge the loser loop formula. "Okay," they say, "I'll show you. Even though I already know there's no way I can succeed in achieving my grand dream goals, I'll give it a shot anyway, just to prove you wrong. I'll show you the reason I haven't succeeded has nothing to do with my past results. I just know I'm not going to be able to succeed at this. Things like that don't happen to people like me. I wasn't born under a lucky star. But it doesn't matter. I'll try again anyway and prove to you that it won't work!"

They go and try to achieve their goals already knowing that they're going to fail. Those loser thoughts can only produce passionless actions—actions that match the way they feel. Passionless actions will never produce the wonderful results that you want. So, after another one of their half-hearted attempts at going for it, they say, "See? I told you so! I told you it wasn't going to work, and it didn't. I tried to do it, and it didn't work. Ha, ha! I proved you wrong!"

The truth is they didn't prove me wrong. They proved themselves right. By remaining in the loser loop, they proved that they are losers.

———

Let's do a little experiment. Do you have a pen or pencil sitting on a table nearby right now? Try to pick it up.

Did you pick it up?

If the writing instrument is in your hand, you have failed, and if it's still lying there on the table, you have also failed. We use the word "try" when we have no intention of succeeding after exerting a small attempt. To use "try" is to give an excuse to quit when you're not getting the result you want. "Oh, I tried to do it." There is no such thing as trying. You either do it or you don't.

Remember: The true winner at life understands that it doesn't matter how many times you get knocked down that counts. What counts is how many times you stand up. As long as you stand up one more time than you were knocked down, you're a complete and total success.

The reason the majority of people don't experience the quality of life they would like is because they quit just before they are about to succeed. They say things like, "I just couldn't see the light at the end of the tunnel." What they don't understand is that there might be a bend in the tunnel, and if they had taken just one more step and turned their head to the side, they would have seen that the light they were looking for was right there all along. You may have already noticed that life isn't a straight line. It's a series of twists and turns. The key to having holistic success is to just keep walking in the direction of your grand dream goals, and eventually you'll get there.

When you quit, not only do you fail at getting the prize you were searching for, you also wipe out all the efforts you've already put in. When you quit you throw into the garbage all the actions you have already taken. How is that ever going to get you the happy life you yearn for?

The Power of the Subconscious: Pleasure and Pain

To really understand how all this works, let's have a quick look at how your brain processes information.

The most powerful part of your mind is your subconscious. It's your subconscious mind that stores all your memories, life experiences, and education. It also has control over your entire nervous system.

Very simply, your subconscious mind pictures whatever you are focusing your thoughts on and then connects that image with the emotion you're experiencing at that moment. The important thing to understand is that your subconscious mind doesn't have the capacity for judgment. It doesn't judge whether what you're feeling is right or makes sense. It just connects whatever emotion you're feeling with the image produced by your thoughts.

Your mind has another feature you need to know about as well. It's an instinctive defense mechanism, and it's designed to get you to move toward whatever will bring you pleasure and automatically move you away from anything that will cause you pain.

Here's the important bit to remember: this part of your mind can't tell the difference between what's real and what's perceived. It doesn't matter if you're feeling real pain or perceived pain—either way, it is going to get you to move away from it in an attempt to keep you out of harm's way.

Remember: your subconscious mind can't judge whether a situation is going to bring you real pleasure or real pain. It can only go on the information it has stored away from all your past experiences and feelings. Can you see where this is going?

If your emotions about an event in your past are negative, then your subconscious mind has stored thoughts of that event connected with negative emotions, with pain. Whenever you focus your thoughts on that event, your subconscious mind comes up with a "pain" reading and automatically makes you move away from whatever you are thinking about. So if there's a goal you want to achieve, and you're thinking negatively about your past inability to attain it, your mind attaches the image of that goal to the negative feelings you're associating with the non-achievement of it. Your mind then gets you to automatically move away from the goal you want to achieve because it's trying to protect you from that perceived pain. You'll resist achieving your goal without even realizing what you're doing!

Understand that the negative thoughts don't have to be about the goal itself to cause damage. They can be about anything related to the goal, including how you feel about not having achieved it yet. Your mind still makes the connection between what it is seeing (the goal) and what it is feeling, and if the feeling is negative, it automatically signals you to move away from the goal.

Have you ever had the experience in which you were moving toward achieving one of your goals and then, for some unknown reason, it seemed as though you sabotaged yourself? Now you can see where that self-sabotage comes from. Your mind somehow got the message from you that you thought something about that goal was painful, so your mind instinctively moved you away from it in an attempt to keep you out of harm's way. It's like when you go to touch something, then right as you touch it you realize that it's hot. Your hand instinctively jerks away even before you consciously discover that what you were touching was hot. That's the automatic defense system at work.

The opposite is also true, and it can work in your favor when you use it correctly. When you focus your thoughts on a goal and maintain only positive, empowering feelings about the goal and everything related to it, your mind will move you in the direction of that goal. This is really important. When you understand how this works, you have a powerful strategy you can use to attain all your grand dream goals instead of automatically moving away from them without even realizing what you're doing.

Remember that if you're not moving in one direction, then by default you have to be moving in the other.

It's all about how your brain and your subconscious mind perceive the outcome of what you are focusing your thoughts on. If the perception is pain, it moves you away from achieving the result, even though the real result may have been pleasure. If the perception is pain it moves you away, and if the perception is pleasure it moves you toward achieving the result.

Can you see the challenge here? When you're thinking about having a happy, fulfilled life, and then you start thinking about the times in your past when you tried for these goals and failed, what's going to happen? That's right. Your subconscious mind links those two thoughts together and automatically moves you away from achieving the grand dream goals because it assumes those goals are going to cause you pain. That's exactly what happens when you get stuck in the loser loop by telling painful stories from your past.

How about those times when you think about your goals and you're feeling frustrated because they haven't happened fast enough? Your subconscious mind links your goals with the pain of frustration and automatically moves you even further away from achieving them.

How about those times when you think about your goals and you're feeling resentful because other people seem to achieve those goals so much easier than you do? Or when you think about your goals and you're feeling stressed about all the work you think you'll have to put in to achieve them? Or when you think about your goals and you're feeling anxious about whether your friends will still feel the same way about you when you're living your dream life? Do you see how easy it is to tell your subconscious mind that achieving your goals will result in pain? Interesting, isn't it? So what can you do about this?

How diligent are you at making sure you're always feeling positive and empowering when you're thinking about your goals? Are you still thinking in an empowering way when it appears things aren't happening fast enough for you? How do you process the setbacks that sometimes happen?

If your reply to that last question was something like, "What do you mean *sometimes* happen? Setbacks *always* happen to me!" then I suggest you *examine your thoughts*. Is the thought that setbacks *always* happen to you an empowering thought or a disempowering thought?

Thinking your goals are hard to achieve is a loser loop thought. If you think it's going to be hard, it *will* be, because you will act on the thought about it being that way, and that will make it so.

One way to check for loser loop thinking is to listen to your self-talk. That's the chatter that goes on in the back of your mind between you and you, a.k.a., talking to yourself. Monitoring your self-talk is vitally important because it's the way you communicate with yourself that determines the quality of life you have now and in your future. The way you communicate with yourself is the original source of all your life's achievements and, at the same time, the original source of all your biggest disappointments. *Remember; your words are thoughts that you are giving sounds to.*

Think of it this way. Have you noticed that when you're asking a person for assistance, asking nicely usually gets the best results? Wouldn't you agree that it's not just about *what* you ask, it's also about *how* you ask it?

Whom do you listen to most? Undeniably the person you listen to most is yourself. So don't you think you might be more willing to do some new things and take some new actions when you start talking to yourself in a more kind and empowering way?

Achieving or not achieving your goals isn't a matter of how many personal development books you've read or how many seminars you've attended. Just because you haven't achieved what you want yet doesn't mean it's not going to happen for you. What it does mean is that obviously you are going to have to learn and apply some different rules from those you already know. The crucial point to remember is that information alone is never going to be enough to produce the results you want. To get results, you're going to have to follow through on what you have learned and take the necessary action.

———

Before we go any further, let me ask you a question. Why do you think I know so much about the loser loop? (I hope you didn't just answer by saying that I'm a loser!)

I was truly stuck in the loser loop for the two years following the helicopter crash. Every single day of that turbulent time I wanted to stop using cocaine. I wanted to quit smoking. I wanted to be free of the dark depression and the terror of putting a gun in my mouth every night. Being free of these disempowering behaviors was my goal, yet every day I failed in my attempts to achieve this result. Day after day my failures reinforced my belief that I wasn't strong enough to get out from under these dark habits. The more I tried to quit and failed, the more my thoughts that I was weak and the task was impossible were reinforced. Thinking that you're weak and thinking that the task you're undertaking is impossible, are those empowering or disempowering thoughts?

My subconscious connected my thoughts of changing with the painful emotions that flooded me every day. The image of a life free from cocaine, cigarettes, depression, and attempted suicide was connected with the painful emotions of failure and weakness. My subconscious mind automatically moved me away from achieving my goals because it equated the goals with more pain—the pain of having to face more failure and more feelings of weakness.

Every day I wanted to give up all my disempowering behaviors, and every day I tried, and every day I went back to those same behaviors again. Because I had tried so many times to change and failed, I was stuck in the loser loop, with thoughts like, "I can't do this," "I'm just too weak a person to make the change," "I don't have the strength or willpower to make the change last," or, "Look how many times I've tried already before, and they never worked out."

I was also asking some very disempowering questions. "Why does God hate me so bad that he did this to me?" "Why didn't I stay in the 'copter and die like a hero instead of getting off and living like a coward?" "Why am I such a loser?"

Take a look at the thoughts I was having and the questions I was asking myself. Are they empowering or disempowering? Now you can see why I was acting so weak and couldn't make the changes to my life I wanted to make. That's what disempowering thoughts do; they make you weak by stealing your power away. When you ask disempowering questions, you can only get disempowering answers. Energy attracts like energy.

It's obvious that the loser thoughts I was having back then were only making me act and behave in the same disempowering way. And since the Law of Cause and Effect is always working, those consistent actions I was taking could only produce the same consistent loser results.

Now you can see why I call this the loser *loop*. It's a vicious circle, and the longer you stay in it, the less you believe that real change will ever happen for you, and the less enthusiastic you become about the actions you take to make changes to your life.

If you stay in the loser loop long enough, it will eventually disempower you so much that it wipes out any chance that you'll ever live the quality of life you desire. It also renders you a victim—that is, until you make the decision to change it. If you don't, every time you go around the loop, you strengthen the loser thoughts, creating a false sense of proof that they are true. As it gets harder and harder to succeed, you begin to feel your life is on a downward spiral. Whenever you feel as if your life is spiraling out of control, or whenever you see someone else's life spiraling out of control, you're witnessing the loser loop in action.

Changing Directions

You may be thinking, "If the loser loop is such a trap, how can you possibly break out of it? How can you take the first step that will break the cycle and get you on an upward spiral?"

In chapter 6, I told you that the question I am asked most often is, "How did you turn your life around from those dark days into the great life you have now?" I also told you that the answer to that question is that one day I woke up and had a new thought. I described how that new thought led me to take brand-new actions and marked the turning point in my life. From that moment, my life changed forever.

The best part of all of this is that if I can do it with my own life, then so can you. Remember that your life doesn't have to be in the garbage for you to want to make it better. Regardless of where we are in life right now, we all need to evolve. Evolvement is our life's quest.

Remember that your life is not your own. There are people who love you, care about you, and even look up to you. When you allow yourself to get sucked into the spiral of the loser loop, you will take those people down with you. Negative energy is a much heavier, denser energy than positive energy is.

When you live in the loser loop and let your life go down the tubes, you don't take the ride alone. You take other people with you. Your life becomes a black hole with such a powerful gravitational pull that it starts pulling everything and everyone around you into it. Then they start pulling people around them down too. The negative cesspool keeps growing and growing like a cancer killing everything in its path.

In my own life I realized how devastated these people would have been if I had actually committed suicide, and how much pain I would have caused them. I realized how much we teach others by the way we live our lives, and I realized that people could look at my life and think, "If he can make it, then I can make it too." Once I really absorbed the impact of that thought, I knew that I had to change. I couldn't let a miserable life be my legacy.

You have to think about, "What lesson am I teaching with my actions?"

My next new thought was, "I don't care how many times I've tried to change and failed. Today is the day that I make *the decision* to change and succeed." It's at that moment of decision that all real, lasting change happens.

The Winner's Formula

Let's take a look at the winner's formula to see how it differs from the loser loop and to understand how you can apply the winner's formula to achieve your grand dream goals.

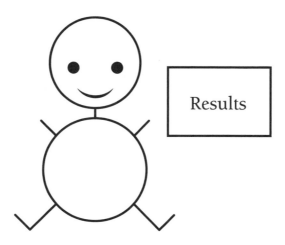

In life we all have results. Everything you do creates a result. Even if you don't take an action that will also produce a result, but it probably won't be the result you were looking for. It's like going into a shooting range. Wait a minute, isn't that the same way I started talking about the loser loop formula?

If you noticed that, you are correct. The truth is, all truly successful people have had more failures in life than unsuccessful people have, and the reason is because they have made more attempts at succeeding than unsuccessful people have.

A winner knows it doesn't always work out as planned every time they try something new. So what? The most important thing to understand is that a winner

> *"Failure is the opportunity to begin again more intelligently."*
>
> HENRY FORD

doesn't care when results don't match the ones they had planned on getting. They're not afraid to lose. **Only a loser is afraid to lose.** When you're committed to finding a way, you will. When you're focused on finding a good excuse in case you fail, you will. Seek and you shall find!

Losers are focused on instant short-term gratification. Winners are focused on creating a holistically successful life, and they are willing to *do* what it takes to get there. It's in the *doing*, not in the *having*, that we develop.

What a loser calls a failure, a winner calls a learning experience. Losers spend their time telling their failure story to anyone who will listen, getting them all stuck in the drama glue, while winners are busy preparing for their next drive to the top.

Winners look at each of their experiences to see what they can learn from them and to see how they can use these insights to develop, knowing that development will eventually lead to achievement of the results they desire.

If you're thinking you want to start a new business, but you're too scared to because so many businesses fail, I can teach you the guaranteed way to make sure your business never fails. Do you want to know what the strategy is? It's this: don't go into business. As you can see, this is also the guaranteed way to make sure you never succeed in business either.

If you want to trade shares in the stock market and are afraid you're going to lose all your money, there's a way to guarantee against this happening: don't trade in the stock market. This also guarantees you will never make money in the stock market. If you're afraid to fly because the plane might crash, don't fly. And if you're afraid of dying, don't live.

The truth is everything in life has risks. Things don't always work out the way you want them to or the way you planned. Welcome to life! The challenges that come along with life are what give your life its real value. It's what you can possibly lose that gives what you have so much worth. How exciting would skydiving be if there wasn't any risk involved? And what if you really want to experience skydiving but let your fear stop you from doing so, only to be struck dead by a coin falling out of someone's pocket as he's skydiving? Then what?

There are even risks in standing around doing nothing. If you live like a hermit and hide in your home because you're afraid of the risks and dangers in life, you're already dead. Boats are safer tied up to the dock, and that's not what boats were made for.

Remember that life isn't fair, and it never has been, so stop expecting it to be that way. Your life will instantly get easier the moment you stop trying to make it some thing that it's not. Life doesn't turn out the way it should. It turns out the way it does. It's what you do with it that will make your life what it is.

The funny thing about life is that when you get knocked down and are empowering about even that, you'll notice another view of life you weren't able to see before. *It's when we face our fears that we grow the most.* That's evolvement! The only thing you have to do to be successful at life is stand up just one more time! Take one more action. Make one more phone call, ask for help from one more person, or take one more step. That's the key ingredient that separates the winners from the losers, the minority from the majority.

If you don't want to play the game because you're afraid you might lose, guess what? You've already lost the game, because there is no way to win unless you play.

Remember: the people who get the best rewards in life are the ones willing to *do* what everyone else isn't willing to do. It's not that the majority doesn't know what to do, because they actually do. Knowing what to do isn't enough. Taking the necessary action is the winning step that creates the rewards you desire. The only difference between having a dream and living the dream is the follow-through. The fortune is in the follow-through!

———

The key to making the best out of any situation, even your failures and your losses, is to celebrate them. That's right, celebrate them. When you try something and it doesn't go as planned, celebrate that you're in the game and took your best shot. Also celebrate the empowering learning experience you're gaining.

When you celebrate your losses and failures, you teach your brain that negative feelings no longer go with failure. After a while, your brain creates a new meaning for what used to be looked upon as failure and registers it as a positive learning experience.

As you celebrate and reward yourself for stepping out of your comfort zone to try something new, whether or not you got the result you were looking for, you will become more willing to step out and try again. The more you try it, the better your chances of succeeding.

You already know what's on the other side of the coin. Don't take the action, or quit before you get there, and you are guaranteed to lose.

The choice is yours. Make sure you make it. Remember: the only way to guarantee you won't lose is by not playing.

―――

Winners don't look at their past results to determine what is possible for their future.

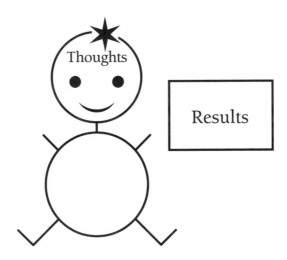

Winners start their journey toward success with positive, empowering, winner thoughts. Winner thoughts are the visionary thoughts about where they're going and what they want in their life.

A winner sees the power in everything by making sure they are empowering about everything.

Adopting these visionary thoughts will cause you to take new actions, and it's those new actions that will produce the results you want.

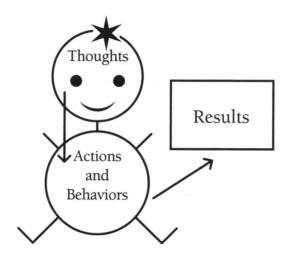

Train yourself to see only wealth, even when your conditions appear to be those of poverty. Fill your mind only with thoughts of abundance. Thoughts about being poor or the current condition of your bank account will never change that condition. Wealth can never be in your life as long as thoughts about scarcity keep occupying your mind. Only thoughts of abundance can lead you to wealth. Remember: this is an abundant universe we live in, and everything you want is coming to you because the Creator wants you to be happy and have everything you want. That's why it was all put here—for you enjoy. There's no common sense in thinking the Creator would put all these wonderful things on the planet just so we can't have any of it. That kind of thinking portrays the Creator as a cruel tyrant, yet all the writings and teachings describe the Creator as pure, unconditional love. Wouldn't you think that Love would want you to enjoy your gift of life to the fullest? If you asked Love, how would Love respond?

Train your mind to see only health, even when it appears that sickness and disease are all around you. How can focusing on sickness ever produce health?

The physical is the manifestation of the mental, and not the other way around. Stop attempting to get the physical to control the mental. It doesn't work that way. Don't let your current results dictate the way you think, because that's trying to work the system backward. That's like trying to have an apple tree so you can harvest the seeds. You have to plant first before you can harvest.

> *"I only see my outcomes and my obstacles will give way."*
>
> NAPOLEON BONAPARTE

Remember: the formula for creation is thoughts become actions that produce the results, and not the other way around. If you let your current results dictate your thoughts, those thoughts can only keep producing the same results you have now. There's no evolvement in that.

Do you really think that allowing your head to be flooded with thoughts about sadness, pain, and loneliness will ever bring happiness to your life or anyone else's? The only way to be happy is to have happy thoughts.

> *"Change your thoughts and you change your world."*
>
> NORMAN VINCENT PEALE

To be wealthy you have to start with only wealthy thoughts, and to be healthy you have to start with only healthy thoughts.

If you focus your thoughts on obstacles, you will move toward having those obstacles in your life. The more you focus on the obstacles, the stronger they become and the harder it becomes to get past them. Quit giving the problems in your life any energy. If you keep giving them energy, they'll grow up and bite your head off. Kill the monsters while they're still small by not giving them energy. Instead, utilize your energy to achieve your outcomes. That's a much more powerful strategy.

As soon as you start seeing yourself as a healthy person, you will start to produce health in your life. Yet again, if you're waiting for your body to be healthy before you start thinking healthy thoughts, then it's just not going to happen, because that's trying to get the physical to control the mental. As soon as you start consistently thinking about where you're going, you automatically start to move in that direction. That's being a visionary. *Wherever your head goes, your body follows.*

To be a visionary, you need to be proactive with your thoughts, not reactive. When you're reactive, you're declaring that something outside of yourself is the cause, and your life becomes the effect of that outside cause. When you react, the best you can hope for is to make the best out of a bad situation. When you're reacting, you're not taking responsibility, because you're not choosing how to respond. Have there ever been times when you reacted to something and later regretted that you did? That's why reacting isn't a strategy for success!

On the other hand, being a proactive thinker is a powerful success strategy. When you're proactive, you're choosing how you want to respond. That's what taking responsibility is. Instead of giving your power away to something outside of yourself, you become the cause that creates the effects you want in your life.

Proactive = Empowering

Reactive = Disempowering

Look at what's above the line and what's below the line. Where are you choosing to live your life?

Where Are You Going to Put Your Gold Medal?

When I started working with the Australian women's beach volleyball team, one of the first things I had Natalie do was to go out and buy a display case for the gold medal she was going to win at the Olympics. When I first told her to do this, she said, "I will, right after the Olympics."

"No, you need to buy it this week," I said, "and it has to be a quality display case because it's where you will be displaying your Olympic gold medal!"

She said, "It's two years before the Olympics. Why would I buy the case now when I don't have a gold medal yet?"

I didn't beat around the bush with my reply. "If you *really thought* you were going to win the gold medal, wouldn't you have a quality display case to keep it in?"

Nat said, "Yes, but what if I don't win?"

I asked, "Is that an empowering or disempowering thought? Are those the thoughts of a winning visionary?"

Those are the thoughts of people stuck in the loser loop. If you ask, "What if I fail?" or, "What if I lose?" then what you are truly thinking about is losing and failing, right? And if that's what you think about, then loss and failure are what you will produce. Always remember to examine your thoughts and ask yourself if the thoughts you're having about your grand dream goals are empowering you to succeed or disempowering you, making it easier for you to fail. They can only be one or the other.

If you're thinking that asking questions about losing is a good way to prepare yourself in case it happens, you are not running the complete race right up to the finish line. If you are preparing to lose, then you will lose, because if that's what you're thinking about, that's what you'll create. As I explained to Nat, "When you take the actions that a gold medalist takes, then you will get the results that come from taking those actions. That's a gold medal! Wouldn't you think that a gold medalist would have a case to display her medals? Of course she would. If she does, then so will you."

I told Nat to put the case in the place in her home it would occupy when the gold medal was displayed in it and to allow nothing else inside the case except gold. This would train her mind every time she saw the case to expect to see only gold sitting there. She borrowed some gold medals from some of her athlete friends and put those in the case, along with a gold medallion she already had. Often she also had the Australian national anthem playing, as they would be playing that when they awarded her with her gold medal at the Olympics.

THE FORTUNE-TELLER | 239

I also had the girls meditate every day with the national anthem playing while imagining themselves up on the podium at the Olympics receiving their gold medals. What we were doing was creating more and more visionary thoughts about what they were going to achieve. By making sure they were filling their heads consistently with winning thoughts, we were also helping guard against letting other thoughts in. Remember: if you don't consciously choose positive, empowering thoughts, then negative, disempowering ones have a chance to slip in and wreak havoc in your life. If you don't make the conscious choice, then the choice will be made for you.

Proof Is in the Pudding!

As the Sydney 2000 Olympics began, the results for Natalie and Kerri were very much the same as they had been in Atlanta four years earlier. They were doing exceptionally well, beating all the teams they were facing during the preliminary matches. When they got into the gold medal match, things became more challenging.

They were playing the Brazilian team, which was known to be the best in the world, and the score for most of the first match seemed to confirm that. At match point, the Brazilians were up by five points, and the Australians were one point away from losing. This is where most people would say, "Oh shoot, we're about to lose!"

Knowing what you do now about the power of your thoughts and the effect they have on what kind of actions you take, do you think saying, "Oh shoot, we're about to lose!" is a winner thought or a loser thought? If you said loser thought, then you've been paying attention. Thinking, "Oh shoot, we're about to lose!" will never get you to produce the necessary actions to create a win.

Consider this: if Nat and Kerri had thought about how they lost the gold at the Atlanta Olympics while they were playing at the Sydney Olympics, what kind of results do you think those thoughts would have produced?

Since they had trained their minds to focus only on the results they wanted, even though they were five points behind at match point, they didn't give up and they didn't give in. As a matter of fact, they knew it was time to try something new, because what they had been doing up to that point had produced a five-point disadvantage. They knew what they needed to do was make a little adjustment, and to do that they knew they needed to start with having a new thought.

Natalie knew she had to check in with her emotions and get her passion turned up to a higher level, so she started waving her arms in the air and got herself all pumped up. Then she got Kerri to do the same. Together they got the audience on their feet, and in a matter of seconds, there were 10,000 people up and cheering. The energy in the stadium was at fever pitch. You could see the energy fill the Australians with passion and power.

Right then a look came over the Brazilians' faces as if to say, "Why is it we don't feel like we're winning just yet?" Sure enough, the Australians, point by point, started coming back, and they won that match. They repeated their performance in the second match and won that game, bringing them victory and the gold medal.

> *"You must form a clear mental picture of the things you want; then you must hold this picture with a fixed purpose to get what you want, with an unwavering faith that you will get what you want . . . closing your mind to all that may tend to shake your purpose, dim your vision, or quench your faith."*
>
> WALLACE D. WATTLES

Remember: the race isn't over until you cross the finish line, which means that if you haven't achieved your grand dream goal and the time you set for the achievement of that goal is drawing near, don't give up! *Examine your thoughts!* Are the thoughts that you're having going to bring you closer to achieving your GDGs or take you farther away from achieving them? Remember that there is no neutral. Check in and make sure that all the thoughts you are having are empowering, winner thoughts. A visionary is always a visionary and not just when it's easy or convenient.

When you lock your focus in on the new things you want to experience, and you make sure all your thoughts about all aspects of your goals are positive and empowering, you'll automatically start to move in that direction.

Remember that our brains are wired to move us toward joy and away from pain.

Plant Positive Seeds and Pull Negative Weeds

If you don't consciously put into your mind the positive thoughts you want, then the negative thoughts you don't want have the ability slip in and cause havoc. Not only do you have to make sure you are putting positive thoughts into your mind, you also have to make sure you are weeding out the negative ones that come up along the way. And when you want to cast off those old, negative thoughts, do it in a kind and empowering way. If you cast them off in a negative way, you're still participating in a negative way.

When some old, negative thoughts come up, just say to yourself, "That's an interesting thought, and I choose not to have it anymore. What I choose to think about is this . . ." and then add a new, empowering thought to the end of the sentence.

Stay focused on your vision for your future, and don't let anyone or anything distract your focus.

Make the commitment to play full out and follow through to the end. Lock your focus into achieving your goal no matter what is happening around you and no matter what people are telling you. Act as if the finish line is actually five or ten meters farther than it really is.

Let me explain.

Have you ever seen a race in which the leader, just before breaking the ribbon at the finish line, pushes his chest out as if striking a pose for the cover of the sports magazines? When you're running with your chest out and arms spread wide, are you running at your fastest speed? Probably not! That's the posture of someone slowing down in anticipation of crossing the finish line. Is that what a real gold medalist would do? If he's hungry he doesn't.

> "All that a man achieves and all that he fails to achieve is the direct result of his own thoughts."
>
> JAMES ALLEN

If you watch the gold medalists, you'll see they keep running at full speed long past the actual finish line. Why would they do that? It's to ensure they cross the line at full momentum because they know that the difference between gold and fourth place can be as little as 1/1000th of a second, and they may lose the gold if they don't play full out beyond the finish line.

As you know, Nat and Kerri won their gold medals at the Sydney 2000 Olympics. At the medal ceremony, the girls were standing on the top podium, about to receive their gold medals. The Australian flag was being raised on the center flagpole, and the Australian national anthem was being played. Natalie bent down so the presenter could put the gold medal around her neck, and as she stood up and looked around the stadium, I saw a unique look flit across her face. It wasn't just the look of extreme joy you might imagine. It occurred to me, as I watched, that it was a look of familiarity, as if this wasn't a brand new experience for Natalie after all.

Moments after the ceremony was over, I asked Nat about it. She said, "As I was getting my gold medal and I looked around the stadium, it was just like I remembered it!"

Think about this for a moment. How could Natalie remember a moment she had never lived before? The answer is because she had lived it over and over again in her visionary winner thoughts. Natalie and Kerri rehearsed the experience of standing on the podium receiving their gold medals hundreds of times, over and over, for the two and a half years leading up to the Olympics. They had done it so many times that their subconscious minds didn't know the difference between real and imagined. Remember that when you think like a gold medalist and you act like a gold medalist, the result is a gold medal. When you decide to make your life golden, you now know how to do that.

Remember:

Focusing on the past creates pain!

Thinking about the present creates more of the same!

Thinking empowering thoughts about the future creates the gain!

Be a Visionary

Remember at the beginning of this chapter when I asked if you would be excited if you were able to see your future and know you were going to get to live the life you've always wanted to live? You would be immensely excited, right? That's why being a visionary is so important in creating the life you desire. It's that *excitement* about your future that activates your brain to move toward achieving it. When you really *see* in your mind what it is you want and you get *excited* about experiencing it, your mind automatically gets you to take the actions to create it!

To be a visionary doesn't mean you only look toward the distant future. A true visionary is someone who starts every day by looking forward to what he or she is going to achieve that day, as well as in the distant future. Visionaries focus on the future while experiencing the now. When you start to look forward to what you're going to achieve each day, you'll start to achieve more every day.

What are you willing to give, or give up, in order to have everything you want in life?

Are you willing to become aware of the negative disempowering thoughts you have throughout the day?

Are you willing to take responsibility every time you have a negative, disempowering thought and transform it into a new, positive, empowering one?

To have the holistically successful life you desire, it's critical that you do both these things. The more you find yourself having disempowering thoughts and make the effort to change them into empowering ones, the more habitual it will become, until your normal way of being is to think only empowering thoughts.

Remember that the more you think empowering thoughts, the more power goes to the source (you), the brighter your light becomes, and the more life is attracted to it. You get the future you empower.

Examine Your Thoughts

Make sure you're consciously both planting positive seeds (empowering thoughts) and pulling negative weeds (disempowering thoughts).

Both are necessary in order for you to move your life to next level. The more you check in with your thoughts to see if they are empowering or disempowering, the more you have the opportunity to weed out the negative ones and replace them with positive thoughts.

A powerful strategy for making sure you are planting positive thoughts in your mind on a consistent basis is the use of daily positive affirmations. An affirmation is simply a formal and solemn declaration of what you want to believe and feel. It's an effective way of placing the type of thoughts in your head that lead to the actions that produce the results you want.

If you can't find an affirmation to express what you really want to say for yourself, then write your own! Make sure you read your affirmations out loud to yourself every day so you can be sure your mind is filled with the thoughts that will empower you to reach your true potential in life. Keep in mind, however, that just reading them every day isn't enough. It's *how* you read them that counts. Remember that your brain takes its cue from your emotions when it determines what to do with new thoughts. It moves you toward things you feel positive about, because it knows they will bring you pleasure. And it moves you away from negative things, because it determines they will cause pain. So if you read your daily affirmations with a dull voice or low emotional energy, the exercise can turn out to be counterproductive for you, as your brain may read your low energy as negative or painful and push you away from what you really want. To make sure there's absolutely no confusion in your brain as to which emotion you attach to your affirmations, read them with passion and excitement every single time. Read them as if you truly believe that reading them is going to create the life and grand dreams goals you desire, because when you read them that way, it will.

And remember that doing this once in a while isn't enough. You can't go to the gym once and expect to be in shape for the rest of your life. It has to be consistent. So stay conscious of it, hold yourself to a higher standard, follow through, and do it. The rewards are truly worth it.

Take this first step and start putting your visionary skill into practice. Think about it. If you're not going to take the action and do step one, why would you think you're ever going to do step two?

The Story of Farmer John

Farmer John was looking through his barn to see what seeds he still had left for this year's crop. What he planted last year hadn't produced a successful crop and hadn't had much appeal at the market. It had been this way for Farmer John for the last few years. He seemed to be stuck in a rut.

As he was looking through his barn, he found a bag of "X" seeds. "X" was what he had planted last year, and all the years before. Farmer John told himself that *this* year was going to be different. He dreamed of having a successful crop this year. He fantasized about all the wonderful things he was going to experience once he sold his crop at the market and became wealthy in return. It had been the same every year. Every year Farmer John has had these dreams, and every year he ends up putting them on the back burner because his crop of "X" hasn't sold well enough.

Farmer John picked up his bag of "X" seeds and walked out onto his field. He once again dreamed about how things were going to be different. He took one "X" seed from his bag and planted it in his field. He watered that "X" seed and nurtured it, and it wasn't long before he had grown an "X." It looked just like the "X" he had grown last year. He wasn't very happy about this because it reminded him of how poorly it had done at the market last year, and how once again he has had to put his dreams on hold as a result.

As Farmer John stood there, he once again dreamed about how things could be if only his circumstances and conditions were different. He reached into his bag of "X" seeds and planted a whole crop of them. Then he watered and nurtured those "X" seeds until they grew big and strong. He harvested his crop of "X" and brought it to market, only to be disappointed once again. What he had grown was more of the same thing. He had planted the same type of seeds, so he had just gotten more of the same.

Seeing how disappointed and down Farmer John was feeling, Farmer Bob asked what was troubling him.

"When I planted one 'X' seed, I got one 'X' to grow, and when I planted lots of 'X' seeds, I just got a lot more of the same thing," said

Farmer John. "And I didn't want a whole lot more of the same thing I had before."

Farmer Bob understood Farmer John's challenge and told him that he too used to have a lot of "X" growing in his fields and hadn't been happy about it either.

"That's when I decided to get some 'Y' seeds and plant them," Farmer Bob revealed. "It turned my life around."

"Y" is a much better crop. The wealth it created for Farmer Bob gave him the freedom to realize his dreams and have the wonderful experiences he had always wanted.

Farmer John heard Farmer Bob's story and listened to his advice. He went back to his farm and planted a crop of "X" seeds. That next harvest season, Farmer John was once again disappointed because he still was growing the same thing. Farmer Bob had tried to help him, but Farmer John was too lazy to take the new action and start planting some new seeds.

In this story "X" represents the thoughts you're currently having. Remember: everything starts with a thought, and thoughts lead to actions, and actions create results. So the moral of the story is if you want to stop producing the same old results, you're going to have to start with some new thoughts, right now. Not next year, or the year after. Now!

You can't look at your current situation and think those same old thoughts are going to help you achieve something different in your life. You can't look at your current bank balance and think it's going to help you create the wealth you want. You're going to have to start, right now, thinking about what it is you want in life. Focus your thoughts on where you are going, not on where you have been, or on where you are. Be a visionary. As Farmer Bob would say, "When you stop planting 'X' (your old thoughts) and start planting 'Y' (your new thoughts), your dreams will start growing into reality. Believe me, I know. Look at my life

> "We are what we think. All that we are arises from our thoughts. With our thoughts, we make our world."
>
> BUDDHA

and what I have produced! I know many other successful farmers who are reaping rewards from planting 'Y' too." It comes down to this: you can't grow wealth when a scarcity mentality is occupying your mind, can you?

Are you a Farmer John who is going to read this and go back to your old ways, or are you making the decision to be Farmer Bob and start planting your new crop? Remember: what you plant determines what you will grow!

12

The Three P's of Power

Imagine My Alarm

I've come across so many people in the world who complain about how bad their childhood was and about what terrible parents they had. If you haven't personally met anyone who blames their parents for their problems, all you have to do is turn on daytime TV and you'll see an abundance of people on talk shows using their painful childhood stories to justify their miserable lives today.

My parents, I discovered, condemned me to death from the moment I was born, and the story gets even more shocking. As it turns out, they were actually arranging my death before I was born. So if you think your parents were cruel to you, top that! My parents were setting me up to die. From the moment I was born, my death sentence was signed. To make matters worse, I didn't find this out until later in my life. The whole time I was growing up, I thought my parents loved me and wanted me to live. Instead they had given me an incurable disease, one that would eventually kill me.

When I confided in people about how my parents condemned me to death, they said, "That's terrible!"

I said, "Maybe."

Imagine the thoughts that would run through your head if you found out your parents had willingly given you a fatal disease guaranteed to take your life. What would you do if you found this out? (How would you respond?)

Do you want to know what I did?

I thought about it for a while and then decided that since my time was so limited, I was going to really live and make every moment count. The reason I say it was worse that I found out later in life is because if I had found out sooner that I was really going to die, I would have made the decision to really live sooner.

Death is forever, so if you want to live, now would be a very good time to do it, right?

The fact is that when you were born, your parents condemned you to death just as mine did me. And if you're a parent yourself, then you did the same to your children. You signed their death sentence.

The moment you're born is the exact same moment you begin your journey toward death. You can't have one without the other. There is no life without death. The same two people who started your life also started the clock ticking away the seconds of your life, and at some point time will run out for you.

For me, the best gift I was ever given was the realization that I am going to die one day, because it got me to stop procrastinating about the things I wanted to do in my life. It was the same time that I started living the dream.

Once again, I have Mike, Geoff, Don, Gadi, and Jojo to thank for that realization. Before Mike died in my arms, I thought I was invincible and would live forever. Then, as I felt the life going out of his twenty-nine-year-old body, I was forced to see that life is fragile and, without any doubt, is going to be over some day for all of us. No matter when that moment of death comes, life still won't have been long enough. There will inevitably be many things you wanted to do that you don't get to.

It was that thought that got me to wake up and start living my life by a different standard. I realized there isn't anything in life frightening enough to stop me from doing what I truly want to do. Life is a race in which your outcome is to experience as much as you can before time runs out.

I know firsthand that after this life we all go somewhere else that is beautiful and wonderful, yet I also know the person I am right now, and the person you are right now, is a one-time thing. We will only be in this *form* for this one trip, so while you're here, make each moment a valuable, fulfilling moment. Make each one count by filling your life with as many incredible experiences as you can. Instead of living your today as if it's just another day in your life, live it as if your entire life is in this day.

While we are only in this form for this one trip, there is a carryover. Whatever you plant in this life becomes the seedlings that will start your next journey, and since you don't know when this one will end, make sure you're always planting the seeds you want to start your next life with. When you live this life to the absolute fullest, just imagine how the next one is going to begin as a result, and the possibilities of where it can go from there. Now that thought excites me!

By following a life plan in which I'm planting seeds for both this life *and* the next, I get to have an incredible life this time *and* I'm guaranteed the next one will be even better. How awesome is that?

Yet just for a moment, let's look at the worst-case scenario. Let's say I'm completely wrong about all of this. Let's say you're living your life to the absolute fullest and by some outside chance there is nowhere to go after this life. Even if there is no life after this one, as long as you live this one to the fullest, you are still guaranteed to have the best life you can have. Either way you win.

Yet if there is a life after this one, and you don't go for it this time, there's not much of a chance for you next time either. Think about it. If you knew that you could live your dream life during this lifetime and you still didn't go for it, why would you think you'll do it any differently in the next one?

Out, or On Your Feet?

My mom and dad got divorced when I was three. For most of my childhood, I lived with my mother and stepfather. When I turned twelve, I moved in with my dad. He ran a pretty strict ship. He enforced a curfew for me to be home every night by midnight. I followed his rules until I turned eighteen. I felt that since I was legally an adult and had graduated from high school, those rules shouldn't apply to me anymore. Night after night, for a few weeks in a row, I got home past my dad's curfew.

One bitterly cold December night, I strolled home around 2 A.M. after dancing the night away at a club with my girlfriend. As quietly as I could, I slipped my key into the outer screen door dad always kept locked. Even though we lived in a very safe neighborhood, my dad always insisted that both the inner door and the outer screen door be locked when we went out.

I hadn't had much to drink, but it felt like I had because I couldn't get the key to unlock the door. I tried every which way, finally taking the key out to see if I was using the correct one. Considering I only had three keys on my key ring, one of which was my car key, there weren't many to choose from. So I tried once more with what I thought was the right key. That's when the outside light came on and I thought, "Oh no, I've woken up my dad by fumbling with my keys in the lock."

Sure enough, my dad opened the inner door of the house and looked at me through the screen door with a familiar "I'm not happy" look on his face.

"While you were out, I changed the locks on all the doors, including the garage door," he said.

I figured staying up so late must have been affecting my thinking, because I just couldn't understand what my dad was really saying.

"Dad, why would you change all the locks? Can you let me in? It's freezing out here!"

"Do you know what time it is?" asked Dad, still not opening the door.

"Yes, sir. It's 2 A.M."

"And what time are you supposed to be home?"

"Midnight. I'm sorry. Time just got away from me. Dad, I still don't understand why you changed the locks. Can you let me in now? It really is freezing out here!"

My dad explained that he changed all the locks at midnight

when, once again, I wasn't home on time. I couldn't believe he had gone to all that trouble just to teach me a lesson!

"Okay, I've learned my lesson, Dad. Can I come in now before I freeze to death?"

He just stood there looking at me through the screen door. Then, choosing his words carefully, he delivered his message in one clear and concise sentence, "You don't live here anymore!"

"What do you mean?" I asked.

He didn't budge. He just stood there looking at me and said, "You knew the rules."

"Dad, we live in Chicago! It's the middle of winter and there's snow on the ground. I have no money and nowhere to stay. What am I supposed to do?"

He delivered his next line with surgical precision. "You should have thought about that before you decided to break the rules, again!"

Without saying another word, he closed the door, turned off the light, and walked upstairs. I stood there shivering in the driveway. I knew he would wait a few minutes so I would feel the impact of his lesson and then come back and let me in.

Half an hour later, I was still shivering in the driveway. I was wrong. He wasn't coming back to let me in.

Where was I to go? My girlfriend followed strict moral rules, so I knew I wouldn't be allowed to stay at her place, either. I didn't even own a car I could sleep in, so until I could get enough money saved from my job to afford a place to stay, I spent the next two weeks sleeping in a field, under a pine tree, wrapped in a sleeping bag and an old army blanket.

When people found out about what my dad did that night, they were mad and upset. They said, "That's awful that your dad did that to you!"

I said, "Maybe."

How would you respond if that happened to you?

How would Love respond?

It took me a few weeks to figure it out, and, when I did, I decided to look at this situation as one of the most powerful and loving things that my father ever did for me.

My father wasn't kicking me out of the house to be mean or hateful. He did it to teach me responsibility. He was showing me through his actions that no matter where you go in life, there are going to be rules that have to be obeyed. When you don't obey those rules, there are consequences you will have to deal with.

Once I let go of my anger, I could see that it hadn't been easy for my father to do what he had done. He loved me so much, but he was frustrated because he couldn't figure a way to get me to learn some of the life lessons he thought I needed to know. He knew that if I didn't change my ways, I would be on a collision course with disaster. His last option was to deliver some tough love to me.

That's what happened that night. The way I look at it, my father didn't kick me out; instead he kicked me onto my feet.

With that one action, my father taught me that if you want to survive in the world, you have to take responsibility for your life. If you don't want to follow other people's rules, then you have to make a life for yourself, and even if you do that, there are still going to be some rules you will have to obey. If you don't follow those rules, you'll have to pay the price for those actions.

The truth is that if my father hadn't pushed me out of the nest, I may never have learned to fly on my own. There's a good chance I would have procrastinated and stayed where I was for a lot longer.

But because I did get the boot, it was only a few months later that I decided to leave for Hollywood to follow my dream to be in movies.

I still remember seeing the tears well up in my dad's eyes as I got in my car to make the drive across the country to California. He was torn between knowing what he had to do and worrying if he made the right decision.

I hugged him and told him I was going to make him proud.

By the time I arrived in Hollywood, found an apartment, and paid the first month's rent, I had $200 left to last me until I got my first acting job. It didn't happen as quickly as I expected. It took me three years to get my first role.

The first six months were super tough. I ate only two meals a week. One meal consisted of half a can of soup and half a box of instant macaroni and cheese. Later in the week, when I just couldn't take anymore because I was getting shaky and weak, I would eat the second half of the soup and the rest of the macaroni and cheese. I think the cockroaches infesting my apartment actually ate better than I did.

The neighborhood I lived in was obviously not the best either. One morning, after working all night as an armed security guard for five dollars an hour, I was greeted at the door to my apartment building by five gang members who were determined not to let me in. I had to pull my gun out of my holster to convince them differently. The same week, the security company I was working for refused to pay me the money they owed me.

There I was, 2,500 miles away from my family and what used to be my home, with no friends, no TV, and, most of the time, no money. To top it off, my car caught fire, and I had to abandon it right there on the side of the road. So then I was car-less too.

When I talked to people back home about my mishaps, they said, "Man, you sure are having some bad luck!"

I thought, "Maybe."

The next couple of years in Hollywood weren't much different from the first. I was working every odd job to keep myself fed and to try to keep a roof over my head. For two weeks I worked in the worst neighborhoods in Los Angeles repossessing cars from people who hadn't made their payments, until a guy who worked for the company was shot fourteen times by the owner of the car he was trying to repossess. After hearing about that, I didn't even collect my final check. I never went back.

Another job I got was working as a plainclothes security agent arresting shoplifters at a large department store. In my eight months on the job, more than sixty people behaved violently toward me as they were being arrested. Some pulled knives on me, and, in one case, a woman pulled a gun.

One day I was chasing a suspect through the store, and, as I went to tackle him, we both went headfirst through a plate glass display case. Every day as I started work, I wondered if this would be the day my luck would run out and I would pay the price with my life. Everyone who heard what I was going through remarked on what a terrible job I had.

I responded, "Maybe."

One of the jobs I really enjoyed was working at a health club. While I was there, I learned about physical fitness and how to reshape a person's life by helping them shape their body through exercise. Before long I was taking on clients. I always had a curious fascination with human nature and why certain people get better results than others and what it is that gets them motivated to take the actions that get those results. Combining the peak performance strategies I was learning with what I was taught about physical fitness, I quickly learned how to help people get massive results with their workouts and eating regimes.

One of the people I met and trained in the gym was John Herzfeld. John is an award-winning movie director who, at the time, had just won an Emmy for a television movie he had written and directed.

Every morning at 6 A.M., I would meet John at his house so we could go to the gym to train. John took a personal interest in helping me become a better person. He insisted I expand my vocabulary because he always said that having a good, strong vocabulary builds good, strong character. Every morning when I picked him up to go to the gym, he would give me two new words that I would have to look up in a big dictionary he had.

John instructed me to carry a pocket-sized notebook at all times to write down these two new words with correct spelling, their definitions, and an example of how to use each in a sentence. Later in the day, he would call me from his office and test me on a word in my notebook, saying, "Spell it and use it in a sentence." If I got it right, he would say, "Good job," and then hang up. If I didn't get it right, he would let me know it.

He also forced me to start reading books. John is an avid reader himself and said that reading makes you wise. Before John came into my life, I had never read a book and had no real interest in making myself an educated person. I didn't think I needed it to become an actor. I couldn't have been more wrong.

The first book he made me read was *Think and Grow Rich* by Napoleon Hill. It changed my life more than any other book I have ever read. John would call me from the studio to ask me what page I was up to and what was happening in that section of the book. Sometimes I would make something up to hide the fact that I hadn't been doing my reading for a couple of days. He always knew when I wasn't being truthful. John would get mad and blow his top. He would yell at me over the phone, accusing me of being a liar. And every time he did, he was right.

As I look back over my life, no one has been more influential in getting me to evolve than John Herzfeld. He groomed me to be successful. He helped shape me into who I am today, which, in turn, has produced the incredible life I now enjoy.

You might say I was very lucky to meet John at the gym that day. I say, "Maybe."

For the next few years, I worked for John as his assistant. He had me on call twenty-four hours a day, seven days a week, and he had a tendency to work me seven days a week and all hours of the day and night too! I was his go-to guy. Anything he needed I did. I'd walk his dogs three times a day. I'd pick up his dry cleaning, clean graffiti from his fence, and do any number of other odd jobs. For all this he paid me only thirty-five dollars a week.

I was making ten trips a day back and forth from his house to his typist to get his new script pages typed up, and that alone cost more than thirty-five dollars for gas in my motorcycle.

I worked so many hours for John each day that I didn't have time to take on another job to earn extra money, so there were periods of six months at a time when I was actually living in my car.

Once John had me stay on guard in my car all night long in front of his house, every night for an entire month so that I might catch whoever was spray painting and vandalizing his wooden fence. I even spent Christmas Eve and New Year's Eve nights watching John's.

Many of the people who knew John and knew how much he was paying me were quite angry about his behavior. They constantly advised me to ask for more money or quit. They used to say, "Don't you see how John is using you and taking advantage of your good nature?"

I said, "Maybe."

How would you have reacted if you had been in my shoes?

How would Love respond?

One day John called me. The call was a gift that changed my life because it was proof that dreams really do come true when you decide to make them come true. He cast me in a movie that he had written and was about to direct called *Two of a Kind*, starring John Travolta and Olivia Newton-John.

I had to wait a few months until work began, so I had to find another job to survive in the meantime. Through a friend I got a construction job building a soundstage at Laird International Studios, where *Gone with the Wind*, the original *Batman* series, and many other well-known motion pictures and TV shows were made.

While working on the construction crew, I got to meet a lot of famous stars, including Ann-Margret and Treat Williams, who were filming the remake of *A Streetcar Named Desire*. How lucky was I to land a job where I got to work around and meet all those famous people?

Well, maybe.

Actually, I found it very frustrating. Here I was, wanting to work as an actor, and instead I was doing construction while having to be around people who were actually working as actors. And the last thing anyone there really wants to hear from you is that you're another wannabe actor just like everyone else in Los Angeles.

Every day I would come home from work filthy, covered in dirt and grime, and exhausted from physical work I didn't enjoy doing, and every day I was getting more and more frustrated. When friends saw how tired and frustrated I was considering my small salary, they would say, "Get out of there! It's a terrible job."

I'd say, "Maybe."

One day I was in a bad mood from the moment I walked onto the job site. By lunchtime I was already covered from head to toe in cement dust from walls we were demolishing with sledgehammers. I walked into the studio commissary, bought my lunch, and went to find a table as far away from everyone as I could get. I was feeling so aggravated that I just wanted to be left alone as I ate my lunch. Not more than two minutes later, two men walked into the commissary and looked around as if they were looking for someone before walking directly over to my table. Being in the anti-social mood I was in,

I did my best to pretend not to notice them walking toward me so they wouldn't try to talk to me. It didn't work. These two men I didn't know and had never seen before went out of their way to walk over to me and start a conversation. Why I don't know!

One of them was doing most of the talking—not about anything in particular, just small talk—asking me my name and where I was from. Because of my mood, I was giving him short answers so he'd get the hint I wasn't in the mood to chat. That didn't work either. They both kept asking me questions about my life. The second man asked me what I was working on. I told him we were tearing down an old soundstage and building a brand new one in its place, which I thought must have been quite obvious from my filthy appearance.

He said, "Kurek, I know you said you're doing construction, but you look more like you should be an actor."

When I answered him, my frustration really kicked in. "Thank you very much. Like everyone else in this town, I'm an actor who's doing something else to pay my bills."

Then I went on to say, "I do have a small part in a film coming up in a couple of months starring John Travolta and Olivia Newton-John."

The more talkative of the two men spoke up. "When you see John Travolta, please say hi to him for us. We're good friends with him."

He pointed to the other man and said, "He directed *Urban Cowboy*." Suddenly I knew exactly who the second man standing in front of me was: James Bridges.

James Bridges is a director who has made many big movies, including *The China Syndrome*, starring Jack Lemmon, Jane Fonda, and Michael Douglas.

All of a sudden I wasn't feeling so anti-social anymore. Instead I was feeling a little stupid and embarrassed for not recognizing him.

I asked the first man, "Sir, aren't you an actor? I know I've seen you somewhere before."

"I used to be, but now I'm a producer," he replied.

"When you were an actor, what did you work on that I may have seen?"

He said, "I used to play Jimmy Olson on the original *Superman* TV series."

My jaw dropped open. Of course! He was Jack Larson. If I hadn't been in such a mood I would have instantly recognized him too. He looked exactly the way he had when he was on the series.

I apologized to them both for the mood I was in and explained to them why I was feeling so frustrated. They said they understood and that they had enjoyed our twenty-minute chat and had to go back to work.

Just as they were about to leave, Jack Larson stopped and turned back to look me in the eye. He said, "Kurek, you and John Travolta should become good friends. You'll make great friends with each other, and I think both of you could use a friend."

I thought to myself, "Great. What am I supposed to do? Just walk up to John Travolta and tell him we're supposed to be great friends because Jack Larson said so?"

Jack continued, "Remember what I said, and please make sure you say hi to John for us when you see him." He turned around, and they walked away.

You might think that as an actor, I had a lucky break meeting Jack Larson, a successful producer, and James Bridges, a famous director.

Maybe.

The following week I went down to the set where they were filming *Two of a Kind* to visit John Herzfeld. I stood in the background waiting for them to begin filming a scene, and in walked John Travolta. Instantly the room lit up with his energy.

For the next two hours, I watched them film the scene they were working on, and then they broke for lunch. John Travolta and Olivia were on their way to their dressing rooms, and I got up my courage to approach them.

I introduced myself to John and then passed on the message from Jim Bridges and Jack Larson, telling him they said hi and sent their best to him. To my surprise, he was excited to receive their message and asked me how I knew them and where I had met them.

As he walked away to get his lunch, I stood there, numb, thinking about how cool it was that I just had a three-minute conversation with him. I really felt like pinching myself to make sure I wasn't dreaming it all.

The next couple of months passed, and the time finally came for me to get to work on the movie. I thought the day would never arrive!

I played a police officer with only one line of dialogue near the end of the movie. My character tries to stop John Travolta from jumping onto a fire escape in a bid to save Olivia from the bad guy. I didn't care that I only had one line because I got to work for two and a half weeks with John Travolta and Olivia Newton-John while filming the scene.

John has an awesome sense of humor. He's a very funny guy who always makes everyone laugh. And being the crazy guy I am, John and I really hit it off and got along great with each other. After only a couple of days, we were eating lunch together, hanging out and spending a lot of time talking about our lives. We noticed similarities, and it wasn't long before we became friends.

One day we were talking about getting together later in the week for dinner. John asked me where I lived so he could pick me up. Whenever I tell this story to people, they always say, "Man, you're so lucky you got to go to dinner with John Travolta."

I say, "Maybe."

When John asked me where I lived, I had to think about it for a moment before I answered. Finally I answered, "I live in Hollywood, Studio City, Burbank, at the beach."

Confused by my answer, he asked, "Kurek, how do you live in all of those different places?"

I smiled at him and said, "I live in the Hotel Cadillac."

"I don't understand. What and where is the Hotel Cadillac?" he asked.

"When you pick me up, you'll understand," I explained.

I told him the street where the Hotel Cadillac was situated, and we decided on 7 P.M. the following day for him to pick me up for dinner.

The next day, at the appointed time, I was standing on the curb when his stretch limo came round the corner and pulled up beside me. John got out of the back of the limo, looking puzzled.

"Kurek, where's this Hotel Cadillac?"

"I'm leaning on it. Welcome to my home. It's a 1972 Cadillac Coupe DeVille."

John was still confused.

"I live in my car. It used to be my mobile home, but it broke down, and so this is where I live." John was in total disbelief, so I asked him if he would like a tour of my home. He said he would. I opened the trunk. "This is my wardrobe," I said, and showed him the separate piles of my clothes, all clean and neatly folded. John asked if he could sit in my car. I opened the back door, and he climbed in. I continued the tour. I pointed to the front seat and told him it was my entertainment room. The windshield was my big-screen TV. I also explained to him that he was sitting in my office that at night converted into my bedroom. He saw all my blankets folded neatly on the seat, and just sat there for awhile. That's when I noticed tears welling up in his eyes.

"What's wrong?" I asked.

John said he had never personally known anyone who was homeless and living in his car. "It's terrible that you have to live this way," he said.

I said, "Maybe."

"Why do you have such a great attitude about this?" John asked me.

"John, at least I have a car to sleep in," I began, "and it's a Cadillac, so it's nice and roomy. I could be living next to my car, sleeping in the gutter. Now that would be a drag."

"You're in great shape, and you're always clean shaven," John observed. "Where do you shower?"

"I go to the gym every day."

"If your car's broken down, how do you get to the studio every day?"

"I bicycle there."

John was still very concerned about me being homeless and living in my car. "Kurek, I don't feel comfortable with you living like this. I have a big house in the Hollywood Hills. You can stay with me for a while until you get on your feet. As a matter of fact, I insist that you do."

Now how cool is that? John Travolta invited me to live in his house! I must be the luckiest guy on the planet, right?

Maybe.

I thought about John's offer for a moment and decided against it. Later I'll tell you why I made that decision.

———

As the years in Hollywood went by, I started landing more and more acting jobs, until finally, in 1989, I struck gold. As I told you in the first chapter of this book, I was cast in two big-budget movies, both of them featuring big stars I always wanted to work with.

Other actor friends of mine told me I was the luckiest guy they knew.

I replied, "Maybe?"

When I landed in the Philippines to discover a bunch of my friends were working on the same film, including one of my best friends, Mike Graham, was I lucky?

Maybe?

As you know, on the movie set in the Philippines, a helicopter crashed while filming, and I lost five of my friends, including Mike Graham.

So, what do you think? Was I lucky to land that role?

Maybe.

So many people have remarked what a terrible experience the helicopter crash must have been.

Maybe.

I know you're thinking, "Kurek, how can you possibly think that what you went through wasn't a terrible experience?"

And if you're wondering why I keep saying "maybe" after each of my stories, it's because I have been demonstrating the first "P" of power—perception.

The First "P" of Power Is Perception

The helicopter crash, my father changing the locks, living in the Hotel Cadillac, John Travolta's offer to stay at his house, and all the other stories I've described to you were just events, and that's all they were—events. Events by themselves don't have any real meaning. We give the events of our lives their meanings through our perception of the events.

So how can any event be good or bad, when it all depends on how you look at it? Actually, there isn't anything that is good or bad. It's only your perception that makes it so. You might see an event as bad on the day it happened and then, looking back later, see it as good. It's still the same event. What makes it good or bad is the way you choose to see it.

Even though two people can experience the same event at the same time, it doesn't mean that they will have the same interpretation of that event. One person might look at it one way and the other might look at it another way. Have you ever had a situation in your life in which you saw something one way and the other person you were with saw it another? How can that be when it was the same event?

When you think about it, you'll realize that one person's reality is not the same as another person's reality. In fact, there's no such thing as *reality*! Your reality is only your interpretation of an event. Someone else's brain interprets the same event in a different way. Reality is what you make it to be. When you change the way you look at the world, the world you're looking at will change. It's as simple as that.

See how powerful this is! This is why perception is the first "P" of power. It's your perception that determines how you see and respond to the world, and you have the power to change your perception at any time. When you choose your perception of an event, you choose how you experience that event and how to respond to it. And how you respond to it creates your result. That's the power of perception.

Events have no real meaning. It's the way you perceive the event that gives it a meaning. And it's what that event means to you that will determine how you decide to react to it.

In chapter 8, we talked about the Law of Polarity, which states that everything in the universe has two opposite sides. Where there's a top there has to be a bottom. You can't have an inside without there being an outside. Where there's a left there has to be a right. Every problem has to have a solution. And for every event that happens in your life, there is always more than one side to it.

When you look at the events in your life, which do you pay the most attention to, the "good side" or the "bad side"? The positive or the negative? The empowering or the disempowering? You can use your power of perception to choose which side of an event you want to see. The choice is yours, but if you don't make it, there's a good chance you'll get handed perceptions by someone else, and you will be stuck with the consequences of those perceptions.

For example, if you watch the news or read the newspaper, you are being forced to see someone else's negative perceptions of the world. The way the news is presented alters our perception of the world and the people in it. And it's our perception of the world and the people in it that determines how we think and feel about the world and the people in it. And it's how we think and feel that determines how we react. The news is filled with average people doing average things. It shows average people focusing on their problems or on other people's problems and then shows how they react to those problems. This creates even more problems for more people, which they, in turn, react to! The interesting thing is that the people who are usually in the news are the same people who usually watch the news. Now there's something to think about! The challenge with watching the news is that what you're seeing is not the whole story. It's only one side of the story, and it's usually the negative side. Rarely do you see good stories about good people doing good things. Why? Because reporting on the good stories don't get good ratings. There's no drama glue in the good stories.

When you consistently see the negative versions of stories being presented, you start to believe they're the whole story. And because you think they're the whole story, you start to form an opinion about what they mean. Think about it. After watching news stories about people being robbed, raped, and murdered, then seeing other stories about people slaughtering thousands of other people during wartime, do you think there's a chance it might have some influence on the way you view the condition of the world? After seeing a lot of those stories, do you think you might think the world is in bad shape and only getting worse, and that people are becoming more insensitive and uncaring? Maybe you've seen stories about some-place in the world where our troops are involved in a war, and because of that, you form the opinion that the people on the other side are all the "bad guys."

Can you see that these are nothing more than interpretations? They're only your perceptions. And just because you think one way or another doesn't make either one of them so, yet it will determine how you react, and it's that reaction that produces the results you're getting.

Do you remember in chapter 8 when I was talking about Jesus and Buddha, and I said they were empowering about everything? Well, this is how they achieved that: they choose an empowering perception about everything that happened in their lives. No matter what happened, they always looked for something positive about it, and because they looked for it, they found it.

The truth is that we can't go back and change what happened in the past. What we can change is the way that we look back at what happened. Always choose the perception that makes you feel the best and brings you the most peace. When you do that, you are being empowering about everything, and that's what will surround you with the light that attracts everything you want.

You may wonder how there can be any perception of the heli-copter crash I went through that could get me to feel good about it and bring me any peace. The truth is that it was changing my per-ception about the crash that initiated the biggest transformation I experienced during that period of my life. I changed my perception by asking myself one small and powerful question: "What's great about this?"

The first answer I got back was, "Nothing!"

Not content with that answer, I decided to ask again, "If there is something great about what happened, what is it?"

My answer: "I don't know!"

Certainly not happy with that answer, I asked again. I figured I would keep asking the question until I got an answer I was happy with.

So then I asked, "If you pretended that there was something great about what happened, what would it be?"

That's when the magic started to happen. I actually got a positive answer to my questions.

I instantly felt grateful when I realized that at least I had five friends to lose. How lucky am I that I got to know those five outstanding human beings while they were here on the planet? There are so many people who will never get to do that. I started to think about all the lonely people out there who don't have anyone they can call their friend and yet I had five great ones. And they'll never really be lost because they are always in my heart. I also felt pretty special knowing that when I die, I will have an awesome welcoming party waiting for me.

> *"Ask, and you will receive."*
>
> MATTHEW 7:7

That's when another magical thought crossed my mind. I realized how grateful I was for being there during the crash because I know, without a doubt, that all the care and attention that could have been given to the guys during the time of the accident was given to them, because I was one of the people giving it.

I also felt so happy that my best friend, Mike, died in my arms and not in the arms of a stranger. Having that thought brought me a lot of peace.

The more times I asked the question, "What's great about this?" the more empowering answers I received. And with each answer I got, the better I started to feel. *A shift in perception will trigger a shift in personal reality*. That's the power of choosing a positive perception. When you feel better, you act better, and better actions always produce better results.

Anything that happens, anything anyone does, and even the reason you think they're doing it is all based on your perception. The world that you see and experience is all based on your perception. When you change the way you look at people, the people you look at will change. When you change the way you look at situations, the situations you're looking at will change. And when you change the way you look at the world, the world you're looking at will change.

Some other great positive perception questions to use are:

> "How can I look at this situation in an empowering way?"
> "How am I going to grow from this experience?"
> "What am I grateful for?"
> "What is the blessing in this?"
> "How would Love respond in this situation?"

By asking these types of questions, you change what you're focusing your thoughts on. And remember: it's those thoughts that determine how you'll act, which produces what you get. The Law of Attraction states that whatever you focus your attention on, you attract to you. So if you're feeling upset, it means that you're only looking at one side of the coin. Look for the other side, and you'll find it.

The best part about this is it works on everything, including all the things you've been perceiving as "the real big stuff."

What's the difference between a terrorist attack and a heart attack? These days it seems the news is filled with people angry that people are dying as a result of terrorism. The truth is that there are a lot more people dying from heart attacks than there are from terrorist attacks, but you don't see many people upset about that. It's just accepted and expected that millions of people will die as a result of not taking care of themselves.

Personally, I'd rather die from something exciting, like being eaten by a shark or having my parachute not open, instead of rotting away in a hospital bed from a disease I got from not taking care of myself. At least if you die doing something exciting, you'll have a great story to tell in heaven, right?

Yet so many people still ask me how it's possible to have an empowering perception of something as terrible as a terrorist attack.

They ask, "How can you possibly see anything good in an event like the one that happened on September 11, 2001, when two planes were intentionally crashed into the World Trade Center in New York City, a third plane was intentionally crashed into the Pentagon building in Washington, D.C., and a fourth plane crashed into a field in Pennsylvania while civilian passengers were fighting with terrorists to regain control of the hijacked plane? Approximately 3,000 people died in these attacks."

When it happened, people were angry and wanted revenge, while others were scared. People were talking for years afterward about how bad the event was.

Still I thought, "Maybe."

It's true that the people who did this cowardly act took the lives of a lot of very good, decent people. I have a lot of compassion for the 3,000 people who lost their lives and for all the families and friends who lost someone.

> *"If you want to change the world, change your attitude! "*
>
> DEEPAK CHOPRA

The fact is that we cannot change what happened. What's done is done. What we can do is change what the event means to us. We can take responsibility for our own lives. Remember that responsibility means the ability to choose how you respond. When we want to, we can choose to not let the terrorists win by looking at the event in a different way. We can even choose a way of looking at it that helps us live our lives even better than we did before. We can choose to have what happened mean something to us that will help us improve our lives.

I choose to see what happened that day as a reminder that we never know when our lives will be over, that no one can promise us tomorrow, and that since we never know when our lives will be over, we need to start living our lives to the very fullest every moment of every day. You can choose to never waste another moment of your life by doing anything just for the sake of "killing time." When you think about it, we don't really have any time to throw away. It's way too precious.

I believe I am doing all those people who lost their lives an honor by using the events that happened that day to inspire me instead of ruin me, to make me a better person instead of a hateful person. It all comes down to which perception you choose to have. Maybe their deaths weren't in vain if the result is that we all learn how to love more and fight less. Imagine how much good would come out of that event if, instead of getting angry and vengeful, we decided to appreciate more, to be more grateful, and to just be happier for no other reason than because we choose to be.

Give yourself the peace in knowing that the laws of nature are always in effect, and that includes the Law of Circulation. You reap what you sow. You can't hide from the universe. The people who hijacked those planes and killed those innocent people will be held accountable for their actions. That's the perfect working order of the universe.

Think about it this way. Yes, the terrorists killed 3,000 of us, and there are billions of us still left. If we buy into their scare tactics and become scared ourselves, the terrorists will have won because they will have achieved their desired effect. Getting us to live in fear is what terrorists hope for. The great thing is that it's actually very easy to foil their plans. All we have to do is choose a perception that empowers us all, and we all become empowered. The result is the exact opposite of the terrorists' intention. No matter what happens, you always have the ability to choose what any event means to you.

Which meanings are you going to give to the events of your life—ones that empower you or ones that disempower you? It's your choice. Instead of living today as just another day, live it as if your entire life is in this day!

There's one more part to this. Think about how much hate must have been in those terrorists' hearts to commit such an act. How much hate would it take to plan this attack, train for it, and carry it out? How much hate would it take to say good-bye to your family and friends knowing you're going to murder thousands of innocent people? Hate destroys lives—yours and everyone's around you. Hating anyone is never a good thing, because when you hate someone, you are focusing your mind on hate, and in life you get what you focus on.

As a matter of fact, if you hate the terrorists for what they've done and you want them killed out of revenge, then that makes you a terrorist. Remember: it's that same hate and that same need for revenge that turned those people into terrorists in the first place.

Take a step back and remember what life is all about. You came into life with nothing, and one day you will leave and take nothing with you except for the love you gave, the love you received, and the experiences your soul got to have. So make all your experiences golden by choosing a positive, empowering perception for everything that happens in your life.

> *"When the doors of perception are cleansed, man will see things as they truly are . . ."*
>
> WILLIAM BLAKE

For a moment, imagine your life is over and you're on your way to the pearly gates of heaven. As you get closer to the entrance, you see the Creator standing in front of you, and on each side of the Creator is a big, empty bin.

"Before you can enter heaven," the Creator reveals, "you have to sort all the days of your life into these two bins. One is for the good days you had, and the other is for the bad." How would you judge which of your days were good days and which were bad? How would you divide up your days? (Now you know why this moment is sometimes referred to as Judgment Day.) I know how I'll respond.

"I can't do it. I need a different bin," I'll say.

"Oh yes," the Creator will smile, "and what kind of bin might that be, Kurek?"

"I need one for incredible days," I'll explain, "because I didn't have good or bad days. They were all incredible, and I'll need one big bin for all of them."

"How can you say that?" the Creator will test. "I gave you loads of challenges in your life. I gave you a helicopter crash in which you lost friends. You suffered from depression and endured all kinds of pain for years. How can you say they were all incredible days?"

"God," I'll say, at peace with my reply, "they were all incredible days because they were all part of that most magical gift you gave me to enjoy, that gift called life. They were all incredible because they were all a part of being alive, and to me, life is the most incredible experience to have, and I am grateful for each and every one of them."

A warm and loving smile will appear on the Creator's face. "You graduate. Come on in and welcome to my kingdom."

If on your judgment day you have any days to put in the "bad day" bin, you will have failed the test, because the only way to fail this life is by being unhappy and wasting days of your life by labeling them bad days.

The secret to mastering this life you were given is to be happy. It's about having a life filled with nonstop, back-to-back, glorious, joy-filled, blissfully happy experiences, and the only way to do this is by transforming all disempowering moments into empowering ones by seeing the good in the days you might otherwise have seen as bad. Change the way that you look at your life, and your life will change.

The Second "P" of Power Is Perturbation

I figured that moving into John's house wouldn't teach me how to change my conditions. For me, moving in with John would have been the easy way out, and in the long run, it would have done more harm than good.

If I had taken him up on his offer, it would've taught me that whenever you're in trouble, you should wait for someone else to bail you out. The problem with that is that sometimes there isn't anyone to bail you out, and because you haven't developed the skills yourself because you didn't need to, you're too weak to help yourself.

It also would have stolen my driving hunger to succeed, and one of the things I learned when my father locked me out of his house and kicked me onto my feet was that driving hunger pushes you forward and helps you to develop the skills you need to get the results you desire. Pain can sometimes be your friend because it can be the motivational fuel that gets you to move away from it and toward the pleasure you desire.

It was more important to me to learn strategies to change my own conditions and circumstances than it was to be supported by

John Travolta. It's the challenges in life that force us to develop our-selves the most, and once we learn those new strategies, we get to use them for the rest of our lives.

Perturbation is the experience of pushing through the challenges blocking your path to achieve your grand dream goals. To get through those challenges, perturbation forces you to reinvent your-self and expand who you are. Going through challenges is the quick-est and most efficient way to reinvent yourself to become the new and improved you.

Think about it this way. In order to move to the next levels of life, you're going to have to become more personally developed, because the you that you are now is the one who is doing what you're doing now, and that's why you have what you have now. When you personally develop yourself, you'll instantly start to do new things that the old version of you wasn't doing and that always will produce new results that you weren't getting before.

To get through your challenges, you're going to have to come up with some new ideas. You're going to have to learn some new things and take some new strategies on board. And you're obviously going to have to take some new actions too because your old actions can only produce the same old results, right?

Here's where it gets exciting. Once you come up with those new ideas, learn those new strategies, and take those new actions, you then have the opportunity to keep using and doing those things for the rest of your life, and you're going to get consistently better results because of that.

All real growth happens when we move toward our fear. By facing your challenges, you're forced to learn how to expand who you are, what you know, and how you do things. And that's the recipe for creating a much happier and more fulfilling life.

Remember that the rewards are always in proportion to the test. So the more you are getting tested, the grander the rewards you will receive once you get past the challenge, and I believe that the Cre-ator would never give me a challenge that I couldn't handle.

That's the power of perturbation.

———

There's a story about a man who was walking through a field when he saw a butterfly trying to work its way out of its cocoon. The butterfly was struggling, fighting to make its way out of the little hole that had appeared in the cocoon. The man could see the hole was much too small for the butterfly to get through, yet still the butterfly kept struggling to get out. The man watched for hours as the butterfly fought for freedom.

The man started thinking the butterfly would never make it on its own, so he decided to give the little creature some help. He pulled out his pocketknife and cut away the rest of the cocoon.

The butterfly emerged instantly, only there was something strange about the creature. Its body was swollen, and its wings were small and shriveled up. The man stayed and watched the butterfly as it crawled around on the ground, unable to fly. He waited for the moment its wings would grow and expand to support its body. Sadly, it never happened. The butterfly spent the rest of its life unable to fly, just crawling around the ground, never living the full life on the wing for which it had been intended.

What the man hadn't understood was that by judging a situation as wrong and trying to change it, he caused more harm than good. The struggle required for the butterfly to free itself from its restricting cocoon is the Creator's design for forcing fluid from the butterfly's body into its wings. This way the butterfly can fly as soon as it is free from its cocoon.

———

When we're perturbed, or challenged into action, we move through the resistance, gaining strength with every determined move until we make the final shift and break through the barrier we had perceived. Then we are both free and strong because it was that challenge that forced us to grow and expand. This is what shapes us into being who we want to become.

I always say, "If you want to learn how to swim, take your boat into the middle of the ocean and jump in. You're either going to learn to swim or you're going to see a lot of good-looking fish on the way down." That's the power of perturbation.

Now you know what it means when people say, "If it doesn't kill you, it will make you stronger." It's the challenges in life that give our life value. *Without perturbation, there's no appreciation.*

Sometimes struggles are exactly what we need in our lives. If we don't have challenges, we become weak and crippled; unable to fly to a higher level. We also become bored with it all. For example, most big lottery winners find that their good luck turns bad fast. Many file for bankruptcy within a few years. Others commonly suffer attacks by their family members or friends who feel they deserve a share of the winnings.

In 1988, a man who won over $16 million survived a murder attempt by a family member wanting to collect the rest of his winnings. The man went on to spend or lose all his winnings. He was living on social security benefits when he died.

Another person won $31 million in 1997 and, after spending big, he committed suicide. After his death the remaining funds were insufficient to pay for his estate taxes.

Another lottery winner, a woman who won $11 million, is serving time in prison, penniless, convicted for a drug- and alcohol-induced collision that killed one person and paralyzed another. Most lottery winners simply do not know how to handle the money, and they make bad investments or spend relentlessly instead of investing and living off the earnings.

What happened to these winners? Why did it all go so wrong? Their wins were easy. There was no perturbation, and without the power of perturbation, there's no appreciation. It took them no effort to go down to the shop to buy the ticket, so they didn't have to learn any new skills. But they needed to learn new skills, because if they already had the skills required to handle such huge sums of money, they would already have created that amount of money in their lives.

Many winners who end up in poverty are there because that's where they were before their big win. If someone is earning $20,000 a year, it's because that's all he or she is worth—not to me, but to themselves. That's what they believe they're worth, so that's where they're at. If they thought they were worth more, they would find a way to create more money to match that worth. If a person earning $20,000 is challenged by the power of perturbation to gain a higher sense of worth and the strategies needed to create that worth, they'll earn far more. That lack of perturbation is why most lottery winners end up right back where they started, or worse.

Remember: the rewards are always in proportion to the test. No test, no rewards! That's why I love challenges—because they force me to grow, and when I grow, the rewards grow too.

Think about it this way. What if you were a golfer, and every day you played golf with the same person, and you always beat him by a huge margin? Wouldn't you get bored? If you won each time by a huge margin, there's a good chance your skills would diminish because you were never really pushed to keep yourself sharp. You would coast along for so long that you would stop evolving. And we all know what happens when you stop evolving. You start dissolving!

Now imagine playing Tiger Woods every day. Let's face it: if you're golfing with Tiger Woods, there's a very good chance he'll beat you every time, right? I would be excited about that kind of challenge. Imagine how many powerful golfing skills and strategies you could learn by playing with Tiger Woods. Think about how your drive to improve your game in the hopes of some day beating him, or at least narrowing the margin between your two scores, would improve your skills. Do you think your golf game would improve if you got to spend an entire year playing golf with Tiger Woods every day?

That's what perturbation is, and that's why it's so awesome to be challenged. It's the best thing that can happen to you. As soon as you are challenged, you are given the opportunity to improve the quality of your life in all areas. Perturbation forces you to tap into your dormant resources. Dormant resources are the skills and tools you have inside you that you haven't utilized yet. A soon as you do, you instantly start to get better results.

By celebrating my challenges, I'm also using the power of perception. Instead of looking at the challenges in my life as being something bad or something I dread facing, I look at them as being the best gift I could ever be given. Because I'm excited about the fact that facing challenges always reaps me huge rewards, that excitement empowers me to face them head on, and it gives me the necessary energy to find the answers more quickly and effectively. And at those times when it feels like it's taking a long time to find the answers that will get me through my challenges and I start to get a bit frustrated, I get excited that I'm frustrated.

Frustration is empowering when you use it to push you into taking action. Being unsettled or uncomfortable can be a very good thing because it means you still want to evolve. If you get frustrated about the fact that you're frustrated, that's disempowering and robs you of the energy you need to succeed at your task. Just because it doesn't happen as quickly as you'd like doesn't mean that it isn't going to happen. God's delays are not God's denials.

You always get what you ask for, and it rarely comes in the package that you expect it to show up in. When I was a young child, I dreamed I could someday live the life I now live. I dreamed I'd be in a position to help people improve the quality of their lives.

Then came the helicopter crash. What I didn't know at the time was that the crash was exactly what I had been asking for, as it was the experience I needed to get me to where I am today. It was the catalyst that forced me to change the way I was running my life and go in search of new skills and tools.

When you turn away from your challenges, the challenges become more powerful. The challenges win, and you lose! That doesn't sound like much of a strategy for success, does it?

Facing your challenges makes you more powerful. When you face your challenges, you become empowered, which makes you more powerful. That's when you win, and that's when you win the most!

The Third "P" of Power Is Procession

We start our lives at a place called birth and end up at a place called destiny. The line between those two points is called life. As I'm sure you're well aware, life isn't a straight line. It's more a series of twists and turns. I'm just using a straight line in the diagram because it's easier to demonstrate the point I'm making.

We won't really know what our destiny is until we are about to take our last breath and look back over our life. The reason I say we

end our journey at our destiny is because death isn't the end; it's the beginning of the next chapter.

Where you're sitting right now is the center of the universe, because in whichever direction you turn to look, you have the infinite universe in front of you. Since there is no real up or down in space, and the planet is round, each one of us is positioned to be on top of the world. From where you are at any moment of your life, you have the ability to do and be anything you want to. I've heard Deepak Chopra say that we live in a field of infinite possibilities, which means we can go anywhere and do anything we desire. Yet if we choose to do nothing, we will stagnate and rot.

That's why we set goals. *Goals give our life direction.* If you don't pursue goals in your life, then your life has no direction, and you stagnate because you're not in motion. Everything needs to be in motion to evolve. Goals get us to move in a chosen direction, and, to achieve those goals, we have to take actions. Actions are like pebbles being thrown into a pond.

Each pebble that hits the pond creates a ripple, that action activates the Law of Cause and Effect. The first ripple creates the next

ripple, and that ripple creates the next ripple, and so it goes. That's known as the ripple effect, or the processional effect. When you throw a stone into a pond, the ripples expand out until they reach all the shores. Once the ripple touches the shoreline, the energy is reversed, and the ripples head back toward the center. And you'll notice the energy from every action you take expands and comes back bigger than it went out. It evolves!

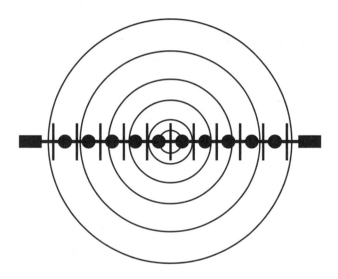

The ripples you create can only be one of two things—positive or negative. What those ripples provide feedback. Another way to describe what the ripples are is the term "Karma."

When you get negative feedback, it's a sign that the actions you're taking are inappropriate and need to be changed. Remember: the seeds you're planting dictate what you're growing and harvesting. You'll also want to remember that the energy you put forth expands before it comes back, which means that when you participate in a negative way, it comes back to you twenty-fold.

When positive processional ripples come back to you, it's a clear sign the actions you're taking are positive actions.

The processional effect are those ripples that come back to you, and procession is a "P" of power because when you do great things for yourself and others, the more you do the more great things come

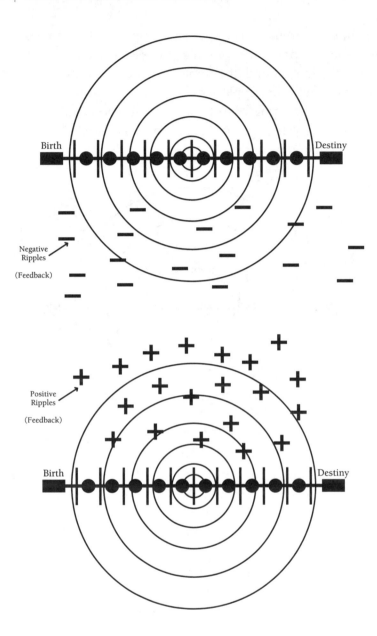

back to you. How easy is that? It feels good to do positive things, so the payoff is immediate. The positive waves that come back to you are even better.

Remember that *it's never about the goal and it's always about the growth*, because when you go after your grand dream goals, it forces you into perturbation, which causes you to personally develop. That's the purpose of having grand dream goals. They give us a direction in which to move, and that movement creates evolvement. And remember that evolvement is our life's quest.

The big payoff from pursuing the goal is bigger than the goal itself. That payoff comes from the waves of the procession. Whatever you put forth comes back to you in like kind. That's why it's so important to never give up when going after your grand dream goals. You have to keep putting the positive energy out there so that it can come back to you. If you don't consciously send out positive energy, then, by default because there is no neutral, you are sending out negative energy. And we already know what happens when you send that out. It always comes back amplified.

When you take positive actions, procession magnifies the effect and brings you huge rewards in return for your efforts. Here's an example: Years ago, when I first got to Australia, I was having some challenges with the company that brought me here. I had been in Australia for about a year, and I hadn't been paid in a long time. I used up all my personal savings trying to stay afloat. Pretty soon I was down to my last twenty dollars. I was twenty dollars away from being homeless in two countries. I couldn't even afford to go back home to the United States to be homeless there. I called my oldest brother, Jeff, and told him about my situation. Being the awesome big brother that he is, he offered to send me a plane ticket back to Chicago and offered me a room at his house for as long as I needed to get back on my feet. I weighed my options, which were few, and I decided I would take him up on his offer.

Here's the challenge. I hadn't lived in Chicago for over twenty years. I love the city, and I can't stand the winters. For me this move would be like starting my whole life over again at the age of thirty-eight. I wanted to avoid moving back there like the plague, but I didn't really have any options. At least, that's what I thought at the time.

A couple of weeks before I was scheduled to leave, I started tossing out many of my belongings to lighten my load back to Chicago. I felt like I had failed and was going back with my tail between my legs. As I was going through some files to see which ones I needed to keep, I came across a business card from a man named Dean who had seen me speak at a seminar I had given months earlier. That night Dean had said that if I ever wanted to do some public seminars, he would be interested in producing and promoting them. He had never done it before, and he said he had always wanted to start a seminar company. I was just about to throw his card away, but I hesitated. The reason I hadn't called him before was because I wasn't really sure if he was serious or not, and, if he was, I didn't know if he knew what he was doing. I sat there for a moment looking at his card wondering if I should give it a shot and call him. I teetered back and forth debating whether I should call him or toss the card.

My head was filled with internal chatter. "I'm not sure he'll even remember me. Because he hasn't heard from me, he's changed his mind." Blah, blah, blah!

The other half of my brain was saying, "You won't know unless you make the call."

Needless to say, I made the call. To my delight, not only did he remember me, he was still interested in doing the public seminar with me. The next day I went to his office. We agreed that I would give a one-day personal development seminar.

The next thing I did was call my brother Jeff, thanking him for his kind offer and telling him I wouldn't need it. I said, "I'm digging in my heels and moving forward. I didn't allow John Travolta to carry me, and I'm not about to allow myself to be carried now either." The next thing I knew, we were on our way, promoting the seminar, and for the next couple months, I was Dean's houseguest, sleeping on the floor of his apartment.

He and his team set up back-to-back introductory seminars for me to give to anyone who would hear me speak. The seminars were each an hour long. The agreement was that we would do the seminar for free for companies in exchange for allowing us ten minutes at the end to promote our upcoming public event. I ended up giving five free seminars a day, six days a week, for eight straight weeks.

At one of those free seminars was Natalie Cook, who asked me to help her win the gold in Sydney.

At another seminar, I met a stunningly beautiful woman named Marie, who became my wife.

At the full-day public seminar we were promoting, we sold 365 seats, and I broke the world record* for firewalking by walking along 266 feet (81 meters) of coals burning at 1,200 degrees Fahrenheit (649 degrees Celsius), creating a huge media profile for me that has produced huge results that have come back to me many, many times over. (*It's not an official world record in the record book because I didn't have the officials there to judge it. However, there were over 360 people, as well as plenty of members of the media, there to witness it. For me it wasn't about breaking the world record; it was about showing people that you can achieve anything that you set your mind to.)

The moment I took that one new action of phoning Dean, I set into motion a massive processional wave. If I had walked away from the challenge, the challenge would have gained power and won, and I would have lost. Instead, I faced the challenge and won because winning comes from pushing through your challenges. Everything in my life now is a result of that processional effect, and those rewards are still coming into my life every day. Great things happen when you refuse to quit and instead drive forward toward your grand dream goals.

Remember that the Law of Circulation is always in effect, so make sure to be conscious about the pebbles you throw into the universal pond, because whatever you send out will come back to you many times over. Use the principles of procession to your benefit by diligently being positive and empowering about everything. With the three P's of power—perception, perturbation, and procession—you now know how to do that.

One last thing. Remember those two men I met at the studios when I was doing the construction job? About a year after working with John Travolta on Two of a Kind, he called to tell me about the next film he was doing. He told me to call the production office to audition for it because he thought I was perfect for some of the roles. Then he said, "Hey, Kurek, you already know the producer and director, Jim Bridges and Jack Larson."

I said, "John, they won't remember me. I only met them for twenty minutes that one time, and that was over a year ago."

John assured me they'd remember me and told me to make the call. I did as I was told. I called the production office and asked to speak with James Bridges. The receptionist asked, "Whom may I say is calling?" I told her my name, and she said she would check to see if he was in.

I was preparing myself to hear the standard "I'm sorry, he's not in. I'll have him call you back." Can you imagine my surprise when Jim Bridges got on the phone? Not only did he remember me, he was excited to hear from me. He remembered everything about our meeting a year ago. He told me to come to the office that afternoon so he could introduce me to the casting director.

At 2 P.M. I arrived at the studio lot and walked to the production office for my audition. As I opened the door and went in, Jack Larson was standing there talking on the phone. He looked at me and smiled as he put down the phone. "I told you to become good friends with John Travolta," he said, grinning.

As it turned out, the film they were doing was *Perfect*, starring John Travolta and Jamie Lee Curtis. I was hired to work on the film for twenty-two weeks. I made more money on that film than I did on any other.

How lucky was I to get that job, right?

Maybe!

————

If you want to see some great photos of me with John Travolta and Jamie Lee Curtis, and other stars with whom I have worked in my acting career, go to www.howwouldloverespond.com or www.kurekashley.com.

13

Bliss or Blisters: Mastering Responsibility

In the last chapter, we discussed the power of your perception and discovered that everything we encounter in life is nothing more than an event and that events by themselves don't have any real meaning. We give meaning to the events of our lives.

For example, let's say a couple has been married for twenty years, and then one day the husband comes home from work and informs his wife that he has fallen in love with his young secretary and is running away to start a new life with her.

> "Whatever is begun in anger ends in shame."
>
> BENJAMIN FRANKLIN

How would you feel if this happened to you? How would you react?

In all my years of working with people, helping them to improve the quality of their lives, I have come across quite a few people who have had this kind of experience. Sometimes the husband is the one who leaves, and sometimes it's the wife. Either way, it's pretty much

285

the same event. Yet the way each individual reacts is quite different. There are usually two different responses. We will refer to the people who respond the first way as group A. Group A doesn't do so well with the news that their partners are running off with someone else. They feel their world has come to an end. They're usually very angry and hurt at their partners for "doing this to them." People in group A take this experience and label it as depressing, and so they get depressed. They also typically get together with all their friends on a regular basis to talk about what happened and how bad they feel about it. At first their friends listen to the drama-filled stories and add their own commentaries, agreeing with the hurt partners and making them feel even more justified for the way they're feeling. (Remember that justification is below the line!) The friends then all start sharing how bad their lives are too. Birds of a feather flock together.

Some group A people who feel they got dumped by their partners end up in deep depression for years and begin taking antidepressants to try to alleviate their pain.

Does this scenario sound familiar? Do you know anyone like this?

Then there's group B. Let's say these people were also in a relationship for twenty years and they, too, were informed by their partner that they were running away to have a relationship with someone else. A group B person has a different reaction to the news from a group A person. Instead of getting depressed, he or she yells out, "Freedom! Yahoo! Party, party, party!" as if this is one of the best things that has ever happened to him or her.

Think about it. What's the difference between these two types of people? They both encountered the same scenario, yet each had a completely different reaction to it. Why is that? It's because they each had a different perception of the event, and it's your perception that determines what an event will mean to you.

If someone breaks your heart, what's the quickest and easiest way to get over it (or to get even)? That's right: Be happy! You'll get a completely different reaction from the person leaving when you're actually happy about it. And even if you don't, at least *you're* still happy!

It's like when someone gets fired or loses his job. Most people just go out and look for a new job, but there are other people who get so upset they load up a gun and try to kill everyone they used to work with. They are reacting differently to the same kind of event.

So, as you can see, events by themselves don't have any true meaning. They're neither empowering nor disempowering on their own. It's your perception of events that gives them meaning. If you label an event as disempowering, it becomes disempowering. When you label it as empowering, it becomes just that.

And what determines your perception of an event is a filter system in your mind known as your emotions. It's your emotions that determine how you perceive all the events in your life. Have you ever noticed that you have a more positive perception of things when you're in a good mood than you have when you're in a bad mood? Have you also noticed that you have a completely different set of actions and behaviors when you're in a good mood than you do when you're in a bad mood? That's because when you're in a positive mood, you perceive things more positively, and because of that, you take better positive actions. And by now you know that when you take better actions, you automatically get better results, right?

Have you ever done or said something while you were in a bad mood that you later regretted? Let me ask you another question. Have you ever had a big, heated argument with someone you love and care about? I call those arguments "the mortar attacks" because when you're in the middle of one, you no longer care what the other person is saying; you just want to say something worse to them than they're saying to you, right? Then comes a point during one of these arguments when you think you are Albert Einstein, and you are so proud of yourself because you have just thought up the atom bomb of all comments. You know this is going to hit your mark with precision and impact. It's probably the first time in argument history when you are going to let the other person finish what they're saying without interrupting them because you're thinking, "Go ahead. I'm just going to wipe you out anyway, so have a good time." Then it's your turn, and you unleash the comment of destruction you're so proud of. At first you're happy with the carnage you cause—that is, until a moment later, when your brain finally catches up with your mouth, and you think, "Oh no! What did I just do?" That's when you realize you've gone too far. You've passed the point of no return. This comment is going to cost you forever because it is going to be brought up again and again by the person you hit with it. Sound familiar?

During arguments like this, why was it that at one moment you're proud of yourself, and a moment later you're not? Think about it. There are even times during an argument when you're saying to yourself, "Shut up, and don't say any more. You're getting yourself in trouble." But what happens? You just keep yapping away and getting yourself into deeper and deeper trouble. The reason it happens is because when you are in a bad, negative, disempowering mood, you do not have access to the personal power you do when you're in a happy, positive, empowering mood. While displaying those negative, disempowering emotions, you don't have the ability to tap into the same resources, skills, and tools you do when you are in a good emotional state. That's why you say and do things while in a negative mood you later regret.

That's why it's critically important to the achievement of all your grand dream goals that you become the master of your emotions. When you're in control of your emotions, you're in control of your actions, and it's those actions that create your results. This is where responsibility is created. When you are in a better emotional state, you have a better ability to choose how you respond.

By suggesting you become the master of your emotions, I'm not talking about becoming an unemotional droid chanting out in a robotic voice, "I am happy, I am happy." I believe your emotions are the colors on the artist's palette the Creator gave you to paint your life with. The key is for you to choose the colors. When you're in reaction to what's happening in you life, the colors get chosen for you.

Sadness, fear and depression all have their place in life, and it's important not to get consumed by them. When my dad passed on, I didn't want to miss the experience of missing him. At his funeral I gave myself permission to feel and experience whatever came up. Then, after his funeral, I decided my time would be much better spent enjoying quality time with my mom and my stepmother, Pauline, since they are both still alive. I didn't want to miss that opportunity simply because my dad died. I had allowed myself to experience my moments of grief, and then I started to enjoy life again.

Prisons are filled with people who lost control of their emotions. They got emotionally charged and reacted. I'm sure there are many people in prison who deeply regret their actions too.

Buddha said, "There is no way to happiness. Happiness is the way." He meant there is nothing outside of yourself that will make you happy if you're not happy within yourself first. So instead of trying to achieve happiness, happily achieve. When you're happy, you're positive, and when you're positive, you're empowering. The more power that goes to the source, the brighter your light gets and the more life is automatically attracted to you. It's easy to achieve whatever you want when you're happy. Everything in the universe grows in the light of happiness.

Remember that happiness is our ultimate goal. Why do you want to be financially free? Because you think it will make you happy. Why do you want to have a nice car? Because you think it will make you happy. Why do you want a great relationship? You guessed it—happiness! The best thing about being happy today—even if you don't have the nice car, big house, and great relationship yet—is that at least you're happy. Happiness in itself is a great reward.

And since everyone likes spending time with positive, happy people and since there are so many people who choose to walk around all day being unhappy, that just makes your happy light shine that much brighter, which means even more people and more opportunities will be attracted to your light. How easy is that?

> "Choose the path of least resistance."
>
> BUDDHA

Think about it this way: when you're happy and peaceful, you're in harmony with the natural flow of the universe, which makes going through life easy and makes getting the results you want easier too. If you choose the path of negativity and disempowerment, you are going against the flow, which creates resistance. Resistance creates friction, and friction causes blisters. The longer you stay unhappy with anything or anyone, the more out of harmony you are with the natural flow of the universe, and the only thing it produces is more blisters. So it really comes down to making the decision, what do you want, bliss or blisters?

Here are ten guaranteed ways to be and stay consistently happy. When you do that, you truly are a master of responsibility.

Ten Guaranteed Ways to Be and Stay Happy

1. PHYSIOLOGY

Physiology is just a big sounding word that means the way you carry your body. It's also known as your posture. Your posture sends signals to your brain telling it what emotion you're feeling.

Let's do a little experiment so you can see this for yourself. Stand up the way you would if you were feeling happy and confident right now. Breathe the way you would if you were feeling happy and confident right now. Put the look on your face you would have if you were feeling happy and confident right now.

If you're actually taking the action and doing this exercise, you may notice that you're standing straighter and more upright. Your shoulders are pulled back. Your breathing is full and deep, and there's a smile on your face.

Now let's change the emotion and see how your posture changes. Stand the way you would if you were feeling depressed right now. Breathe the way you would if you were feeling depressed right now, and put the look on your face you'd have if you were depressed right now. Did your posture change? Are your shoulders more rounded and hunched over? Is your head facing down? Have you noticed that your breathing is shorter and shallower than it was when you were in the happy posture? I'm guessing you don't have a smile on your face anymore either.

To become the master of your emotions, you need to choose the posture that matches the emotion you want to feel.

Checking in with your physiology is a very easy and effective way to be happy and stay happy. The easiest way to do this is by asking yourself questions such as, "How would I stand/sit if I was feeling totally happy right now?" and "How would I breathe if I was feeling happy right now?" It goes without saying that smiling tells your brain you are in a good mood too.

Have you ever noticed that when you skip it's impossible to stay in a bad mood? Skipping is a strategy that guarantees to put you in a great mood ever time you do it. Right now I can hear you thinking, "Oh yeah, I can just see myself skipping through the office at work! People will think I've gone crazy or I'm stupid!" Let me ask you something. Are these people that you're so concerned about looking bad in front of, are they paying your bills for you? Are they taking care of your family? Are they helping you fulfill your dreams? No? Well, since they're not, why do you care about what they think of you? To be holistically successful, you have to learn to be free of other people's opinions.

Honestly, if these people whom you're so concerned about judging you had holistic success in their own lives, they certainly wouldn't be worried about what *you're* doing.

Change the way you carry your body, and you will instantly change the way you feel.

2. Choose What You Focus On

Imagine you are holding a coin flat between your first finger and your thumb. Let's call the heads side of the coin the right side, and the tails side the left. Which side of the coin makes up the coin—the right side or the left side? If you answered both sides, you are correct.

Let's take an imaginary saw, cut the coin in half, and throw away one of the halves. Does the portion of the coin that's remaining still have a left and a right side to it? If you answered yes, you're correct again.

Let's take the imaginary saw and cut the coin in half again and throw away one of the two halves. Does the piece you have in your hand still have a left and right side to it? Of course it does.

Our example demonstrates the Law of Polarity, which, as we discussed in chapter 8, states that everything in the universe has a polar opposite side to it. For example, you can't have a top without a bottom. You can't have an outside without an inside. If there's a left side, there has to be a right side. It also means that all your life's problems

292 | HOW WOULD LOVE RESPOND?

have to have solutions, and all your challenges also have opportunities attached to them.

How you feel about a situation is determined by which side of the situation you focus on. Focus on the negative side, and you'll feel bad about it. Focus on the positive side, and you'll feel great about it. The choice is yours. Remember that no matter how thin you slice it, there are always going to be two sides to a situation, so whichever side you choose to focus on is going to create what you get. Change what you focus on, and you change the result.

While the majority of people are caught up focusing on the problems of the world, the successful people are focusing on the solutions and opportunities.

Have you ever had an experience that seemed, at the time, to be the worst and most painful period of your life? Maybe something traumatic or sad happened, like the loss of a loved one. Maybe you had an experience that was so dark and consuming that it felt there was no way out of your pain and it seemed you would never recover from it. There you were, going from day to day in that dark and painful time of your life when it seemed there would never be another sunny day for you to enjoy. Then as time passed, and whether it took days, months, or years, the day finally arrived when you felt your life was back on track.

Then something wonderful happened—that moment when you looked back on that dark and painful time of your life and started to see it in a different light. You began to see it as the time of your life when you learned the most about yourself. Maybe it was the time you feel you evolved and grew the most. Maybe it was the event that taught you the most about gratitude and compassion. What really happened was that, as time passed, you made a perceptional shift. Your perception shifted from seeing that period of your life as the most painful to seeing it as the most powerful time of your life. You realized it was a transformational time for you. Have you experienced this?

For me, the helicopter crash and its aftermath was the most devastating time of my life. It felt so bad it almost cost me my life. Once I got clear of the depression, I could look back at that same event as the most powerful transformational growth period of my life. The event that seemed so devastating at the time is the same event that transformed me into who I am today and created the incredible life I now enjoy.

What determines how long you suffer during such a period in your life depends on how long you focus on the negative portion of the story. The sooner you stop telling the negatively perceived version of your story, the sooner you will free yourself of its drama glue and the pain that goes hand in hand with it. In fact, you don't have to wait for years to go by to start feeling better and stronger. You can make the shift as quickly as you make the decision to start to feel good.

The easiest way to change your focus is by asking new empowering questions, such as, "What's great about this?" "How can I look at this in an empowering way?" or, "How would Love respond?" When you start asking better questions, you get better answers, and it's those new answers that instantly start to change your focus. Remember that when you focus on the painful side, you'll feel pain. When you focus on the sad side, you'll feel sad. You can do that, or you can choose to start focusing on the positive, empowering side, because when you do that, you'll become positive and empowered!

Oh, and by the way, "why" questions are not empowering questions. "Why did this happen?", "Why did they do that to me?", and "Why did he or she cheat on me?" are not empowering questions. They're disempowering. When you ask why, all you get is more pain you don't want because the answers can only make you feel worse. Asking why someone did something you didn't like or appreciate is an activity of your ego. When you ask "why" questions, you're just reacting to a perceived wrong against you. Instead of reacting to what happens in your life, start being proactive and start looking for a new meaning in the things that bother you. Seek, and you will find. When you stop being reactive, and start being proactive, you become the co-creator of your life.

Here are some great empowering questions, "What's great about this?", "How can I look at this in an empowering way?", and "How would Love respond?"

You get what you focus on, so if you want to change what you're getting, change what you're focusing on.

3. Utilize the Law of Relativity

This is an easy yet powerful strategy. The Law of Relativity states there is nothing in the universe, big or small, good or bad, until you compare it to something else. You can probably see already why this is such an easy strategy to use. All you have to do is make sure that when you're comparing yourself or your life with someone or something else, make the comparisons with things that make you feel good.

Most people compare themselves to people who are doing better than they are, and it's that comparison that makes them feel as if they haven't accomplished much. How would that make you feel— empowered or disempowered? Use the law in your favor, and only make comparisons with things that make you feel great.

I keep reminding myself how far I have come already, and how much I have evolved since the days of the helicopter crash. Every time I do, I feel great, and I'm inspired to keep the evolution going forward.

4. Stop Telling Disempowering Stories

"There is no life in your life story;
there's only story!"

Promise yourself from this moment forward that you will never, ever, ever tell the painful or sad stories from your past again. *If it doesn't serve you, then don't say it!* Every time you talk about painful times of your life, your brain replays the video of the experience and you're forced to relive it. You already had to endure it once—why would you want to go through it again and again? Does that sound like a good strategy for improving the quality of your life?

No matter how bad you think your childhood may have been, it's never too late to look back at it with great memories. When you stop telling painful stories about your childhood, you'll stop feeling pain. Instead, start telling good stories, and as soon as you do, you'll start to feel good.

After the helicopter crash, what was getting me into so much trouble was the fact that I kept repeating the worst parts of the story, and every time I told it, I was forced to relive it. It's funny how we have a tendency to forget to tell the good parts of a story. The reason that happens is because there's no drama in telling positive stories, and people love getting stuck in drama glue. Telling disempowering stories keeps you stuck in the drama glue.

If you don't have any good stories, make them up. Remember that your subconscious can't tell the difference between something that's real and something that you vividly imagine. If you tell the positive story enough times, you'll start to believe it happened. I will do whatever it takes to get myself to feel good, because I know that when I'm feeling positive, I think better and I act better, and it's those better actions that create better results. And when I have better results, I feel even better!

5. LIVE WITH CDI

The average person overestimates what he or she can do in a day a week or a month, and they underestimate what they can do in a year, five years, and a decade.

CDI stands for **C**onsistent **D**aily **I**mprovement. If you make the commitment every day to improve the quality of your life by only 1%, at the end of every year, you will be at least 365% improved. Think about how happy you are going to be with those kinds of consistent results day after day, and year after year. Think about how good you're going to feel with 365% improvement in your health and fitness. How excited are you going to be this time next year with 365% improvement in your financial situation? There's no limit to how happy you can get when you make sure to improve your level of happiness by at least 1% every day.

Remember that evolvement isn't a destination. It's your life's quest! You don't actually reach a place of being evolved because, if you did, you'd immediately start going backward. Why? Because you wouldn't be moving forward anymore. Remember: everything is always in motion. It's either growing or decaying. There will always be more to learn and growth to experience. So our goal isn't to get to the place where we know it all. Our goal is to continually evolve. I would worry if I thought I really did know it all because when that happens, death follows. When you know it all, you no longer have a reason for being here as a human because your mission while you're here is to keep evolving. And where there's no mission, there's no life to be lived!

We all have the same birthright to be happy, healthy, and wealthy, and it's not just our right, it's our responsibility, our obligation, to be so. It's our duty to continuously evolve and make the best of ourselves and our lives. When we advance ourselves, it contributes to the growth of the universe. When we evolve, the universe evolves, and that's the price we owe for the gift of life we were rewarded with. When we work on ourselves, we inspire others to do the same, and, through our results, we also show them it's possible. This, too, is our responsibility, because if we're not part of the solution, then we're part of the problem.

Living small doesn't serve the world or contribute to its evolvement. When you play small by not going for your grand dream goals, what are you teaching everyone else you come into contact with? You're teaching them that living in scarcity is acceptable, when it's not. The worst lie we tell ourselves and teach others is that when we become adults it's okay to sell out and give up on your dreams. The reason this is so bad is because it promotes stagnation and rot. It's the catalyst that creates so much unhappiness for the majority of adults, and it steals the hope of our youth because that adult way of life is all they think they have to look forward to. When you give up on your dreams, you die. You may still be physically alive, but you're dead inside. It's the natural order of the universe for you to want to develop into the best "you" that you can be. The strategy for doing this again comes down to asking a magical question: "How can I make it better?" Ask that question, and the answers you get will be strategies. Take action with those strategies, and you will achieve your desired result every time. Imagine how excited you are going to be waking up every day knowing you'll be improving by at least 1% in all areas of your life. And some days you may go wild and make it a whopping 2% or more! Does it really matter, as long as you're evolving every day? Remember that evolvement is our quest because it is the natural order of the universe for everything to seek to reach its highest potential.

When you live with CDI, your life gets better and easier every day that you're alive. How happy does that thought make you?

6. Let Go of Your Judgment, and Have Fewer Rules

All conflicts in life are rules conflicts. If you go back and analyze any argument or disagreement you have ever had in your life, you'll notice every one of them was a result of a conflict in rules. Your rules were in conflict with the other person's rules. All wars that have ever been fought on this planet were the result of rules conflicts. One side says, "Mine is the right God and yours is the wrong God," and then a war over religion begins. Or the people of one country feels it doesn't have enough resources so, according to their rules, it's okay to go and take from another country. The invaded country believes this action is against their rules, so they fight back. All conflicts in life are the result of opposite sides both thinking they are right because, according to their rules, they are.

Judgment is the need to be right. When you let go of that need, life immediately becomes easier and happier. When people have too many strict rules about everything, they get tightly wound up, giving them way too many reasons to get upset. Their rules get them fired up, and then they react. That's a prescription for an angry, stressful life.

Remember to choose your battles wisely. Don't fight every fight just because it comes your way, because if you do, you'll be so busy fighting all the time that you won't have any time left for enjoying your life. Release yourself of the need to be right and the need to make others wrong.

The difference between perception and judgment is that perception is having a point of view while judgment is thinking that your point of view is right.

Remember to ask yourself, "Is it more important to be right or kind?" How would Love respond to that question? You'll notice that when you always choose "kind," it's easy to stay happy and peaceful. As Love, are you willing to trade in the judgment for a positive perception?

7. BE FULL OF PEACE AND FREE OF STRESS

Let's look at the meaning of these two words, "stress" and "peace," so you can clearly see the different effects they can have on you, the achievement of your grand dream goals, and your happiness.

> "We choose our joys and sorrows long before we experience them."
>
> KAHLIL GIBRAN

When your body experiences stress your thoughts are turbulent and at dis-ease. *It's the dis-ease of your mind that creates the disease of your body.* One in three people develops cancer these days, which is amazing when you consider that 100 years ago, the number was dramatically less. What's really perplexing is the fact that we have way more medical advances now than we did 100 years ago. We have healthier restaurants, more knowledge about cancer, more vitamins and nutritional supplements, and more places to go to get regular exercise. With all these advancements in health, fitness, and science, why is it more people are developing cancer than ever before? It's because so many people are regularly stressed.

Remember that the most consumed drugs on the planet are anti-depressants. Why are so many people taking anti-depressants? Because they're depressed! So many people are depressed over so many things that it stresses them out. Stress is mental dis-ease, and wherever your head goes your body follows.

Stress
↓
Dis-ease

Another way of saying your mind is experiencing dis-ease is to say your mind is not at ease.

Stress
↓
Dis-ease
↓
Not at ease

Have you ever noticed that when you're feeling stressed out, you don't have your best thoughts? Have you also noticed that when you're stressed, you don't take your best actions, either? If you're taking poor actions the only thing poor actions can produce is poor results, right? When your mind is not at ease, you're making achieving your goals not easy to achieve. Not at ease means that things are not easy.

Stress
↓
Dis-ease
↓
Not at ease
↓
Not easy

And the last part of this is very simple to understand. If something is not easy, it means that it's difficult or hard to do.

Stress
↓
Dis-ease
↓
Not at ease
↓
Not easy
↓
Difficult/hard

Remember that stress is the result of having stressful thoughts. As you can see, it's anti-productive when you participate in a stressful way because you are making it harder on yourself to succeed, while at the same time getting far lesser quality results.

Let's look at the other side of the coin for a moment and discover a more effective way to create the life you desire for yourself. When you're at peace, your mind is at ease.

Peace
↓
At ease

When you're at ease, you're making things easy. Have you ever noticed that when you're feeling peaceful, you have a tendency to have better-quality thoughts? Have you also noticed that when you're having peaceful thoughts, you also have a tendency to take better actions? When you take better actions, don't you also get better results? Hmm, now there's something to think about!

Peace
↓
At ease
↓
Easy

To be at peace is to be surrounded by and immersed in the light. We already know what happens when we are in the light— life is automatically attracted to us. How easy is that?

Remember that stress is the number one killer on the planet. When you're stressed, you weaken your immune system, making your body more susceptible to disease. Stress can cause heart attacks, among other unhealthy conditions, and even death.

When you're happy, not only does it strengthen your immune system, it also gets your body to produce interleukins, the most powerful cancer-fighting agent there is. Being happy creates better health results. When you're in a happy, positive, empowering mood, you think better, which means you act better, and we all know what better actions create—better results!

When the people you work with are stressed out, do you think they're being their most productive? Are they having their best thoughts and making their best decisions? Stress at work can kill your business. And it doesn't stop there. Given the opportunity, stress can also kill your relationship. No one enjoys being around stressed-out people because it makes them feel stressed out too.

Have you noticed that when some people die, their loved ones have R.I.P. inscribed on the headstone on their grave? R.I.P. stands for "Rest in Peace." Have you ever wondered why R.I.P. is written on so many people's gravestones? Maybe it's because what put that person in the grave was the stress they experienced during their life. And since they didn't have any peace in this lifetime, their loved ones are hoping they get the message so they can get some peace in the next.

It's fitting that being at peace means you're immersed in the light, because when you're in your light, you are enlightened, and when you look throughout history at all the people considered to be enlightened (Martin Luther King, Jr., Gandhi, Mother Teresa, Nelson Mandela, Jesus, and Buddha), you'll notice they were all peaceful people. And because they were peaceful, the masses saw their light and were attracted to them to help them with their causes. They made a positive impact on the planet and continue to do so, even though all but one of them have passed on. Would you like to make a positive impact on the lives of people you love and care about, as well as on your own life? Would that bring you happiness? Remember what Jesus said: "Even the least among you can do all that I have done, and even greater things." Do the same things they did, and you will get the same results.

Are you fired up by inspiration or pushed by stress?

8. Be Empowering about Everything

If you didn't get it the first time, go back and read chapter 8.

It doesn't take any effort on your part for the great things in life to be attracted to your light, because it doesn't take any effort to be empowering. It just takes the commitment to be that way. It's actually easier to be empowering than it is to be disempowering, because being empowering feels good, and all the rest of the rewards just naturally gravitate toward you without any effort. It all starts with making the decision to be that way. When

> "If you want others to be happy, practice compassion. If you want to be happy, practice compassion."
>
> THE DALAI LAMA

you are being empowering about everything, it's easy to always be happy!

9. PRACTICE FORGIVENESS ON A REGULAR BASIS

Anger, hate, jealousy, and envy are all activities of the ego. When you feel them, you are declaring your separateness from the universe. Remember that forgiving doesn't let the other person off the hook for what he or she has done. Karma is the only way to clear that debt with the universe, because you reap what you sow. Just because you feel someone has wronged you doesn't mean you need to be the judge, jury, and executioner. The universe and karma will take care of that. It's your ego that needs to see those people who you feel have wronged you get punished. Just let it go, and forgive them. As soon as you decide to forgive them, you begin the process of healing. If you don't forgive, you don't heal. The wound stays open. If it stays open long enough, it can fester and become infected. Remember that it is the dis-ease of your mind that causes the disease of your body.

The following quote is from one of my favorite films that I think really hits the nail on the head. The film is *K-PAX*. The lead character, played by Kevin Spacey, is an alien visiting Earth from another planet. In this scene he is explaining to a psychiatrist, played by Jeff Bridges, some of the observations he has made since being here.

> Every being in the universe knows right from wrong. . . . You humans, most of you, subscribe to this policy of an eye for and eye, a life for a life, which is known throughout the universe for its stupidity. Even your Buddha and your Christ had quite a different vision, but nobody's paid much attention to them, not even the Buddhists or the Christians. You humans! Sometimes it's hard to imagine how you've made it this far.

Remember that forgiveness is for you and is not about anyone else. Forgiveness is a full-time job. Forgive the people in traffic who have cut you off. Forgive the people in the news who have misbehaved or done inappropriate things. Forgive yourself for not forgiving. The moment you forgive, you free yourself of that negative energy, and you instantly begin to heal. Heal the world through the power of love.

You get to choose whether you hang on to the anger, hurt, and rage, or free yourself from it by using forgiveness. How would Love respond?

10. BE GRATEFUL

I've saved the best for last. I don't feel I have to say much more on this subject because we have already gone over it so much throughout this book. Just remember that gratitude is the way you tell your Creator, "Thank you for everything, and I'm ready for some more." If you don't have gratitude, the Creator will say, "Why would I give you anything else when you don't appreciate what I have already given you, which is everything?"

Keep in mind that your very worst day is someone else's very best. There are people who would do anything to have your worst day. Being grateful for everything is an easy way to stay empowering, and you already know what that brings!

Make sure to ask the magic question, "What am I grateful for?" every morning when you wake up, and every night before you go to bed, because when you start and finish every day by filling your heart with gratitude, being and staying happy become effortless.

Bonus Strategy!

Spend more of your life being timeless. The reason we are captivated and entranced as we stare into an aquarium is because our spirits are reminded of our timelessness. Creatures that live in the sea have no awareness and no consciousness of hours and minutes. To them, time doesn't exist. As humans who spend most of our lives bound by time, our spirits connect with whatever we encounter that reminds us of our true selves, which are timeless.

Time is a man-made creation and we measure it by the rotation of our Earth. Make sure to spend more quality moments connecting with nature. Stick your feet in a stream. Take a swim in a lake or an ocean. Meditate in the middle of a field or under a tree. However you do it, make sure to check back in with nature on a regular basis, and, while you're doing it, leave your watch at home. Or be like me and choose to never wear a watch. It's a very liberating feeling.

I don't celebrate my birthday either, because instead of having just one special day, I choose to treat every day as a celebration of my birth. How happy do you think you will be when you start celebrating every day?

When You Plant Happiness, Your Happiness Grows

Don't give others the power to determine whether you're happy or not. Save that choice for yourself. (And here's a bonus: the more you smile, the tighter the upper muscles in your face get, so it's like giving yourself a natural face lift.)

When someone tells you that you have inspired him, or that you're inspiring, what he's really saying is that you have helped him see his own light. Nothing feels better than that.

Build your happiness muscles by making happiness your habit. When you take responsibility for keeping yourself happy, you won't have to think about it anymore. It will just be what you do.

The world you see around you is nothing more than a reflection of the world you see inside yourself. When you change your internal world, the external world you experience will instantaneously change too.

When you come to think about it, it really is quite easy to be consistently happy, and when you're happy it makes everything else in life easy too.

14

The Seven Essential Ingredients for Creating Holistic Life Success

1. Desire

The first essential ingredient you need to transform your life into your grand dream life is *desire*. Just wanting it or hoping for it isn't powerful enough to make it happen. Wanting and hoping don't have the emotional power necessary to make you take action.

Wanting, by itself, isn't enough to produce your grand dreams goals because it's missing the key component that turns your dreams into reality. That missing component is passion. When you add passion to wanting, you have desire, and desire is so much more than wanting. *Desire is want backed up with passion.*

> "We must be the change that we wish to see in the world."
>
> GANDHI

Have you ever noticed that although there are plenty of things you want to experience in life, you still haven't gotten around to doing them? The truth is that most people wish really big and expect very little, and in life you get what you expect. When you expect miracles, they happen.

Remember that the formula for creation is T→ A = R (thoughts turned into actions produce results). There is a way to supercharge this formula to make it even more powerful. The supercharged formula for creation is ET → MA = UR (emotional thoughts turned into massive actions produce ultimate results).

Since desire is wanting backed up with passion, desire is an emotional thought that moves us to take massive actions, and that's when our GDGs become tangible and real. *Desire is possibility seeking its own expression.*

2. Passion / Enthusiasm

In his book *The Science of Getting Rich*, Wallace D. Wattles says, "Getting rich is not the result of doing certain things. Getting rich is the result of doing things in a certain way."

> *"Whatever thy hand findest to do, do it with all thy heart."*
>
> JESUS CHRIST

When Wattles talks about being rich, he's not just referring to money or financial wealth. He's talking about having an *enriched* life.

When you look back on your life, you'll notice that everything you have ever been great at, you were passionate about. When you want to be great at doing something, get passionate about it. That is the "certain way" of doing things that Wattles is talking about.

To make your GDGs a reality in your life, you have to go after them with passion and enthusiasm. The word enthusiasm is derived from the Greek word *entheos*, which means "having the God within." Do you think you'd be more powerful and better able to achieve your GDGs with God in you? Are you seeing how this is all connected? Remember that the more power that goes to the source of the light, which is you, the brighter your light becomes, and the more life is attracted to it, automatically!

Remember that simply reading your affirmations every day isn't enough to create your grand dream life because it's not about reading the words; it's about *how* you read them. If you're not reading them with passion and enthusiasm, you're just wasting your time. The same goes for reading your goals. They have to be read with passion and enthusiasm.

And when you take actions to produce your desired results, you need to back those actions with the emotional power of your enthusiasm too. Having passion for what you're doing is showing your love for what you're doing. That is the "certain way" that produces your desired rewards.

3. Belief

A belief is an idea you have references for to make it appear to be the truth. Yet just because you believe it doesn't make it a fact. People can have opposing beliefs, and beliefs can change when you learn or experience something new. For example, do people from different religions have different beliefs? Of course they do. So whose beliefs are the truth? Practitioners of many religions believe they alone are "right," that their beliefs are the real truth, and all others are "wrong." Which religion is right? The answer is none of them, because beliefs are not right or wrong. And as soon as a person changes religions, he also adopts new beliefs.

Remember that your subconscious mind doesn't have the ability to determine if something is real or not. All it can do is work from the input you give it. It assumes this to be the truth. Since your subconscious mind has control over your entire nervous system, it determines what actions you take or don't take.

If you wrote down a lie on a piece of paper and carried that piece of paper with you everywhere you went, reading it numerous times a day, you'd start to believe that lie after a while. Do you know anyone who tells so many stories about their life they actually start to believe them?

The strategy to get your belief system on board to help you achieve all your grand dream goals is simple: fake it until you make it. Keep telling yourself with absolute certainty, over and over, how you are going to have everything you desire in your life, and find as many references as you can to make it seem like it is really going to happen. When you do that for long enough, your subconscious mind will believe it, and that's when it will activate your nervous system to make it happen.

In chapter 9, I described how I instructed beach volleyball team partners Nat and Kerri to say to themselves and anyone else who would listen that they were the gold medalists from the Sydney 2000 Olympics. They did this for two and a half years leading up to the Olympics. They said it so many times, and for so long, that they believed it. When you believe you're a gold medalist, you start to act like you're a gold medalist. When you take the actions that a gold medalist takes, that produces what? Gold! And that's exactly what Nat and Kerry produced for themselves—gold medals.

4. Courage

There are two main reasons why you need courage to be holistically successful. The first is that no matter what you know, no matter what you learn, you will still have fears, uncertainty, and doubt. The truth is, everyone has fear, doubt, and some uncertainty. Who said those things were bad? Fear and doubt are neither good nor bad. Fear can either break you or make you a champion. What counts is what you do with the fear. Having courage doesn't mean you don't have fear. Having courage means you have fear and you move forward in spite of it.

The other reason you need to have courage to holistically succeed is because some people will try to shoot down your dreams and knock you off your path. They will come up with reasons why you won't make it and why it's not possible. Some of these may be people you work with. Some may be friends or acquaintances. Some may be family members. One of these people may even be your partner. Sound familiar?

Understand that most of these people aren't doing this to be hurtful or malicious. There's no point in being angry with them. They're just acting this way because of their own fears. As soon as you make the decision to go for your dreams, you become confrontational to people who aren't going for theirs. In their world, it appears easier to try to call you back to the hole they live in than it is to get up and take the necessary actions to get out of the hole and create their own dream lives. If you think deciding to stay in the hole with them is going to help them, it isn't! The only way you can help them make positive changes in their lives is to lead by example. If they don't follow your lead, they were never going to anyway. Does it make sense to throw away your dreams for someone who was never going to go for theirs?

The only way to inspire your family, your friends, your community, and the world to be happy, healthy, wealthy, and successful is by being that way yourself first. Knowing this, what are you going to do with your fear—use it to drive you forward or let it paralyze you? The choice is yours!

5. Faith

The reason faith is such an essential ingredient to creating holistic success is because faith is the power that gives you light when it seems to be dark. It's faith that turns you into a visionary. Remember that every great achiever on Earth was or is a visionary. Faith is the ability to see things before they are physically there, and to see them even when no one else can. You need faith to see your dream in your mind and to hold on to that vision right up until it becomes reality. That's how you become a visionary, and that's the power faith gives you.

A common question people ask me is, "How do I get faith?" Most people understand that faith is needed, but they don't know how to get it. The way you get faith is by having *gratitude in advance*. Think about it this way: if you had already achieved your grand dream goal, would you be grateful for it? Of course you would! When you're grateful for it in advance, your brain expects your grand dream goal to be accomplished, because why else would you already be grateful? Remember: in life you get what you expect. Gratitude in advance creates that expectation, and that's known as faith!

One of the best things about having faith is the more faith you have, the less doubt you'll have. So if you're ever feeling doubtful about your ability to do something, increase your level of faith, and the doubt will diminish.

If you look at Jesus' life, you'll see he had unwavering faith that he could perform miracles, and he achieved that unwavering faith by thanking the Creator in advance of receiving the gift. He would say things like, "Thank you, Father, for giving me the power to heal this person." That gratitude gave him unwavering faith that he could perform the miracle and then he went and did just that.

And remember: Jesus also said, "Even the least among you can do all that I have done, and even greater things."

6. Action with Follow-Through

Without consistent action your dreams are just fruits that will die on the vine. Remember: the people who have the best rewards are the ones who do what average people aren't willing to do, and it's in the doing that we develop the most. Every action you take toward the achievement of your grand dream goals is an investment in their fulfillment. Every one of those actions is like a pebble being dropped into the universal pond, creating the processional ripples that will carry even grander rewards to your life.

> "There are two mistakes one can make along the road to truth—not going all the way, and not starting."
>
> BUDDHA

Do a 98% great job, and that 2% you didn't follow through on will wipe out all the good efforts you put in. It's like quitting two inches away from crossing the finish line. There aren't any medals given out for that. The fortune is in the follow-through.

> "Those who have the ability to take action have the responsibility to take action."

7. Self-Acceptance

Have you ever done anything bad or inappropriate in your life? (By the way, lying qualifies!) Have you ever stolen anything? (That includes the pen from work you didn't pay for!) Have you ever acted in a way that didn't represent the good person you want to be?

For most people, the final essential ingredient, self-acceptance, is the most difficult to achieve. The reason it's so tough for people to have self-acceptance is because, in the back of their minds, they have this nagging thought they aren't worthy or deserving of having a truly wonderful and magical life because they've done bad or inappropriate things in their past, maybe even their recent past. Well, guess what? Everyone has done things they aren't proud of. Everyone has made mistakes. And everyone deserves to be forgiven and given another chance.

Thinking you are not worthy couldn't be further from the truth! We all deserve everything we want to experience while we are here on Earth. Why do you think the Creator put it all here? So that he could tease and torture us by not allowing us to enjoy it? Does that make any sense? Of course it doesn't!

How does a child learn to walk? By falling down. When your child first tries to stand up and then topples over, do you get angry at him for falling down? Of course not! Most parents celebrate their children's attempts to stand up. When the child stands and then falls over, the parents say, "Oh, look at my precious little angel! He did a boo boo!"

Since the time you learned to walk, have you ever tripped or fallen down? When this happened, you didn't think you were a failure and want to cut off your legs, did you? I didn't think so!

When your children make mistakes in life, do you forgive them? I'm assuming you do. So why would you think the Creator doesn't forgive all His children the same way? It makes no sense that the Creator would set us up to fail by giving us the opportunity to make choices and then, when we do, punishing us for the rest of our lives for making a disempowering choice. Where is it written that we

> "If you're not making mistakes, then you're not doing anything. I'm positive that a doer makes mistakes."
>
> JOHN WOODEN

are supposed to be perfect? And if we were supposed to be perfect, then why didn't God make us that way from the beginning? Do you think God makes mistakes?

As soon as you're perfect, you can expect the Grim Reaper at your door, because there is no reason for you still to be here. Our time on Earth as humans is a learning experience, and we do some of our best learning when we make mistakes. *It is our imperfectness that makes us perfect human beings.*

If you ever want to find your way around a new town, get lost. The more times you get lost, the better you'll learn your way around.

It's now time to forgive yourself for whatever wrongs you feel you have done in your past so that you can heal and move on. Which sounds more empowering: hating yourself for making an inappropriate choice, or forgiving yourself and growing from the experience? How would Love respond?

And if you believe you don't deserve to be forgiven, too bad! Remember that being holistically successful is not only your birthright, it's also your obligation. It's the debt you owe to the universe for the gift of life you were given. It's the natural order of the universe for everything in it to try to reach its highest potential. Evolvement isn't what you should do; it's what you must do. It's your life's quest! When you do great things with your life, you give others permission to do the same with theirs! If you don't do it for yourself, you still owe doing it for others.

Have you noticed that the world needs a little help these days? Well, the only way it is ever going to get better is when all of us decide to take personal responsibility for making it better. When you have your grand dream life, you can show others the path to get there too.

Right now go back to chapter 9, and add this one last identity to your "I Am" list: "I am worthy of all of my goals and dreams!" This is the last of the ten "I Am's" and will complete your list. Make sure you put your ten "I Am's" someplace where you will see them and read them out loud every day. And remember what Wallace D. Wattles says: "Getting rich is not the result of doing certain things. Getting rich is the result of doing things in *the certain way*." So make sure you read your new identities out loud, and with passion. When you do, this is who you will become!

15

A Funny Thing Happened on the Way to the Publisher

I had just finished writing chapters 14 and 15 of this book. As I read through the last two chapters, I realized that the closing chapter was a bit fluffy and not really how I wanted to end the book. It didn't have the impact I wanted it to have, so I started asking myself for ideas about how I could make it better.

My agent, Cathy, had been very excited since reading my manuscript and working diligently to secure a publishing deal for me. Cathy loves what's in this book and agreed with me that the closing chapter still needed some work. She, too, felt that it didn't have the same powerful impact the rest of the book has.

Day after day I came to my office and sat in front of my computer asking for guidance: "How I can make this last chapter as strong and life-changing as I feel the rest of the book is?"

It didn't take long before the answer that I was asking for showed up, and it certainly wasn't in the package that I thought it would show up in. Once again the universe showed me that if you want to make God laugh, you'll tell Him your plans.

I now know without a single doubt that the information and strategies in this book are life-altering, because before this book went to press, I had to use it myself in grand fashion to save my own life and my happiness.

As you'll remember, I started this book with a chapter called "Life Doesn't Turn Out the Way It Should," and, as you're about to read, that concept was forced into me so hard that it shook the foundation my life is based upon. If I hadn't had the manuscript of this book to remind me that life doesn't turn out the way it should, it turns out the way that it does and it's what you do with it that makes your life what it is, I don't know if I would have been able to finish the book or anything else in my life. This book saved my life. What happened was so shocking and earth-shattering, it almost took me off the planet.

I don't know any other way to tell you this than to just come straight out with it.

About a week and a half ago, in the middle of a beautiful day, out of the blue Marie informed me she had made the decision to end our marriage and leave me. When she first told me, it was as if she was speaking a foreign language: I couldn't understand what she was saying. I saw her lips moving, but I couldn't comprehend her words. After all, we have always had an amazing relationship. We have always been very loving toward each other; we don't fight, and we don't call each other names. As far as I knew we had an awesome relationship. In fact, only a few weeks before getting the news from Marie, we were on a plane, and the flight attendant came out with a bottle of champagne for us because she thought we were on our honeymoon. She was amazed to find out that we had been married for six years.

Our marriage was everything I ever dreamed of and better. Together we created a thriving business. Every goal we set for ourselves we reached. Every dream came true. We traveled around the world together, first-class, experiencing so many amazing places. Just by reading this book, you can see how much I love Marie and how I feel about our relationship.

Marie must have seen that what she'd said wasn't registering with me, so she said it again: "I don't want to be married to you anymore, and I am leaving." This time it got through loud and clear. My knees began to buckle, and my heart started racing. I thought I was about to have a heart attack. I had to find somewhere to sit down fast, before I fell down. It was as though the bottom had dropped out of my world and I was tumbling out of control.

I asked Marie to help me understand why she was making this decision and what could we do to change it. She said she didn't want to go for counseling or get help because she didn't feel there was anything she wanted to save or fix. She said, "This decision has nothing to do with you. It's about me and what I want for my life."

I was floored. Our marriage was coming to an abrupt end, and Marie was telling me it had nothing to do with me. I didn't understand why. I felt hurt, sad, abandoned, left behind, and lost.

For the next three days, I was a basket case. I felt like I'd been hit in the chest with a cannonball. My entire world turned upside down and backward. I felt so heavy and tired that walking seemed like a major effort. It was as though my body aged fifty years overnight. Walking down the street, sitting in my office, or even talking with my staff, I would burst into tears. I felt as if I was losing my grip on reality.

Even though this was going on, Marie and I were still being very loving and peaceful toward each other. There wasn't any anger, blame, or hostility between us. Everything appeared to be just as it had always been, except all of a sudden I felt like a stranger in our house. Marie began acting very distant toward me and started making plans to move out. This was so unbelievable to me. I honestly never saw this coming. I thought we had a great relationship right until the minute that she dropped the bomb. I didn't know who I could talk to or what I would say. I didn't know why it was happening; I just knew it was happening.

Because Marie and I were scheduled to fly the States to meet with Cathy and some publishers who were interested in publishing my book, I had to call her to let her know what was happening and that the trip would have to be postponed for a few weeks. Cathy was in shock and in tears when she heard the news.

Then I got hit with some more challenging news. Cathy told me that she couldn't submit my book to any prospective publishers the way it was because of the many references to Marie and how it talked so much about the incredible relationship that we no longer had. She said that I had to rewrite my book. Cathy explained that since Marie and I didn't have our relationship any longer, it would make me look bad by leaving it the way that it was. So there I was, having completed a two-year mission in writing my book, and then I was told that I to do a major rewrite! Though I wasn't thrilled, I finally conceded it had to be done.

So I went through and reread the manuscript, highlighting all the parts about Marie and our relationship. The more I read it, the more I realized I didn't want to take Marie out. She's such a huge part of the book and my life; she was there for all of the experiences I wrote about, and I felt that taking her out of the book would be dishonest and phony. Now I was caught between a rock and a hard place: if I wrote Marie out of it, I would feel as though I wasn't being truthful because she is a part of so many of the experiences that I wrote about, and if I didn't write her out, and we were already divorced by the time the book was published, the information in the book might appear to be a lie.

There I was, sitting in my office feeling very sad and sorry for myself and feeling justified for doing so. Then I remembered what I wrote in chapter 10: justification is below the line and renders you powerless to create the results that you desire. That thought prompted me to glance over at my manuscript sitting on my desk. I looked at the front cover and read the title to myself: "How Would Love Respond?" And that's when it hit me. This was the moment to ask that question, to put it to use.

I thought about it: "How *would* Love respond?" Answers started flowing in my head. Love is unconditional. Love would want Marie to have everything she wants, and Love would want her to be happy no matter what, whether she is with me or not. That's why it's called unconditional love. Love would want me to be happy too.

Later that day I called up my close friend Michael Wernicke to see if he wanted to get together to hang out. I knew Mike would be a good positive influence for me to be around, so I asked Marie to drop me off at his house. As I got out of our car, I was still feeling very down and heavy. As I walked up the stairs to his house, I felt like each of my legs weighed a ton. My body was still weak—the effect of first looking at this situation in a disempowering way.

I understood conceptually that I wanted both Marie and me to be happy with whatever choice she made, and I hadn't figured out how I was going to make that happen yet.

I arrived at Mike's house a little earlier than planned, so he offered me a beer, sat me down at his living room table, and went to take a shower.

As I sat there, I felt so tired and weak that I couldn't find the strength to lift the beer bottle to my lips to take a drink. I just sat there slumped over his living room table staring at the bottle. All of a sudden a question popped into my head: "How can I make this situation with Marie better?" Once I heard it in my head, I repeated it out loud. "How can I make this better?"

I know that every question that is asked has to be answered. That's just how the brain works. Once a question is asked, it feels incomplete unless it is answered. So I continued to sit there expecting an answer to reveal itself.

A few minutes later, Mike came out of his room, showered, dressed, and ready to go out so we could grab something to eat. He saw that I hadn't touched my beer, so he opened one for himself and sat down across the table from me. Then he asked, "Why do you think Marie is making this decision to leave? I've never seen a man more loving and supportive as a husband than you are with her. It doesn't make sense."

It was when he asked his question and said that it didn't make sense that the answer hit me like a lightning bolt. Suddenly it seemed so obvious. I realized that it would be my own book that would save my life and my happiness, and it would do it even before it was published.

I must have chuckled, because Mike asked, "What's so funny?"

I said, "She's not leaving me!"

Mike, looking very confused, said, "What do you mean she's not leaving you?"

"Marie isn't leaving me, dumping me, or abandoning me," I said. "She's going to find herself, and the thing I just realized is that I'm the one who taught her how to do it."

It was in that moment that I understood that Marie had to undertake her own "hero's journey." The hero's journey can be found in any great novel or movie: the main character has a grand goal or an outcome to achieve, and as they set out on the path to reach it, they are confronted with adversity and challenges along the way that they must overcome to complete the mission. Another name for what they have to go through is perturbation. (Remember the three P's of power!)

Because of the helicopter crash and all the other things I have gone through in my life, I have already completed my hero's journey, creating in me a certainty about who I am and what my calling is in life. Throughout our years together as a couple, Marie often asked me about when it would happen for her, and how it would happen, and whether or not she would she feel the same way about herself afterward, and what it would mean she was supposed to do with her life. I always assured her she would find her journey, and it would happen at the right time. The only way to discover it is to keep your heart open to the signs and trust it will show up when it is supposed to.

That's what had finally happened for Marie, and it prompted her to make her decision. Marie realized she needed to get out from behind my shadow and discover for herself who she is. The moment I realized this, I knew I had to rush home to share my epiphany with Marie so that she could be at peace with her decision and know that I was no longer hurt by it. On the contrary: I am very proud of her for making it.

Marie came from a very affluent and loving family who always supported her in anything that she chose to do. Even when she first moved out on her own, her parents were there to help if she had any difficulties. Then she met and married me, and we made our life together a huge success, but it was always based around me and my life's calling. I didn't force it to be that way. That's just the way it turned out.

I apologized to Mike for having to leave so suddenly, and he understood.

As soon as I got home, I raced upstairs and found Marie. I said, "We have to talk!"

I shared my awakening with her. I talked with her about the hero's journey and how I now knew what she was doing and why she was doing it. A big, loving smile came across her face.

"That's what you are so good at doing," she said. "You've just put into words what I've been trying to explain to you for the past few days."

We hugged each other very tight, and she whispered in my ear, "You are my very best friend, an amazing teacher, and the most influential person that I have ever had in my life."

In that moment I realized that this is what I had asked for too. I had been asking the universe to give me the skills to be able to connect with more people so that I can help them find their way to the light. I have already had my experiences with drugs, suicide, poverty, and depression, and I transformed those situations into something positive and empowering. I now have another connection with people in that my marriage has come to an end, and I turned this situation around too, using the strategies in the pages of this book.

And from this experience with Marie I learned the most powerful strategy of all, one that will profoundly change my life forever. I learned to let go.

The Law of Vibration states that everything is in motion and is constantly changing. It's the human part of us that likes to hold on to things and keep them as they are. As humans we don't like things to change, and that's what causes us so much pain. Normally, when someone wants to leave a relationship, the person left behind feels hurt and angry. We often get mad when people change their minds. And it's why we associate death with pain—because we're fighting wanting to change from our human form. With our brains we try to hold on tight to our spirit as it breaks free from the human experience to move on to its next adventure.

All of this is an attempt by our human form to exist outside the natural order of the universe. Our spirit knows that in the universe nothing lasts forever because everything is always changing, always evolving. Our physical human form is the smallest part of who we are. It can be measured by the physical space that it occupies within the universe. Our spirit, on the other hand, is limitless. It has no boundaries. When you get spiritual you learn to let go. Letting go gives you the ultimate freedom.

It took me more than two years to recover from the helicopter crash. By comparison, the end of my marriage to Marie is a thousand times more devastating—and it took me a few weeks to heal from it. It's funny how when you remember to be grateful, it's hard to feel hurt or upset.

There was a day that I was feeling sad and lonely and so I went for a walk down by the river. As I was walking along the sidewalk, I saw a woman who looked to be in her mid- to late thirties who was strapped into her wheelchair so that she didn't fall out. A man who seemed to be her father was pushing her wheelchair, and he looked so happy to be spending time outside in nature with the woman. She was very severely handicapped. Her legs were deformed and only as thick a broom poles. But despite all the challenges that she was obviously handed in life, she was smiling away as she was being rolled along the riverside. She seemed unable to talk, but that didn't stop her from smiling and making happy sounds.

Right then and there I had to find somewhere to sit down. I'd just had another one of those thoughts that was going to change my life forever. It came in loud and clear and instantly I understood its meaning and the impact it would have on my life. I said it out loud to myself: "A least I had a beautiful wife to leave me." As I looked at that woman in the wheelchair, I realized that there was a good chance that she had never and would never go on a date. She would never be romantically kissed by someone. She probably wouldn't ever be engaged or married. I have had so much more in my life than that woman has ever had and will ever have. I have nothing to complain about or feel bad about. Even if I had an accident today and ended up in a wheelchair, I still have already had an amazing life that she has never gotten to experience.

I realized that the Creator had just sent me another one of His messengers to remind me about compassion and gratitude. I was once again reminded that what I perceive as my worst day is someone else's very best day. They would do anything to have what I was thinking was a bad day, because for them that would be a holiday from the life that he or she has to live every day.

As I watch them stroll down the pathway, through my eyes I sent her my love and thanks for the wonderful gift that she had just given me. All of a sudden my burdens were lifted, and my sadness was transformed into elation and joy.

Now I truly know what it feels like to be empowering about everything.

The truth is that there is no truth; there is only perception. Instead of focusing on what I lost, I'm grateful for the wonderful seven and a half years Marie and I shared and the friendship we will always have. She will always be my friend and I will always be hers. She has taught me so many wonderful things and improved every aspect of my life. She allowed me, for the first time in my life, to experience the sensation of unconditional love. That's why I no longer feel hurt by her decision. When you feel *unconditional* love, there won't be anymore hurting because pure love can't hurt. It can only heal.

> "Whoever does not love does not know God, because God is love."
>
> 1 JOHN 4:8

It just goes to show you, just because you work on yourself and you have a lot of skills and tools to improve the quality of your life, doesn't mean that all of a sudden your life will be perfect and without challenges. As a matter of fact, I can promise you that you are still going to have problems. The only people I know of who don't have problems are dead people, and to me being dead is a problem. When you want to make God laugh, tell him your plans. Remember that it is our imperfectness that makes us perfect human beings.

Because of what just happened in my life, I now feel completely free. Nothing could have been more devastating to me than my marriage ending, but by using the tools in this book, I am not devastated at all. And if I can handle this situation using these strategies, I know they will work on everything else as well.

I don't want anyone to be angry with Marie. She did nothing bad or wrong, and she did nothing to me. She did everything the right way, the way it should be done. She made a positive decision for her life and is following her calling to find herself. It wasn't an easy decision for her. Most people would sit back and enjoy the ride, ignoring what their hearts were telling them to do, but not Marie. She is everything I always knew her to be. Once again, Marie has found a way to get me to hold myself to a higher standard, both as a person and as a teacher. Now I truly know how Love would respond.

Because I am a public figure, I understand that there are a lot of people who are watching us to see how we handle this situation. Everyone around us has seen that Marie and I are handling this like everything else we have done together—in a positive and empowering way. Many of our friends have commented, "You guys even do breaking up good!"

If I can't be positive and empowering in my own life, how can I teach others to do it in theirs? The reason I decided to add this story to the book and share with you what Marie and I are going through is because I want to show you that I am a real person just like you. I want to show you I am not some bulletproof person whose life always turns out perfectly. I have real-life challenges that hit when I least expect them to, just like you. What's going to give you the incredible life you desire depends first on the results you actively create for yourself and second on the way you handle what happens in your life. You can handle it in an empowering way or a disempowering way. The choice is yours!

Remember that life doesn't turn out the way it should. It's not fair, and it never has been fair. When you accept that it's not fair, your life instantly get easier because you'll stop wasting so much energy on trying to make life something that it won't ever be. Life turns out the way it does. It's what you do with it that counts.

So if you're not happy with the way your life is going, change it. When you change the way that you look at what happens in your life, your life will change.

If you're not satisfied with the condition of the world and you think it needs some help, take personal responsibility for making it a better place. But if you keep saying, "I alone can't make a difference," then you'll be right, because as soon as you say "I can't," your brain stops looking for strategies to make it better. Thinking that way renders you powerless and throws you into learned helplessness.

Instead of focusing on the hate in the world, focus on the love. You can never be happy when you're wishing others pain. All we have to do is teach each other about love, and the rest will fall into place. The easiest way to do that is by loving yourself so much that love abundantly starts to flow from you. Start to be more loving and kind to yourself so that you can be more loving and kind to others. Train yourself to find something that you like about everyone you encounter.

> "It is not the strongest of the species that survives, nor the most intelligent that survives. It is the one that is the most adaptable to change."
>
> CHARLES DARWIN

If you've ever pondered the question, "How can there be a God when there is so much suffering going on in the world?", when you choose to identify yourself as Love, the question will longer have any relevance because with the identity of Love you become one with the source.

When you change the way you look at everyone else, the people you're looking at will change.

Let's say a friend of yours loaned you a really nice car and asked you to take care of it while they were away. When they come back and ask for their car back, would you make the attempt to give it back to them in the same shape, if not better than the way that it was given to you? Of course you would, right?

Remember that your body is the vehicle your Creator gave you to transport your soul through life. So when you're asked to return it at the end of your adventure, make sure it's in the same shape, if not better than the way it was when it was given to you.

Be kind to yourself by remembering that life is not about being perfect; it's about getting better. It's your imperfectness that makes you a perfect human being. Evolvement is our life's quest.

"Every day when I wake up, I am born,
and every night when I go to sleep,
I die. So what am I going to do
with my life today?"

Think about how you want to be remembered! On average, a person gets about 4,000 weeks to live. How do you want to invest yours? If you know how you want to be remembered, you may want to start living your life that way now.

Let go, and have the peaceful acceptance that you are worthy of all of your goals and dreams. All your dreams will come true when you make the decision to make them come true.

Remember the message: everything in this life is borrowed, and at the end you have to give it all back. The only thing you get to keep is the love you gave, the love you received, and the experiences your soul got to have.

As soon as you adopt the identity of Love, you will never again have to ask, "Where is the love?" for love will always be with you wherever you go, and in everyone you encounter, forever.

God bless, and have a most outstanding day!

———

Write down ten things you have learned from this book that will have the greatest positive impact on your life. (Are you going to take action and do this exercise, or are you going to be like the majority, who say they will get to it one day?) This exercise is a powerful strategy for retaining the gems you want to remember and put into action. How do you respond?

ACKNOWLEDGMENTS

Thank you, Dad, you are my hero. You taught me about integrity and taking responsibility. Wish you were still here in the form to see me complete this book. I know you would be proud. Thank you, Pauline, for being the love of my father's life and for always being there for me.

To my biggest fan, my mom! Your love and continuous support has always kept me going, especially when I needed it the most. You are an amazing lady. I love you, Mom!

To beautiful Marie, thank you for all our adventures, for always holding me to a higher standard, and for being the facilitator of so much of my quantum evolution. I wish you all the happiness that you desire and that all your dreams come true. You deserve it.

John Herzfeld, you are the most influential person in my life. You taught me about class. You forced me to read, to get a vocabulary, and you inspired me to travel. You gave me wisdom. Thank you, John, I hope you are proud of me and what you helped create.

James Carter, thanks for caring so much and for having the talk with me that day in biology class, it started me on my path.

Big Mike Culbert, you live up to your name in stature and integrity. I am honored to call you my friend.

There are so many people who have helped and guided me to become the person who I am today. Just by me mentioning your name I hope that you understand just how much I love you and how grateful I am for all that you have done for me and for my evolution. Madison and Linda Mason, Bobby and Nancy Fraade, Dr. Dave Schwartz, Mike and Nolles Pelly, John Travolta, Sylvester Stallone,

Gunnar and Matthew Nelson, Ricky Nelson, Steve McGlothen, and my dear friend Rochelle Marmorstein.

Peggy McColl, you are a Godsend. You have helped me so much in so many ways to make this book a reality and a bestseller and on top of that you brought me to Cathy. Thank you!

My Agent Cathy Hemming, the best literary agent on the planet, thank you for believing in me and in the book. Love you heaps!

Glenn Yeffeth, Adrienne Lang, Yara Abuata, Leah Wilson, and the entire team at BenBella Books, you guys are awesome and a joy to work with. I am honored to have my book being published by you. You're a class act all the way!

Steve Harrison, thank you for being such a great friend and incredible teacher. Anyone who wants to learn how to get free publicity needs to go to your program. I highly recommend it!

A very special thank you to author and master wordsmith Jane Teresa Anderson for helping me structure this book and for helping me find my writing talents and style. I couldn't have done it without you. www.dream.net.au

A very, very special thank you to Regi Dittrich. You are super amazing, a massive value to my business, and have been so much a part of making this book a huge success. Thank you, thank you, thank you! You're a legend.

To you, the angel Johanna. You appeared, surrounded in light with your white-feathered wings amongst the olives and grapes. At first I couldn't believe my eyes; I thought I was hallucinating, standing before me was a real live angel. I have never before encountered a soul as pure and sweet as yours. Then you touched my hand and reignited the dream in me that I, too, can fly. I haven't touched the ground since.

ABOUT THE AUTHOR

Originally from Chicago, Kurek Ashley has taken himself from $20 away from being homeless twice to being a millionaire living on the Sunshine Coast of Australia, working in more than 13 countries around the world and speaking to more than 10,000 people a year at his powerful workshops.

Kurek is regularly interviewed for stories on his own life and his methods for teaching personal and professional development in magazines, newspapers, television, and radio. He is the author of three top-selling personal development audio programs—*Fire Up Your Life*, *Massive Momentum*, and *The Power's in the House*—and creator of the Life Success Club.

Join Kurek's Life Success Club

Continue the momentum of the empowering strategies from *How Would Love Respond?* and develop successful habits that propel you forward toward your personal, professional, and spiritual goals. Journey beyond these goals to realize your massive potential using practical step-by-step strategies.

Kurek Ashley's Life Success Club gives you the opportunity to experience a full year of resources and coaching with Kurek so that you can create the success results you want in your relationships, health, finance, business, and career. Personally and professionally develop all areas of your life to new levels.

Take action to unleash the unstoppable you—experience Kurek personally and experience profound change in your life. Join us by visiting **howwouldloverespond.com/lsc.html**

How Would Love Respond? Workbook and Home Study Toolkit

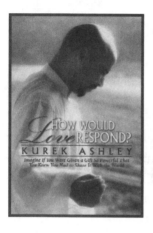

Inside this workbook are the actions that follow the inspiration and empowerment you will experience from the book *How Would Love Respond?*

Journey through your own personal processes of transformation, empowerment, inspiration, perception, perturbation, and procession with exercises that will recreate your life so that you become the person you want to be, living the life you deserve.

Your steps through the book are easy, yet intricate in their structure to reinforce and recap your learning and transformation experience. Your workbook is available at:

howwouldloverespond.com/workbook.html

How Would Love Respond? Screensaver

**Get this amazing screensaver free
when you buy the book**

Each of the screensaver frames is alive
with animation, combining breathtaking
images with powerful messages, specially
sequenced for maximum stimulation. The wisdom in these
frames is ancient, yet sadly forgotten in modern times.

When you have read *How Would Love Respond?*, be reminded of
the powerful and transforming messages so that they integrate
with you daily.

Create your success habits through consistent reminders of the
gifts within this book.

This FREE download is easy and automatically activates your
screensaver function. Get it at:

howwouldloverespond.com/screensaver.html

Kurek's Events, Workshops, and Seminars

If you REALLY want to start making changes in your life—instantly—then Kurek's live events, workshops, and seminars are definitely the programs that will propel your life to the next level. Kurek doesn't do fluff or motivation. Instead, he will drive you to experience three things:

1. Kick you off your ledge so you will spread your wings and fly.
2. Give you the action plan, strategies, tools, and resources so you don't drown once you take that first step.
3. Keep you inspired and empowered to always keep moving forward.

Keep up to date with events and special offers, by registering at:
howwouldloverespond.com/events.html

Kurek Ashley - Speaker

"The life tools and strategies that Kurek has to offer are priceless. Kurek has unleashed my power—I now feel unstoppable and powerful. You are awesome!"
—Natalie Cook, Olympic gold medalist

Kurek is in demand worldwide as an event speaker, on TV shows and radio. His energy, passion, drive to action, and raw emotion cause immediate change to the lives of his audience and co-hosts.

Results are spontaneous. Kurek has been regarded as the divine messenger of the gift that each of us can tap in to, and his practical and real-life strategies have been applied to create ultimate results in many corporations across Australia, the USA, Hong Kong, Singapore, Canada, and New Zealand.

Kurek delivers with his heart and soul and takes his audience members out of their comfort zones to create one of the most profound learning experiences of their lifetimes. See for yourself what Kurek can do for your next event:

howwouldloverespond.com/speaker.html

Sign up for FREE Power Up Your Month Newsletter

Our free e-newsletter is the best way to keep up with what's happening. It's a mix of inspirations, strategies to fire up your  life, interesting reflections on what's happening around the world, special offers and bonuses, and firsthand news about events in your area.

We welcome you to our community where you will be inspired monthly and informed ahead of time.

Join us at kurekashley.com

FIRE UP YOUR LIFE

6 x CD Audio Program with 52-page Workbook

Take your life to the next level with this best-selling audio series. Overcome obstacles and loser thoughts, set new goals, and push your comfort zone with this transformational six-hour program designed to give you a step-by-step action plan to design the life you truly deserve!

Visit **howwouldloverespond.com/products.html** for your copy

MASSIVE MOMENTUM

7 x DVD Program with 100+page Workbook

In this powerful and unique program, Kurek Ashley will take you on a personal journey to create Massive Momentum for Serious Success in seven specific areas of your life. By using the manual included in this program, you will learn tools and create action plans to excel you toward that next level in your life!

Visit **howwouldloverespond.com/products.html** for your copy

THE POWER'S IN THE HOUSE

Single DVD

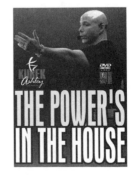

Join Kurek Ashley for two hours LIVE in New Zealand as he makes you laugh, makes you cry, and makes you take a seriously good look at yourself.
This visual display of explosive energy, raw emotion, and life-changing strategies for personal and professional development will change your life in an instant. Go to:
howwouldloverespond.com/products.html